LIFE

THE GENTLE SATIRIST

LIFE

The Gentle Satirist

by

John Flautz

Bowling Green University Popular Press
Bowling Green, Ohio 43403

Library of Congress Catalog Card Number: 72-88414

ISBN: 0-87972-043-3

Printed in the United States of America.

Photographs courtesy of Mr. Henry T. Rockwell of New York

CONTENTS

CHAPTER I

AH, SWEET HISTORY OF *LIFE*

Society, Politics, Literature, Drama. On the cover border design that founder-editor John Ames Mitchell drew in 1882 for the first issue of *Life*, his projected new magazine of humor, these four words appear set off in circles. These were to be *Life*'s topics, and presumably they were Mitchell's best effort to distill the multifarious topics of small-l life. Along with Art, which was always Mitchell's first consideration, they provided *Life* with five reasons for existence. For thirty-five years and sixty thousand quarto pages of print and illustration, through hundreds of fads and fashions, through the settlement of the West and into the first World War, through a generation and more of different contributors with differing ideas, Mitchell kept *Life*'s head pointed directly toward the five.

The early definition of boundaries and goals for *Life* may well have been the most telling decision of its career. The temptation for a magazine of humor to scatter its energies must be overwhelming. An editor desperate for something funny to print must long to throw policy out the window when he finds humor in a form unusual to his magazine. Americans think of humor as a catch-as-catch-can affair, applicable everywhere, and it seems folly to set it about with fences and aim it in one direction. In the end this belief is more relevant to American humor than are *Life*'s selfbuilt fences. However, its fences and direction made *Life*. Without them *Life* would have been the veriest hodge-podge. With them it was not always good, but it was a unit, an entity, a personality. A drawing, a joke, an opinion from *Life* bore the magazine's stamp almost as surely as if the whole production had been the work of one individual. And John Mitchell was the first keeper of the boundaries. *Life*'s personality was primarily the one he chose to give it.

A good illustration of this is found in his treatment of S. W. Gillilan's comic verse, "Off Agin, On Agin, Gone Agin, Finnegan," one of the most famous pieces ever to appear in *Life*. Gillilan made his reputation with it, and used it as the cornerstone for a career as a comic lecturer. It was funny as few things submitted to *Life* were funny. But Mitchell, over the decision of his managing editor, relegated it to the back pages.[1] The move didn't harm the verses, and it helped *Life*. Mitchell said they weren't in *Life*'s vein, and he was right. But few editors have such conviction that they will hide quality on the back pages because unity comes first. After Mitchell's death in 1918, *Life* actually improved in some departments, but its vigor dissipated and its personality withered.[2] The unifying force was gone, and it slid inexorably toward oblivion.

John Ames Mitchell was a man with deep roots in America's past. His mother's family, the Ames family of Massachusetts, was both old and wealthy. His father's family was not so prominent, but his income had been sufficient to send young John through Phillips Exeter Academy and the Lawrence Scientific School at Harvard. Born in New York City in 1845, John Mitchell had shown great promise as a draftsman, and had spent most of his thirty-seven years as a student of architecture and art in the United States and France. He had also practiced architecture with William Robert Ware in Boston. Despite his thoroughly American heritage he had once seriously considered settling in Paris. His Mother had died shortly before *Life*'s founding, and it was with money which she bequeathed to him that Mitchell capitalized the new magazine.[3]

Life was, however, by no means a one-man operation. It was Mitchell's brain-child, and Mitchell functioned as editor-in-chief and publisher. He chose every illustration and spot-drawing that went into the magazine for thirty-five years. But he left to other men the job of choosing words to go with the pictures, and although *Life* was primarily an illustrated magazine, Mitchell's idea of illustration was decorative rather than explanatory. The words, not the pictures, supplied the humor, the opinions, the blood and bone that gave substance to the pretty face Mitchell chose for *Life*. Mitchell retained the last word, but his co-workers were far more than helpers. They included co-founder, editorialist and sometime managing editor Edward S. Martin, Business Manager and Treasurer Andrew Miller, Dramatic Editor James S. Metcalfe, and, a little later, managing editor Thomas L. Masson. Into this formidable array of M's two other names intrude briefly—John Kendrick Bangs, Associate Editor for four years in *Life*'s infancy, and Robert Bridges, who signed himself "Droch," literary columnist for some seventeen years at the end of the century. Bangs did not quite fit the pattern of *Life*; Masson, who succeeded him, was much more in harmony with *Life*'s personality. Droch fitted the personality as closely as sunburn, but in 1900 he quarreled with Mitchell for some undetermined reason and left the magazine angrily, never to return. Compared to other magazine staffs of its time, *Life*'s was remarkably stable.

Andrew Miller's contribution was financial and silent. His name appears only once in every issue—on the masthead, as Treasurer. *Life* kept its business and editorial functions separated. As managing editor, Thomas Masson was a prodigious worker with a talented eye for material that fit *Life*'s needs. He thought of himself as a professional humorist, and felt it his duty to take no strong stands, since any stand might have to be reversed immediately for the sake of a joke. Thus, although his contribution to the magazine in sheer bulk is enormous, he followed *Life*'s personality but did little to form it.[4] He believed that what *he* wanted was beside the point. James S. Metcalfe did the column on drama, the most controversial and troublesome department of *Life*. No great critic, he was a champion gadfly and a circulation booster. He was also fearless and honest. His column was *Life*'s liveliest and its longest-lived feature. Edward S. Martin was an apostle of common sense. He preached it and believed in it. His observations on all possible subjects are both shrewd and amusing. However, he was possessed of a few convictions that no amount of common sense could shake, and these convictions became *Life*'s convictions, partly because the other members of the Sanctum, as the group called itself, agreed with them, and partly because Martin argued them so strongly.

Martin's convictions showed most in politics and literature. His editorials were almost *Life*'s only serious political commentary. His ideas about literature were almost exactly Bridges'. He backed Metcalfe, too, and repeated Metcalfe's opinions when the dramatic critic's attacks on the Theater Managers' Syndicate were damned as anti-Semitic. Masson was always ready with a joke or two to support whatever editorial position Martin struck. The co-operation among the men who ran *Life*, in fine, was far more than ordinarily harmonious. Small wonder that this group, with Mitchell always at the head, produced a magazine as consistently recognizable as an old friend.

This consistency might have been the undoing of another sort of journal. The changes in America between 1883 and 1918 were incalculable. One might suppose that changing public taste would soon abandon a magazine that was too consistent. But the taste of urban middle-class Americans, among whom *Life* found its customers, did not change notably. The cities had grown, but the conditions in which middle-class America lived included the same front porches and grassplots they had included in 1883. *Life*'s readers took their Sunday drives in automobiles in 1918, but they drove them as thirty years before they had driven the family carriages, only faster and farther. Their politics were closer to Chester Arthur's than to Woodrow Wilson's. Mitchell's audience at the end of his life was almost exactly what it had been when he founded his magazine. True, in the last two years, the war years, there began a deep change. But that change was to mean the end of *Life* as well as that of the age in which *Life* flourished.

Many of *Life*'s guiding ideas had faced resolutely backward from its inception, but in its early days its humor was sprightly and scattered. The hoariest tradition might find itself the butt of a *Life* drawing or verse. A little dancing winged boy on the cover design typified *Life* to its readers. The jokes that thirty years of repetition were going to pound into muttering insensibility danced across the pages. When it saw something it didn't like, it tried to laugh that thing to death. It used the lance of scornful laughter where in after years it would use the loaded mittens of peevish insult. It was never "progressive." It always found its butts primarily among those things that were new, fads and crazes, excesses and errors, the ludicrous event and the pointless habit. It always had an addict's craving for mythology and inflexible characterization. To *Life* a young woman was beautiful or she was skinny. A young man was handsome and accomplished or he was rich and chinless. A servant had a paunch. An old man was withered and crotchety, or fat and genial. An old woman was saccharine or pruney. A dog was scraggy and faithful. A mother was perfection itself. Somehow, *Life* invented an enormous number of variations on these, but as it grew older its faculty for observation ebbed away and prejudices increasingly replaced it. It reacted with disgust, not humor, drawing away with a shudder from things that had once made it chuckle and offering as amusement things at which, in a less rancid frame of mind, it would have shuddered.

The changes in the world, which *Life* found troubling, irritated and eventually bored into the hearts of its rivals *Puck* and *Judge*, and, indeed, a whole generation of Americans and Europeans. "Bertrand Russell, on his last visit to this country, remarked privately to a group of younger men that they could not imagine what it was like to grow up in Europe before the First World War with a sense of security that the world has now lost."[5] So says William Barrett. And if the Europe of the period was somnolently secure, what must have been the comparative sense of security in America, isolated by two oceans from the squabbles of less "morally advanced" nations? *Life* chose for a motto, *Americanus Sum*, and in many ways, some of them none too creditable, it was indeed a typical American of its age.

All of this sounds as if *Life* were irretrievably stuck in the mud. Some of its ideas were. But *Life* was itself an enterprise of considerable daring, an illustrated humorous magazine launched by tyros with minimum finances against strong and established competition. Although its ideas on many topics were rigidly conservative, it was neither a worshipper of power nor a "tool of the interests." It told the truth as it saw it; it hid behind the coat-tails of no man or institution; and it never assumed that its readers were anything but sensible, intelligent men.

The story of *Life*'s beginnings is a Babes-in-the-Woods fairy tale that even Mitchell himself could not make up his mind about.[6] He was never quite certain whether he and Martin had been intrepid adventurers into unexplored paths or only two amazingly lucky fools. Mitchell believed, in 1889, that the magazine owed its success to a general artistic revival that swept the country after the Civil War. He said America suddenly became aware that in order to be worthwhile an object did not necessarily have to be ugly, and Americans applied this new idea to everything from picture-frames to horse-blankets. Other magazines of humor were launched, before *Life*, but until the late 1870's, when *Puck* began to circulate beyond the German community for whom it was originally intended, none was successful.[7] Mitchell believed the reason to be that while public taste was improving then, it had not yet improved enough.[8] It was on an afternoon in May, 1882, when Mitchell conceived the idea that became *Life*. He was at that time nearly thirty-seven years old, a Jack-of-all-arts. Saving an enormous capacity for youthful enthusiasm, he might have been any of a thousand aging young men with a certain amount of saleable talent and a promising past.

Mitchell wrote that he was working in his studio that May afternoon on a drawing entitled "Our Continent." The vagrant thought occurred to him that he liked sketching better than painting. To justify the preference, he began to enumerate the reasons why it was better. It was neater. It took a surer eye. It suffered fewer errors to pass. He could do everything with a drawing that he could with a painting, and he could do it more sharply, more quickly, with more detail. It demanded composition, balance, light values—everything that painting demanded except color. Having thus idly convinced himself that drawing was the soul of art, he began to think about it more seriously. He felt it a pity that exhibitions and galleries showed painting, painting, painting. He thought it would be a wonderful thing if there were a way to get the best drawing into the public eye as painting was constantly displayed there.

Somebody, he decided, ought to start a magazine.

The next day, Mitchell visited a friend of his, a publisher identified only as H( ), but almost certainly Henry Holt, who liked the idea. Mitchell's enthusiasm was infectious. Mitchell planned to use the new zinc engraving process to print his proposed magazine, whereas the two established magazines, *Puck* and *Judge*, used color lithography.[9] He had ten thousand dollars to invest.[10] Realizing that the magazine would have to include some written matter as well as drawings, the publisher recommended a writer whom Mitchell calls M( ).[11] M(atthews?) was a man of considerable reputation. He entertained the would-be editor cordially, and for a full day they talked magazine. Mitchell was all but convinced that he held the first copy in his hand. But as Mitchell was leaving, M(atthews?) told him that the idea sounded fine and he was sorry that other commitments made it impossible for him to work on it.

When the publisher heard that the man he recommended had turned Mitchell down, he began to look at the project with an ever more jaundiced eye, and as the summer passed and Mitchell's scurrying in search of talent still bore no fruit, H(olt?)'s first glow of optimism turned to skeptical mistrust. In October, he bowed out, leaving Mitchell approximately where he had been on that first afternoon five months before.

Mitchell now began to search among acquaintances whose experience in journalism was even less than his own—men in their twenties, just out of college. One of these agreed to be his business manager, and for twenty-four hours Mitchell was relieved of at least that much of his burden. The new business manager-elect had a father and a brother-in-law both in the publishing business. When he went home with his new title he talked to them about the proposed magazine and the chances for its survival. The next day Mitchell was looking for a business manager again.

Having failed almost completely to find aid and comfort in New York, Mitchell headed for Boston, which was pleasantly close to his *alma mater*, and where he had family ties. He hoped that a fair crop of promising young men might be discoverable there. A friend introduced him to several possible literary editors and business managers, all of whom listened to him politely and turned him down. Just when he thought he had exhausted Boston the friend came up with another suggestion: Why not ask Edward Martin, the poet? Mitchell had read some of Martin's light verse, and they had mutual friends. Martin seemed a reasonable candidate, but he was technically employed by the New York *Sun*. Mitchell had little hope, by now, that a man with a fair start in one career would tackle the insecurity of his proposed magazine. He wrote Martin a letter and got on the train for New York. He knew he could edit the whole magazine himself if only he had a business manager.

In New York again, he drew pictures furiously and canvassed the artists he thought could work up to the quality he demanded. He drew the cover design, the one that appeared on every issue for years. It remained the standard *Life* cover even after Mitchell had turned to a frequent use of three-color photoengravings for the covers. It had the little circles with the words Society, Politics, Literature, and Drama, and it had a combination of decorative curlicues and comic figures that suggested very well the contents of the yet unborn magazine. He needed a name for the paper, a short name, and he took to scratching down short words on a list. Going over the list one day, he caught the word "life" and decided at once that this was his name. A few days later he found, in Brentano's, an English magazine with that name. He checked on copyright, and came away satisfied that the word was his if he wanted it.[12]

Martin came to New York and decided that he would take over the editorial side of the magazine. By now it was November. He went to work immediately, trying to collect copy from recalcitrant writers. No writer with any sort of reputation wanted to be connected with a magazine that promised to die a-borning, but Martin managed to collect enough copy for a few issues, and some promises. Mitchell said years later during *Life*'s first six months Martin wrote as much of the magazine as all the other contributors combined. In the meantime, Mitchell was still looking for a business manager.

Through the grapevine, he heard that the business manager of "a prominent illustrated weekly" was listening to job offers. He went to see the man, and explained his plans. Mitchell recorded verbatim the conversation that followed. The prospective manager tried to get the facts straight in his mind. According to Mitchell's description, he said, the magazine would be about half as big as *Harper's Weekly*, *Puck*, or *Judge*, and would be priced the same. In order to do that, he said, Mitchell would have to fill his paper with the very best material from the best artists and writers. Mitchell agreed.

> "Well," said the manager, "have you done it?"
>
> "No. The artists are not to be had."
>
> "And the literary men?"
>
> "The same with them."
>
> "That's bad enough. Is your own experience in journalism such as to warrant you in going ahead in such—peculiar circumstances?"
>
> "I have no experience in journalism."
>
> "None whatever?"
>
> "None whatever."
>
> The man of experience indulged in a smile, but a smile of sadness and pity.
>
> "Would you mind telling me," he asked, "just to gratify my curiosity—on what you are building your hopes of success?"
>
> "On the fact of there being an unoccupied field for it. If such papers can thrive in Europe, there must be a place for one in America."
>
> "Previous efforts have demonstrated the reverse, and they have done it pretty clearly."
>
> "But this paper will be a very different thing from any of its predecessors—of a higher grade and far more artistic."
>
> "How can that be when the best men hold aloof?"
>
> "That will occur only at the beginning. I think it will prove an opportunity for talent now unrecognized to come to the front."
>
> Again the business manager smiled the sorrowing smile.
>
> "All that you have said is pure theory, without a single fact on which it would be safe to risk a dollar. Take my advice and drop the business while you can. A year from now you will be amazed that you ever seriously thought of it."[13]

Mitchell didn't doubt that the advice was sensible, but he was in no position to quit now, nor was he in any temper to do so. He set out to find a printer for the magazine, and he decided that his *Life* deserved the best in New York, De Vinne's. But De Vinne's informed him that they printed no weeklies, and again he sorted through a list, this time of printers, approaching one after another and being rebuffed. One turned him down because, it said, it had done the printing for the defunct

Vanity Fair, and it wanted no more large contracts to fizzle and fall through. Mitchell asked what *Vanity Fair*'s circulation had been when it died. Fourteen thousand, they told him. He went out happy for the first time in weeks. He was certain that the break-even point for *Life* would be ten thousand.

The next day he went to Gilliss Brothers, a printing establishment on Fulton Street whose jobs included Columbia University's undergraduate magazine, the *Acta Columbiana*. They were used to inexperienced people with romantic notions, and they accepted the new magazine. Their terms, too, reflected their experience with young geniuses and their publishing ideas—cash in advance.

Shortly afterward, Martin brought in a young man whom he introduced to Mitchell as a Harvard friend and a candidate for the business manager's job, Andrew Miller. He had worked for an advertising agency and for the *Daily Graphic*, and so he understood the market for illustrated publications and how to sell ads. Mitchell gathered him in, giving him and Martin each a quarter interest in the magazine. Now they had a staff, and they set the first of the year, a very few weeks away, as their target date for the first issue. Martin's material was ready, and Miller set to work with surprising success selling ads. The missing element was the most important one—art. Mitchell begged and cajoled, but he found few artists and none who thought of themselves as humorous artists. At last he managed to secure F. G. Attwood, E. W. Kemble, and W. A. Rogers. The three supplied the bulk of the art work for *Life* during its first year and more.

The first number came out on Thursday, January 4, 1883. The three staff members felt positively paternal about it. It sold, too—fairly well. Mitchell, making the rounds of the city, tried to steer conversations toward the new magazine. Generally all he got for his hints was depression. Nobody seemed to like it much. The second week's issue did not sell nearly as well as the first, and the third sold hardly at all. Mitchell and Martin continued to tinker with the content and format. When the returns from the newsdealers came in at the end of the fifth week, there were apparently 6,200 unsold out of a printing of 6,000. The staff was aghast. Not even *Life* could get a larger return than the number sent out. They were not much relieved to find that the extras were leftovers from previous weeks. Miller continued to sell ads, by what means Mitchell did not pretend to know. He later gave Miller credit for saving *Life* in these crucial months.

By March, things looked impossible. There seemed to be no way to the surface.

Martin and Miller went out and saw newsdealers. They talked some of them who had never carried *Life* into giving it prominent display. They walked up to news stands where they were unknown and demanded to be shown that wonderful new illustrated magazine of humor, *Life*. Their circulation ceased to drop. In May and June sales leveled and began to rise—not much, but enough to cheer them considerably. Then Martin's health failed and he left the magazine, turning back his quarter-interest to Mitchell. Mitchell put another thousand dollars of his own money into the magazine in June. He explained that he overheard two newspapermen talking over lunch and they had insisted that the only way to make a publication go was to pour money into it regardless of anything and everything.[14] By August, the increase in circulation was no longer speculative. In September, they broke even for the first time. It was just short of a year since the man of experience had told Mitchell, "A year from now you will be amazed that you ever seriously thought of it."

The magazine gathered momentum gradually for the first few years. Its hallmark was Mitchell's cover design, which wrapped itself around the left and top of nearly every cover while the remaining space was taken up by a captioned drawing. Almost always the drawing was by one of *Life*'s regulars, Attwood, Kemble, Rogers, and, a little later, Palmer Cox, Oliver Herford, and Henry W. MacVickar. Mitchell's *Life* never forgot that it was a magazine dedicated to drawing, and it was sixteen years before it came out with its first three-color cover on the Easter number for 1898, although it had used two-color covers as early as the summer of 1886. *Puck* and *Judge*, of course, illustrated in color regularly. *Life* referred to them, particularly to *Puck*, as "our esteemed colored contemporaries."

The original studio-office was at 1155 Broadway. It was undistinctive and extremely small at best, and *Life* left it for larger quarters as soon as it conveniently could.[15] The magazine moved to an office at 28 W. 23rd St., where, Martin wrote, there were "more light, more elevators, more blue and gold, more roomier wastebaskets."[16] This was in 1887. *Life* was still running twenty-four to thirty-two pages an issue, including ads, but the public had accepted it long since.

Life's next move came in 1894. In the meantime, it had changed its publication day from Monday to Tuesday, although it was dated Thursday. It had branched out in several directions, publishing prints and books of drawings and verse extracted from itself, and it needed a plant of its own. It had grown considerably—its circulation jumped fivefold in 1886, from 32,000 in December of 1885 to 175,322 for the special Christmas issue of 1886. It had experimented with blue and brown ink and found them unsatisfactory. It had upheld with some vigor the dignity of the sewn spine against such publications as *The Forum* and the *North American*, which had switched to steel staples in what *Life* considered blatant disregard for the reader. And it had printed its first half-tone cut, a portrait of William Dean Howells, pasted into a drawing of an infant. The picture was the first of a series titled "*Life*'s Gallery of Beauties." It appeared in January of 1889, and although *Life* stuck to drawings, using photography mostly to go with its drama column, the choice of Howells as the subject for the place of honor is noteworthy. Howells got few enough compliments from *Life*. It proved that they respected him whatever they thought of his literary ideas.

The place *Life* moved to the second time was its very own building, the *Life* Building, on 31st Street between Broadway and Fifth. It was built from the ground up to *Life*'s specifications and needs, and it was to remain the headquarters of the Life Publishing Company until 1936. The building, *Life* boasted, was eight stories high and absolutely fireproof. It had bachelor apartments and artists' studios on the top floor, and the most beautiful architecture in the city, so *Life* said. Mitchell had been a practicing architect, and it is probable that at least the decorative part of the building's architecture owed a great deal to him. *Life* printed one picture of the building while it was in progress, which showed in close-up insert "the most beautiful cornice in New York City."[17] The cornice looks undistinguished, though—Banker's Classic with baskets of stone fruit for supports. *Life* moved in early in 1894.

Building had not been easy. The depression of 1893 caught the building half-completed, and as business fell off, bills piled up. Just when everything seemed clear again, the plasterers struck. Mitchell estimated that the strike cost *Life* twenty thousand dollars by the time the delay and the new wage rates were taken into consideration. It was *Life*'s one real skirmish with labor trouble, and it might have helped to form a policy that was peculiarly *Life*'s when labor problems were in the news. *Life* was generally sympathetic to the cause of the laboring man. It excoriated profit-hungry capitalism, and Mitchell even suggested with some seriousness that revolution, repugnant as the idea was, might be the only answer to the looting of the American economy by the Trusts. But *Life* never had a good word to say for strikes or strikers.

Mitchell experimented from time to time with new methods of art reproduction. Besides being the first American publication to use photoengraving extensively, *Life* was the first to print montage drawings[18] and the first to combine drawing with photographs.[19] Once, a little hesitantly, it claimed to be "the first to introduce half-tones into contemporary periodical literature."[20] But Mitchell never sought distinction by way of novelty. His only aim was to get the best drawing available.

The ability to keep customers happy was an essential part of Mitchell's editorial genius. He was one of the earliest American editors to offer his readers a working share of his publication, to take as well as give, to add to his editor's job the functions of cheerleader and master of ceremonies as well as that of collector and arranger of contributions. From its earliest issues, *Life* sporadically printed readers' letters on all subjects, and readers' correspondence often provided the starting point for Martin's editorials. *Life*'s "Letters to the Editor" column was never as solidly entrenched as its other features such as editorials and the critics' columns, but it appeared often during the later years—one might say "regularly, with notable interruptions." It was among the very first of such columns in an American magazine to carry on the dialogues between reader and editor and reader and reader that subscribers later found so appealing. But Mitchell's primary means of keeping in touch with his public was a device that suggests his editorial modernity even more strongly than does his handling of letters—the contest-by-mail, the forerunner of the opinion poll.

Mitchell must be unique among American editors in his passion for contests. *Life*'s first contest was held in 1898. It was called "*Life*'s Pegasus Contest," and its object was to guess what line by a given poet a certain drawing was intended to illustrate.21 The response was both far greater than *Life* had anticipated and much livelier than its editors might have wished. Every time the winners were announced, losers poured in letters protesting with a great deal of justice that *their* answers were better illustrated by the picture in question. Over and over *Life* explained that it was not how your answer fitted the picture that counted, it was how close it came to what the artist intended the picture to fit. All of this might have suggested to *Life* that its readers were cleverer at illustration than its artists. If it did, Mitchell let the idea pass. What it did suggest was that contests were open avenues to the public mind. From then on, hardly an issue of *Life* appeared without news of some contest, current or to come. *Life* held story contests, essay contests, art contests, clever-answer-to-leading-questions contests, contests to choose the best or the worst novel and railroad and newspaper, and even, in 1917, a patriotic song contest. The readers' responses were seldom noteworthy, but they were always copious. Only one contest, the Worst Novel Contest of 1909, had to close because of lack of public interest before a prize was awarded.22 *Life* itself had lost interest in novels, good or bad, some years before. The failure of this contest merely demonstrated that the instinct which told Mitchell to reduce *Life*'s emphasis on book reviews had indicated the trend of public literary taste as accurately as had the actual public consensus provided by the contest.

Besides being an admirable link between *Life*'s editors and its readers, the contests were revealing in the way *Life* conducted them and the magazine's attitude toward those who questioned its decisions. Absolute foursquare incorruptible honesty was *Life*'s most jealously guarded virtue. Let a critic accuse it of stupidity or crudeness, it laughed and remarked that some people's ill will is complimentary. Let him accuse it of lacking a sense of humor, it smiled and pointed to its ever-rising circulation. But let anyone hint that he suspected *Life* of the least chicanery, and the magazine turned on him savagely. During the Pegasus Contest, *Life*'s annoyance at questioning contestants sometimes got the better of it, and its explanations of the contest aims grew testy. But it continued to run the contests to suit itself, offering as security only the word of a gentleman. This attitude came to some sort of apex in 1916, when one of the judges appointed by *Life* for a short story contest entered it and won first prize. If *Life*'s own judge won the contest, then *Life*'s readers agreed that the judge's entry must have been one of the best in the contest.

The Spanish-American war marked a turning point for *Life*. Politically, *Life* had been strongly against the war, and remained strongly against the territorial expansion that followed. But its politics were never strong enough to change its personality. (Not, at least, until World War I.) By 1898, *Life* had settled into a pattern comparable to the mature life of an individual. Its jokes had been winnowed and the best ones saved to be republished over and over. The only public figure to whom it had ever given its unqualified support, Grover Cleveland, was in eclipse. It had its departments and size settled and its mind made up about everything. The steady growth over the next ten years or more was nearly all advertising— a random issue from 1906 has fourteen pages of copy sandwiched between nine pages of ads fore and eleven aft. The years from the war to the first Wilson administration were dull for *Life*. If it had not had Theodore Roosevelt to provide copy, it might have been bland. But its circulation increased as steadily as its advertising content, and its air was one of plump prosperity.

In 1911 and 1912, *Life* began to put on weight. Editorials went from one page to two. It ran three or four book columns—John B. Kerfoot's "Bookishness," Arthur Guiterman's "Rhymed Reviews," W. T. Larned's "Literary Zoo," and Carolyn Wells's "The Bookstore Girl,"—where Kerfoot alone had done the job since the turn of the century. It added more and more photographs to its drama coverage. Its covers grew rosier and more elaborate. They had been cartoon illustrations, only sometimes witty but always meticulously drawn. Now they were stylized drawings in blocky colors, and finally they melted into the gaudy chromos of Maxfield Parrish and Norman Rockwell. Special numbers became the rule rather than the exception. Nearly every issue was dedicated to this or that event, trend or personality, and Mitchell instituted the practice, revolutionary to the pre-World War era but now nearly universal, of advising his regular contributors of deadline dates for contributions on various topics.23

Life grew from 16-32 pages to 52-64 pages without adding anything significant. This dropsical swelling allowed Martin, as editorial writer, to expand on some ideas he had held for years but always had to pass over quickly for want of space.

In 1909 *Life* began to reach into the past not only for ideas but for material. It reprinted the humor of the nineteenth century on at least two, and sometimes six or eight pages per issue. This was not its own humor but a sort of small anthology. Its circulation was growing so that its ads threatened to overwhelm the rest of the magazine, and it needed something to fill in a half-column or so on the advertising pages. It was beginning to sink in its own good fortune. In 1910 it boasted to a reader who questioned its overuse of ads that "our million readers" were the greatest potential market in the country. In December of 1913 its Christmas issue comprised 246,000 copies.

This steady rise in public favor did not go unnoticed by some authors and publishers with more taste than scruples. *Life* found itself protesting, at intervals, that one or another playwright, poet or publisher had stolen its material. Reprints from *Life* sometimes found unauthorized competition in the field. Charles Dana Gibson, the artist who personified the era and was identified with *Life*, was the plagiarists' most frequent victim. Gibson's drawings or prints were often used as premiums or contest prizes by *Life*, and were, for a while, sold through advertisements in *Life*. At the time, *Life* printed a regular warning to customers that certain persons were removing Gibson cartoons from old copies of the magazine, framing them flat, and selling them as hand-printed prints. Besides this, Gibson's well-nigh sacred Gibson Girl was once taken over intact and turned into a play. The play's producer timed his theft, or so it seemed, to demonstrate convincingly what *Life* was contending at the time—that all theatrical producers were blackguards. Gibson, along with some of *Life*'s other artists, also contributed scenery, quite unwittingly and without remuneration, for more than one New York play. At least *Life* claimed that they did. In 1893, "A Temperance Town," by Charles H. Hoyt, a successful and prolific playwright, was produced in New York with scenery which James S. Metcalfe described as taken straight from *Life*. In 1896, a review, "A Round of Pleasure," included, according to Metcalfe, not only scenery but jokes taken from the magazine.

In 1912, *Life* sued the New York *Mail & Express* for infringement of copyright, and was awarded $1,043.14. Mitchell wrote that the judgment was for the minimum amount under the law, but that *Life* had fought for a principle and proved its point. The *Mail & Express* had pirated from certain French magazines which had in turn pirated from *Life*. Despite the double remove, *Life* demonstrated its title and its author's title to the material. It was, Mitchell said, "a clear definition by the courts that under the copyright laws of the United States the artist and writer are the owners of what they produce."[24] *Life* joyfully announced that it would "take the strongest measures" with future plagiarists; it had campaigned hard for the international copyright law and the suit established a significant precedent under that law.[25]

Life was not wholly guiltless of plagiarism itself, although innocent of any dishonorable intent. In 1889, in successive issues, *Life* printed a review of a book by Walter Learned and a poem ostensibly by one Frederick Peterson. Then the editors were embarrassed to learn that Peterson had sold them one of Learned's poems. They apologized profusely, but they insisted that they could not help it.

World War I and Mitchell's death combined to put an end to the *Life* that flourished in America's gilded years and the tentative chip-on-shoulder internationalistic period that followed. Even before Mitchell's death, *Life* had gone sour.[26] Its treatment of the war was jingo-moralistic. It demanded death for the armies of Germany and disgrace for anyone who disagreed. Its state of mind was reflected, too, in a much nastier conservativism. Once *Life* had clucked and smiled when it thought it had caught the Suffragettes or the Jews or the allopathic doctors trying to take over the country from the good Americans. Now it snarled and spat venom. With Mitchell gone, any chance of recovering the magazine's equilibrium was lost. His was the mind that ruled *Life* and molded it into what it was. His successors never grasped the idea that it was not the same magazine without him.

For fourteen more years of declining popularity, *Life* held on as a weekly, and when in 1932 it ceased weekly publication, it continued as a monthly for four years. Its last gasp came in October of 1936, and almost nobody noticed it. Henry Luce bought the name for his proposed new illustrated magazine. Except for this, the last passing of *Life* might have been as mute as it was inglorious. It was an anachronism in many ways on the day its first number was published, though it thrived to print a quarter of a million copies per issue. By 1936 its old staff was gone, and the bright new staff that resuscitated it briefly in the early twenties had moved to livelier hunting grounds. Its circulation had fallen to a handful. It died of sheer exhaustion from trying to keep up with a world that left it half a century behind.

NOTES

[1]Thomas Lansing Masson, *Our American Humorists* (New York: Moffat, Yard and Co., 1922), pp. 127-128.

[2]Robert Emmett Sherwood wrote *Life*'s dramatic criticism in the Twenties, and Robert Benchley wrote its moving picture review. No writers of comparable stature worked on *Life*'s permanent staff during Mitchell's editorship.

[3]Complete biographical details on John Ames Mitchell are to be found in Chapter III, pp. 44-56.

[4]Cf. Chapter III, pp. 65-67

[5]William Barrett, "The Twentieth Century in its Philosophy," *Commentary*, Vol. XXXIII (April, 1962), p. 320.

[6]Nearly all of the account of *Life*'s founding was taken from an article by Mitchell in *Life*, Volume XXI, pages 15-19. An alternative explanation of the genesis of Mitchell's idea is offered by Henry Holt. (*Garrulities of An Octogenarian Editor*, Boston and New York: Houghton-Mifflin Co., 1923, p. 239.) "A friend said to him: 'Johnnie, you have a sense of humor, you can draw and you can write, why not become the Du Maurier of America?' The result was *Life*."

[7]For brief histories of *Puck* and *Judge*, *Life*'s contemporaries and rival magazines of satire, see Appendix.

[8]John Ames Mitchell, "Contemporary American Caricature," *Scribner's Magazine*, Vol. CI, No. 1 (January, 1937), p. 35.

[9]John Ames Mitchell," *Printer's Ink*, Vol. CIV, No. 11 (July 11, 1918), p. 40.

[10]Edward Sandford Martin, "John Ames Mitchell: 1845-1918," *Harvard Graduates' Magazine*, Vol. XXVII, No. CV (September, 1918), p. 27.

[11]The best guess at M( )'s identity is Brander Matthews. Matthews and Holt were acquainted (*Garrulities of an Octogenarian Editor*, p. 114); he was an early contributor to and supporter of *Life*; he was later a close personal friend of E. S. Martin (*DAB*. XXII, p. 434); and in 1883 he was showing an interest in a humorous magazine, collaborating with Henry Cuyler Bunner, the editor of *Puck*, on a book of stories, *In Partnership*.

[12]It was a decision of some moment. Fifty-four years later, the name *Life* was the magazine's last important asset.

[13]*Life*, XXI, 1893, p. 16.

[14]John Ames Mitchell, with Thomas Masson, James S. Metcalfe, and Sinclair Lewis, "John Ames Mitchell, The Man Who Is Responsible for *Life*," (New York: Frederick A. Stokes, n.d.), p. 5. This is a pamphlet, reprinted from *The Book News Monthly* for 1912.

[15]Picture in *Life*, XXI, 1893, p. 16.

[16]*Life*, IX, 1887, p. 330.

[17]*Life*, XXII, 1893, p. 414.

[18]*Life*, XXVII, 1896, p. 121.

[19]*Life*, XXV, 1895, p. 172.

[20]*Life*, LIX, 1912, p. 772.

[21]*Life*, XXXI, 1898, p. 302.

[22]*Life*, LIII, 1909, p. 22.

[23]Kenneth L. Roberts, *I Wanted to Write* (Garden City, N. Y.: Doubleday & Co., 1949), p. 58.

[24]*Life*, LIX, 1912, p. 430.

[25]*Life*, LXIII, 1914, p. 58.

[26]According to Martin, this was Mitchell's responsibility. Mitchell was an ardent Francophile, and he thought the German invasion of France unforgivable.

CHAPTER II

A LITTLE LIST OF SOCIETY OFFENDERS

But *Life*'s real story is one of success, not failure. The life and works of *Life* are the important things, and its liveliest life and worthiest works came during Mitchell's editorship.

Of the five great subjects with which *Life* sought to fill its pages, Art was the most important to the *conception* of the magazine, and doubtless Mitchell's choice of drawings contributed as much to its public appeal as did any other single department. This study must beg off any sort of assessment of *Life*'s art, however, other than to insist that by making draughtsmanship its first consideration, *Life* linked itself firmly to the art of the century in which it was founded. Besides this, and this is offered as literary rather than artistic criticism, although *Life* employed the talents of nearly every competent American illustrator of the age, its drawings were resolutely non-illustrative. They might have been splendid examples of the best available black and white drawing, admirably composed and deftly executed. But they often had only the vaguest connection with the things they were supposed to illustrate. This situation still prevails in popular journalism. It is so flagrant in some forms—the cover illustrations of paper-bound fiction, for instance—that it has become legendary. *Life* certainly had a hand in setting the pattern. The reader who complains that all the young men and women illustrated in his favorite weekly look alike can put part of the blame, at least, on John Ames Mitchell.

One item so obtrudes itself into *Life*'s art that it cannot be ignored—prudery in art. *Life* was by no means a prudish magazine and Mitchell, writing in 1913, maintained that most of the readers' complaints during the magazine's thirty years were about real or imagined bawdiness. But *Life* was doggedly conventional, and its occasional rebellion against over-moralization of art was prompted by annoyance with the prudes, not by any wavering from the moral standard of the community. Mitchell had made his ideas about puritanism clear:

> So then, your glasses fill:
> Drink to this band of brothers,

> Whose pious joy it was to kill
> The cheerfulness of others.[1]

But *Life* invariably fought back hard when some publisher or theater manager offered fare "unfit for the young person." Such an attitude led to some amusing inconsistencies in *Life*'s treatment of, particularly, nudity or semi-nudity in its drawings. One was a notion, widely put into practice during the nineties, that non-human nudity was acceptable where human nudity was not. It turned into a regular passion for mermaids, with a considerable side-interest in wood-nymphs, beginning with Dan Beard's black and white mermaids in 1892, whose fish halves come within a whisper of missing their obstructive functions altogether. It culminated in 1903, when several covers served up mermaids of astonishing nubility in full color and poses of delightful abandon. One 1903 cover by John Cecil Clay depicted the very feminine spirit of the stream being violently embraced and roundly kissed by the very masculine spirit of the meadow. A reaction set in shortly afterward, because by 1906 a *Life* artist drew the Venus de Milo totally without breasts, cylindrical and chaste. In February of 1910 *Life* issued an "Improper Number" with much fanfare, promising to shock the prudish and amuse all admirerers of the risque. It was a tame affair. Its nearest approach to nudity was a drawing of a window shade on which was thrown the silhouette of a woman combing her hair. It was impossible to tell whether she was or was not wearing clothes. A sufficient number of complaints came in about that one to make *Life*'s staff chuckle for years afterward. They believed that they had really struck a blow for frankness.

Earlier, Mitchell related a story of a prim, New England-ish woman who stormed into his office one day to demand an explanation for the indecent drawing he had printed in one number. He had already had some complaints about that number, so he began to apologize to her mechanically, assuring her that he had heard out several others and that he would be more careful next time. As he went on, he could see a growing puzzlement come over his visitor. Finally she interrupted to ask him what picture he was talking about, anyway. He pointed it out. Why, she said, there was nothing about *that* one that anyone could object to. It was this *other* one that she wanted to tell him about. Mitchell used the story to illustrate the impossibility of pleasing all of the customers all of the time.

After Art, on the list of *Life*'s chosen topics, came Society. Society, for *Life*, was entirely the sort that is spelled with a capital. *Life* never used the word academically. It pictured slums and street cars as well as drawing rooms and carriages, but it would have hooted down the idea that the first combination had anything to do with Society. Society, to *Life*, meant the Four Hundred. It found Society over-dressed, over-leisured, and spoiled rotten—at least, Society women and young men. *Life* had too much respect for the money-accumulating faculty to lampoon "successful" men. Its targets were women who flaunted wealth, slackjawed heirs who were temperamentally unequipped to follow their acquisitive parent's example and took to books or roulette instead of finance, and the crude or flagrantly dishonest climber. The underlying assumptions that allow this sort of segregation by sex and age are twofold, and they define an American attitude toward money that persists to this day. The first is the frontier principle that those that do not make money ought not to spend it. The second is the "genteel" principle that a truly capable person makes no vulgar display, which is to say, those that make it ought not to spend it either. *Life* embraced both of these ideas fervently, at least for purposes of humor. Perhaps it should be excused by its humorous purpose from answering for them. However, it is very difficult to understand the simultaneous acceptance of both ideas by anyone, let alone by a majority of the responsible citizens of the country. *Life*'s readers, though, apparently agreed that while making money was admirable, spending it was ludicrous, and *Life* tailored its jokes to suit their taste.

Mitchell had a kind of vested interest in Society humor. His first successful book had been *The Summer School of Philosophy at Mount Desert*, a collection of mildly satiric drawings on resort life. Its success had come at a time when he had been nearly demoralized by his failure, in the art work which he was doing in America, to live up to the standards that he had believed himself capable of attaining while he was in France. *Life*'s attentions to Society, therefore, never flagged. Still, there was a limit to the number of possible jokes about women named Dressta Kyll and Kakklyn Henne, and men named Lord Howe Poore, Heritage Doolittle, or F. Tayleurs Dummy. *Life* reached and exceeded the limit all too soon. Every summer *Life*'s Society moved to Newport; every winter it put on its tiaras and held formal dinners.

It was early decided that the summer resort would be the chief humorous butt, and the expensive resort was funnier than others. This led to a nearly photographic reproduction, year after year, of jokes about Newport and how impossible it was for dowager figures to maintain their dignity in bathing suits, and jokes about how hopeless it was for lovelorn maidens to seek solace at the summer places because all the desirable young men were working through the summer, and jokes about how the maidens would take a monocled dude when nothing else presented itself but leave the dude on the dune when vacation was over and their first loves came back to claim them. In the winter the victualling of the wealthy gave opportunities to draw sumptuous interiors and flowing gowns. Perhaps the most noteworthy of *Life*'s accomplishments with Society was to present it so that it is impossible to tell whether *Life* had any serious reservations about it. About the practices of certain members of Society, yes. About the undue influence Society wielded among weaker

EXPLAINED.

"HOW DID YOU COME TO MARRY YOUR SECOND HUSBAND?"
"MY FIRST ONE DIED."

minds—*Life* once suggested that the theaters closed in summer to gratify the four hundred, who were out of town in that season—yes. But about the essential usefulness or lack of it to be found in such a group, *Life* simply never committed itself. It saw Society as little more than a collection of foibles, in its drawings and jokes, but it never equated Society with real abuses of money, like Trusts, and it very seldom equated Society people with people it believed the world could do better without, like anarchists and Englishmen. In general, its objections to Society were tied up to or overridden by its other strong objections. It picked on all pretentious women, so it picked on Society women. It picked on all economically useless men, so it picked on dudes. It picked on England, so it lampooned Anglophiliac matrons who married their daughters to dukes, and on posturing young men who wore top hats and bit the knobs of their walking sticks. It found love amusing, and so it amused itself and its readers with love among the wealthy. On the other hand, it admired attractive, well groomed young women, and so it admired the attraction and good grooming of the daughters of the rich. Society, while it deserved its place on *Life*'s cover by virtue of the sheer bulk of space allotted to it, neither inspired any of *Life*'s strong opinions nor offered it a proper arena for the exercise of those opinions. Its real importance, compared to that of its four peers, was almost nil.

Another kind of "society," though, deserves a more serious investigation in connection with *Life* and its ideas and policies. If the word meant only High Society to *Life*, it still means to us the entire structure of human life in a given population unit. *Life* would never have called the population of New York City as a whole "society," but by the new definition of society, that was exactly the population it investigated and portrayed. For *Life*, the social phenomena of America that were worth attention were to be found in New York City.

Americanus Sum was its motto, but *Civis New Yorkus Sum* would have been more accurate in many ways. Its New Yorkishness showed most plainly in its concentration on cityscapes and city interiors as backgrounds for its drawings, but it was also obvious in its insistence on fighting with the New York City Street Railway Company, with New York newspapers, New York politicians, New York theater managers and New York literary coteries, all of which could have had only vicarious interest for readers outside the city. *Life*'s ideas about the lives of rich and poor never passed beyond such lives in the city of New York. Its streets were New York streets, its crowds New York crowds. Its horses and dogs were bred to tramp the pavement or forage in the garbage can, not to run in grass and chase rabbits. Its point of view was wonderfully consistent: its lower orders sunned themselves on tenement steps or gossiped over shantytown fences; its upper crust fondled roped pearls at formal dinners or burrowed into the upholstery at some favorite club. *Life* was a New

Yorker about town, a passer-by in the slums, an observer of street scenes, and an accepted, if not intimate, guest of the great. But like some other men-about-town, *Life* had no home. Its whole function was to observe, and its walking boots were never off. It knew no scenes of domesticity, no wives, no children. The child at play in the street, the wife in Society — these *Life* showed in abundance. But never in the home.

Also, true to its century's notions of the life of a man-about-town, *Life* yearned with a seasonal nostalgia for the purity and beauty of the happy rural seat that it imagined it had left behind. Its illustrations of country life depict an endless picnic. Its country scenes are peopled with fauns and nymphs, or if realism was its goal, Bacchantes in poke bonnets and dowdy ginghams. All its farmers looked like Yankee Sam Slick. All its farmers' wives were fat and adorable. When sin threatened to overwhelm *Life* in the wicked city, it inevitably found a word or two of comfort for itself in its daydreams about the virtue of the farms and villages. This idea extended beyond mere theory to the practical. *Life*'s most prized possession, after its honesty, was its Fresh Air Farm Fund. Over a period of more than forty years, *Life* sent thousands of New York children to the country for a two-week summer respite from bad air, bad food, and bad examples. It is senseless to deny the goodness of the cause or the nobility of *Life*'s effort, but the root of *Life*'s charity was a favorite and foolish fiction.

Under Mitchell's leadership *Life* was continually embroiled in crusades and battles, and while some of these were benevolent others were splenetic. But only one that had more than local importance seemed vital to the magazine: its fight against allopathic medicine and against germ theory, inoculation, and vivisection in particular. A second crusade of national scope, *Life*'s fight against the women's suffrage movement, seldom struck the magazine as serious even though it was long and occasionally bitter. A third nationwide crusade, against fireworks, was carried on every July for many years in *Life*'s columns. For the rest, *Life* confined its attention to Manhattan. Its longest and most important fight there was that against the theater managers, which is related in Chapter VII. Next in importance was its continuing resentment of "alien" encroachment into New York. This was perhaps not exactly a crusade, but it colored many of the magazine's other crusades, for *Life* disliked Tammany for its Irishness and the Theatrical Syndicate for its Jewishness. *Life*'s fight against the yellow papers was important. Some of its minor battles were not. Its attacks on the Street Railway Company were confined mostly to cartoons of dead pedestrians strewn around the city streets while the streetcar galloped on. Henry Vreeland, the head of the Railway Company in the nineties, got his picture drawn in *Life* frequently, too, with some sort of uncomplimentary biographical note attached. The magazine's strongest weapon was repetition.

The Tammany of *Life*'s time was Richard Croker's Tammany, honest to a fault by the standards of the Tweed Ring, but dedicated to machine politics, the spoils system, and the use for personal gain of every advantage offered by political life. Some of *Life*'s sympathies followed these lines. It preferred spoils to Civil Service, believing the latter to be the sanctimonious licensing of graft. Croker himself was an avatar of *Life*'s economic hero—the honest, greedy man. The Life Publishing Company even printed Alfred Henry Lewis' laudatory biography of Croker in 1901, and its reason was by no means a great admiration for Lewis.[2] *Life* respected Croker even when it attacked his machine. It was, perhaps, a piece of genuine conservatism on *Life*'s part, as contrasted with the specious conservatism that it so often preached. *Life* wanted no part of an organization that could name whomever it liked for mayor or even governor. It was less interested in the state of the public treasury than in the nomination of worthy candidates for office. It believed in men, not methods. It also believed, when the belief suited its purpose, in the rule of law. When Tammany judges and Tammany juries made what *Life* believed to be a mockery of justice in the New York courts, *Life* tried its best to discredit the whole machine with its satire.[3]

An ugly outgrowth of *Life*'s disapproval of Tammany was a way of seeing Tammany's handling of New York's immigrant population as somehow the immigrants' fault. The newcomers were offered lightning citizenship, protection from an alien and often hostile police force, and—at least for the shrewder ones—an opportunity to get rich quick, which was exactly what America was supposed to offer everyone. Only the Democratic machine had it to give, and it is little wonder that the offer was often gratefully accepted. The machine asked only votes in return, and it got votes when it needed them. A man with the peculiar combination of a quick mind and gang loyalty might, if he allied himself with Tammany, rise to the office of municipal judge almost before he had worn the outer layer of the ould sod off his boots. This playing fast and loose with American institutions could hardly help alarming *Life*, but *Life* expanded the menace from an opportunistic and quasi-legal political machine in New York to an Irish Catholic plot to engulf the world. To *Life* the city government of New York was bad; but worse, it was Irish. "Irish" meant "ignorant and clannish" to *Life*, and insofar as any generic term is inclusive, the accusation fit. Whatever the reason might have been, the larger part of the Irish immigrants of New York were both. But to the ignorance of a people bred to direst poverty and the clannishness of peasants thrown helter-skelter into a huge outlandish metropolis, *Life* would have added the fabled deviousness of the Jesuits and the notorious subtlety of the Borgia Popes. Croker's own deviousness was really more than enough.

"The government of the largest city in the United States is a despotism of the alien, by the alien, for the alien, tempered with occasional insurrections of decent folk," wrote the London *Times* in 1892, and *Life* quoted it with applause, adding that according to another Englishman, Rudyard Kipling,

> In a heathen land three things are supposed to be the pillars of moderately decent government. They are: Regard for human life; justice, criminal and civil; and good roads. Yet in this Christian city they think lightly of the first. . . . They buy and sell the second at a certain price, openly and without shame, and are apparently content to do without the third.[4]

Life certainly was justified in complaining that its city's government did not qualify as moderately decent by savage standards, but Croker's Tammany had not invented the process. Neither was it so thoroughly entrenched that a determined reform effort could not unseat it, as was proved twelve years later. But *Life* preferred to attack Romanism, not Tammany. It believed that reform stood no chance at all against the Popish octopus, so it was obviously useless against Croker. Besides, *Life* saw reformers as white-handed lilies whose whole function was to shake their fingers at better men, men who were engaged in the world's work, which the reformers could not hope to understand. In all, *Life*'s attitude toward New York politics was remarkably ingenuous. It reacted violently to particular miscarriages of political power, but it continued to admire the men who held the power and the methods by which they gained it. To reconcile approval of theory with dismay at result, it had to invent a demon that corrupted—the insidious Roman Catholic Church, which worked its will on the infinite corruptibility of the Irish nation. "Despotism of the alien," the London *Times* had said, and in the face of the alliance of these two alien powers, "decent folk," of whom *Life* was unquestionably one, were nearly helpless. The best thing that good Americans could do to help, *Life* thought, was to attack the Irish and their church whenever the opportunity arose.

Therefore, *Life* took an occasional swing at Tammany and another at some of Tammany's results—biased judges, corrupt aldermanic courts, nepotism in city jobs or city franchise distributing. But it saved its heaviest ammunition to attack the Irish satirically and the Roman Church with deadly seriousness.

Life's attitude toward "alien" minorities in general was certainly a part of its New York heritage. The Irish-Catholic question belongs in the discussion of Mitchell's personal ideas, in the third chapter, since it was Mitchell, not Martin nor any other *Life* editor, who believed in the Catholic conspiracy and imprinted his belief on the magazine. *Life*'s most trenchant anti-Semitism is discussed in the chapter on drama.

Life was never anti-Negro as it was anti-Irish and anti-Jew, but the reason seems to be that the Negro never seemed to *Life* a threat to the proper direction of society by those best designed to direct it, as did the Irishman, whose enormous numbers had been turned to political capital by the unscrupulous, or the Jew, whose urban and mercantile heritage gave him an advantage not enjoyed by other immigrants to New York. The New York Negroes were more thoroughly ghetto-ized than either of the other minority groups that *Life* noticed, and they were correspondingly less important.   Certainly *Life* subscribed to the idea, vaguely founded on an imperfect apprehension of Darwin but made respectable by Thomas Huxley, among others, that the Negro was a lower order of humanity than the Caucasian.   "The Civil War," wrote Martin in 1912, "was fought under the impression [in the North] that the Negro was a black white-man. He isn't."[5] That settled it. Earlier Martin had noted with many misgivings the appointment of the first Negro to Annapolis. It was unwise, he felt, to suggest by this precedent a non-existent equality of the races. *Life* found Negroes, like women, mentally inferior. The quote above is from a paragraph attacking the suffragettes.

Furthermore, *Life* believed in the efficacy of lynching. It did not see lynch law as a specifically anti-Negro weapon but as a weapon of decent people against the laggard and alien-corrupted courts. It had the Tammany courts of New York before it, and it thought it knew whereof it spoke. When a man who abused a horse was pulled from his truck by a crowd and severely beaten, Martin applauded the crowd and called for more. When someone published the fact that the number of lynchings in America had declined to fifty-two in 1913, Martin suspected that Americans were suffering from "diminished virility."

Martin's concern for America's virility and *Life*'s despair at the law's restraint of the "decent" element were part and parcel of a widespread American reaction against immigration in the late nineteenth and early twentieth centuries. *Life* confined its attention to the "old immigration" —Irish, German, Chinese—and took little notice of the "new immigration" of Eastern and Southern Europeans, which really did not begin until after *Life*'s convictions had solidified. The magazine could justify its claims of "Americanism." Mitchell's New England genealogy and Harvard education were rivalled by those of most of *Life*'s staff. It was fashionable in those times to argue the superiority of nations and "races" on a pseudo-Darwinist basis, and in the class to which *Life*'s editors belonged it was fashionable to maintain that social superiority was "racially" innate. The ideas did not originate from ignorant and uneducated men; rather the opposite. In 1916, Madison Grant, who was a descendant of an old American family, a trustee of the American Museum of Natural History, an officer of the American Geographical Society, and the Chairman of the New York Zoological Society, brought to bear an encyclopedic knowledge of European prehistory in *The Passing of the Great Race*. In that book he "proved" the inevitable natural ascendancy of Anglo-Saxon Aryans and the degeneration attendant upon "racial" interbreeding. His conclusion as to American social theory was exactly what *Life* had preached for years to other properly descended, educated Americans. And if such unimpeachable scientific testimony was not enough, *Life* had its own good common sense to distinguish the sober, productive, desirable citizens from those less favored by Nature.

Life's anti-immigrant leanings were among its most consistent opinions. Early in its career, before the real waves of immigration struck New York City, *Life* deplored the Dingley tariff that in effect barred works of art while no similar restraint was imposed on immigrants. This was mainly in 1888, and in the same year it published a cartoon by Gibson which showed the recently erected statue of Liberty stalking away from Bedloe's island, muttering about the "quality of citizens the country is importing." Later it dwelt on the rigorous customs inspection that "genuine Americans" had to undergo when returning from foreign visits, and contrasted it to the facility with which the immigrant was allowed to enter, whatever his state of physical or moral degeneracy. This is further evidence of *Life*'s insistence on the "inherent" privileges of its favorite class of citizens. Perhaps it is creditable to *Life* that it was willing, if only for the sake of argument, to extend its anti-immigrant ideas even as far as defending the American Indians, and in a more practical context the Hawaiians and Filipinos, against the invasion of their homes and the corruption of their ways by white Americans.

On Manhattan Island, the Jews were *Life*'s most frequent target. Mitchell, in 1889, wrote of the Jews' refusal to be assimilated into American society, pointing out that Baron Hirsch, himself a Jew, believed that "the Jewish Question" could only be solved by the disappearance of the Jewish race. Were the Jews ready for that, he asked? This was the burden of *Life*'s anti-Semitism in its more thoughtful appearance throughout the thirty-five years, although it was Martin, not Mitchell, who was for the most part *Life*'s spokesman against non-assimilation of the Jews—or, if not Martin, James Metcalfe in the Drama column. While *Life* never would have suggested a pogrom, its attitude was pure hatred of the Jews rather than desire for ethnological homogeneity. *Life* wanted no part of homogeneity. It was vehement about the purity of blood of its own class. In the second place, it tried desperately to invent new and more alien alienations to blame on the Jews. It maintained that they were Asiatics, and that while it may be possible for America to assimilate Europeans, she has never and will never assimilate Asiatics. Finally, the unguarded remarks about Jews that appeared from time to time in *Life* are uniformly poisonous. Martin, when it was reported in 1915 that Jews in the Kaiser's army had refused to wear the Iron Cross because it was a Christian emblem, commented that it was *not* a Christian symbol but a prize for efficiency in a particularly nasty war, and while he could see why *Christians* ought to refuse to wear it, he could see no reason for Jews to do so. Metcalfe, on the other hand, while he was sufficiently beset by Jewish villains in his professional capacity and did not need to invent others, contributed a murderous anti-Semitic "Christmas Story" in 1892, four years before the Theater Managers' Syndicate, his epitome of Jewish villainy, existed.6

Even *Life*'s fight with the yellow press was tainted with anti-Semitism at the beginning, although the taint was soon removed. Joseph Pulitzer of the *World*, *Life*'s first target and a pioneer sensational journalist in New York, was an alien and a Jew, and *Life* applied the same strictures to his origin and heritage that it applied to the Irish. In the late nineties, though, William Randolph Hearst moved into New York journalism and almost simultaneously the Theatre Managers' Syndicate was formed by the Frohmans, Klaw & Erlanger, and Alfred Hayman. Hearst and the Syndicate supplied *Life* with a more offensive newspaperman and a more aggressively threatening Jewish conspiracy, and Pulitzer was let off.

The responsibilities of the press, to *Life*'s mind, were stern and unyielding and not to be trifled with. One of *Life*'s earliest critical cartoons attacked the *Irish World*, a Dublin paper which had set up a "skirmishing fund" from which were to come rewards for the assassins of English "tyrants." The drawing showed the ragged, bloody-handed assassin being hustled to the gallows by the redcoats, while in their comfortable offices the dapper editors toast their success above a piled table. *Life* scrupulously avoided any pleas for action against even its most bitter enemies unless it was prepared to answer for the consequences of such pleas. It made exception only for those who were, as the Kaiser's armies were in 1917, enemies of the readership at large.

This particular journalistic scruple might account in part for the breadth and duration of *Life*'s popularity. *Life* never gave offense, other than to those distinctly in the minority. It also accounts, though, for a pervasive lack of salt in *Life*'s humor. By *Life*'s definition the great responsibility of the public press to disseminate ideas would be nullified. Indeed, in *Life*'s case, it was. On the other hand the virtues of the idea are obvious. Although *Life* was not a source of public ideas, neither was it inflammatory. While it resisted thought, it also resisted the less appealing prospects concomitant with change. Its best method of avoiding irresponsibility was to hide from responsibility, but it was a method that seldom began anything it could not finish.

In the light of such a principle, New York journalism seemed to *Life* the soul of irresponsibility. *Life* had no very high opinion of any New York paper, although its Worst Newspaper Contest in 1903 was won by a Boston paper, the *Herald*. It considered Whitelaw Reid's *Tribune* a mere political pamphlet. Charles Dana's *Sun* was never quite pigeonholed by

Life, and after Dana's death it passed through so many owners' hands that it hardly paused to develop a personality, but *Life* thought of it generally as cocksure and opposed to good English. *Life* once called Dana a "pavid and pennigerous philanthropist" to go with its appellation of Pulitzer as a "morigerous and moliminous Magyar." Edwin Godkin's *Post* it largely ignored, although it once called the *Post* the "greatest corrupter of literary style in all the land." James Gordon Bennett and his *Herald* produced so much for *Life* to make fun of, with their interminable expeditions and projects, that perhaps the magazine thought it owed them a debt of gratitude.7 Bennett received kinder treatment from *Life* than his flamboyance or the moral tone of his paper would seem to have deserved. He was lumped with Hearst and Pulitzer only once, when *Life* wanted to give all three to Spain along with Mark Hanna, William McKinley, and the Congress. The New York *Times* was in relative eclipse during this period, and *Life* noticed it only when its panting after the Four Hundred became unbearable. *Life* believed that it was nobody's business whether Mrs. John Jacob Astor wore a grey gown shopping or went naked. In all, *Life*'s good opinions of its daily contemporaries were scarce indeed.

But Pulitzer, and after him Hearst, were deep-dyed villains in *Life*'s eyes. It took great pleasure in reporting their troubles. It noted their triumphs only grudgingly. And at least once it led a genuine crusade against them, a crusade that at once proved *Life*'s courage in its convictions and its hopeless enchainment to the receding century.

In March of 1897 *Life* was elevated by sheer accident to the head of a movement to ban the *World* and Hearst's *Journal* from libraries, clubs, and public institutions. It began when the Newark Library removed both papers from its reading rooms. The Century Club of New York, of which Mitchell and Martin were members, heard about the ban and dropped its subscriptions to the papers. Martin reported it in his editorial in the March 18 issue of *Life*, with a few satisfied remarks about how richly the ban was deserved and how nice it would be if all respectable institutions followed suit. The idea caught on and *Life*, which had been only an interested spectator, assumed first the job of publicizing the swelling list of libraries and clubs that either dropped the papers entirely or removed them from their public rooms, and then finally the nominal leadership of the movement. A cartoon by F. W. Richards to which *Life* gave two pages at the height of the campaign shows a clenched-fisted Minerva punting Pulitzer and Hearst all a-tumble down the steps of a vaguely Greek building that might be a club or a library, but displays *Life*'s little winged boy carved over its door. By April *Life* was able to list seventy-four public reading rooms that had banned both papers.

There was no climax to the story. Little by little, the various institutions allowed the *Journal* and the *World* public display once more. *Life* stopped publicizing the affair in late April; there might have been some pressure brought to bear on the editors although there was no legal action. The reason was more likely a lagging public interest. *Life*, despite its lofty ideas, was as much a mass-circulation paper as was Hearst's or Pulitzer's. But though there was no climax, there is a sort of moral. *Life*'s conduct of the entire proceeding was altogether snobbish. It sought to form a league of the best people against the calculated vulgarity of the yellow press. It identified itself with libraries and clubs, with the goddess of classical wisdom and with Victorian architecture, all of which still go together. And it believed, at least for a time, that its efforts made a real difference. It did not see that the yellow journals did not care a rap for the best people, or that seventy-four unsold copies, no matter to whom they were unsold, meant nothing at all to their publishers. *Life*'s great literary hero was Thackeray, and it conceived itself as Thackeray's Captain Shandon conceived the *Pall Mall Gazette*, a magazine written by gentlemen, for gentlemen. Gentlemen were to be found in libraries and clubs, not in saloons and union halls. If libraries and clubs were against a publication, then that publication was doomed, or so the logic went.

Immediately after the club-library war, Hearst replaced Pulitzer as *Life*'s arch-villain of the irresponsible press. In 1898, Hearst began a campaign to raise a fund for a memorial to the dead of the *Maine*. Various public figures contributed, and the project seemed to be coming along nicely, but it found a stout opponent in Grover Cleveland, who was still *Life*'s favorite politician. Cleveland answered Hearst's demands with a flat refusal "to allow my sorrow . . . to be perverted to an advertising scheme for the *New York Journal*." *Life* cheered Cleveland for standing firm against blackmail, and possibly the publicity *Life* gave to Cleveland's refusal helped defeat the scheme. Hearst, of course, got nearly as much advertising out of defeat as he would have out of victory. In the summer of 1899 *The Chap Book* ran an article on the *Journal* and the *World*, from which *Life* quoted extensively with the comment that the *Journal* had now surpassed the older paper in infamy. When the terms of Pulitzer's legacy to Columbia University were made public in 1905, *Life* commended the publisher for his good judgment in holding back his gift until his death. The magazine pointed out that Pulitzer, unlike some other "philanthropists," was willing to forego the pleasure of hovering over his heirs and interfering with their disposition of the legacy. Later, the editorial page of the *World* received greater and greater approbation from *Life*, while the *Journal* continued in disgrace. In 1908 *Life* printed a set of jingles signed "G. M. F." that professed to be character sketches of New York papers. That for the *World* combined compliment with censure:

> A dual personality is this,
> Part yellow dog, part patriot and sage;
> When 't comes to fact the rule is hit or miss,

> While none can beat its editorial page.
> Wise counsel here, wild yarns the other side,
> Page six its Jekyll and page one its Hyde,
> At the same time conservative and rash
> The *World* supplies us good advice and trash.

That for the *Journal* omitted the compliment:

> The common people's champion every time,
> (This, understand, is what it calls itself),
> Its stock in trade calamity and crime—
> Fire, famine, murder, piracy and pelf;
> It may be true its news is never late,
> 'Tis likewise true it's almost never straight;
> Of all false freakish chronicles diurnal
> In twisting truth none can approach the *Journal*.[8]

Life's most famous jab at Hearst, the cartoon by Oliver Herford which metamorphosed the publisher into a prowling black spider with a facial expression that might stand as the very picture of guile feigning innocence, appeared in 1922 and does not properly belong in this history. It indicates, however, that in spite of the editorial transformations which the magazine went through after Mitchell's death, *Life*'s subsequent editors agreed with the founder on the importance and the malevolence of Mr. Hearst.

Life treated itself to an occasional tilt with publications other than the New York papers, too, but nearly always for amusement's sake rather than in any hope of changing the opponent's errant ways. For example, when *McClure*'s muckrakers were riding high in 1906 *Life* grew almost disturbed enough over what it believed to be yellow journalism's aspiration to the dignity of magazines that it showed signs of wanting to begin a new fight, but the signs subsided. In the long run, New York was *Life*'s bailiwick, and if those beyond the borders permitted atrocities against responsible journalism, *Life* washed its hands of them.

Yellow papers and aliens were *Life*'s great enemies in its home city, but it was just as bitterly opposed, on a grander scale, to another group—the doctors of allopathic medicine. *Life*'s scorn for those who allowed themselves to be taken in by the germ theory was magnificent. Its gory tales of the barbarity of vivisectionists and the horrid sufferings of the victims of vaccination or "shots" were enough to make one flee to the jungles where his death would be natural and realtively painless. Hearst, who made more capital out of anti-vivisection than any other drumbeater, undoubtedly took the idea from *Life*. Hearst's argument was that vivisection was too often fruitless and always painful. *Life*'s was that germs did not exist, that vivisectionists cut up dogs because they liked to, and that to give a man a disease to prevent him from getting that disease was an idea so patently lunatic as to deserve no further notice.

Life's anti-allopath campaign, particularly that part which had to do with vivisection, was definitely Mitchell's idea, but it was not until the middle nineties that *Life* took up the cudgel. Mitchell was by then nearly fifty, and one would suppose him unlikely to crusade over a brand-new idea or even, for that matter, to take up an old one with renewed vigor. But again, the irrepressible exuberance that led him to found *Life* came to his aid, as it was to continue to come until the end of his life. *Life* appears in outline to have been a mossbacked sort of paper when public matters were concerned. Privately, it was not. Fat and prosperous though it may have grown, it was always adventurous. Frightening as "the future" appeared to it, as an abstract idea, *Life* nevertheless retained its trust in its private future, its capability to close its eyes and jump. Mitchell was the source of that capability. If it struck Mitchell all of a sudden that a battle needed fighting, the chances were that a battle would begin.

Life's ideas about medicine had always been fatalistic. As contributors or celebrities died, *Life* reported matter-of-factly on the diseases that killed them, and never did it suggest that their lives might have been prolonged or saved by more knowing medication. It believed that a doctor's function was to make disease less agonizing and death less fearful. It believed that cures were effected by letting a disease run its course. Some patients recovered, some did not. By the same token, *Life* made no little profit from the patent medicine ads that it ran, regardless of the effect of the medicine on the purchaser. Whiskey was advertised as medicinal far more specifically than even toothpaste is today. *Life* advertised such nostrums as Dr. Pierce's Golden Medical Discovery, "as peculiar in its curative effects as in its composition,"—which were also good for Dyspepsia, Constipation, Malaria, Neuralgia, Failing Sight, Hay-Fever and Low Spirits. Medically one good purge seemed to *Life* as good as another, and the rest was in the hands of God. It suggested satirically such possibilities as vaccination against being struck by lightning.[9] It could not believe that medicine had power over circumstance.

From these premises it is easy to conclude that a surgeon who causes pain with the questionable excuse of curing something worse, or an allopathic doctor who pretends to kill little creatures which anybody can see are not there, are charlatans. The schools which advocate hot baths or having one's spine cudgeled seem more natural and correct to any man of sense, and *Life*'s good sense was as much a matter of pride as its probity and charity.

Life struck occasionally at vivisection in particular, along with cruelty to animals in general, throughout the late eighties and early nineties. Its real anti-vivisector campaign began about 1895, though, and its accusations eventually became so excited that in a very few years it was reprinting extensively from anti-vivisection magazines and pamphlets without checking either the source or the truth of the statements. For example, in 1896, it printed a long letter from a physician who defended vivisection on the usual grounds of scientific investigation, the greater claims of human suffering over animals, and no needless pain. Then, rather than make any attempt at rebuttal, it simply called him a liar and let it go at that. *Life* believed that "medical science" was nonsense, that all pain was needless, and that anyone who would rather see animals suffer than people did not understand either animals or people. The latter conclusion is attested to by dozens of cartoons and jokes about the fidelity of dogs and the perfidy of human beings.

Life's anti-vivisection sentiments appeared to swell during war time and ebb in peace, which suggests a link between the magazine's general state of nerves and its urge to protect the helpless. As the Spanish-American War came on, the anti-vivisection campaign grew in size and force. After 1898, it subsided to intermittent sniping until about 1914, when it found new impetus. As the war fever grew, *Life* urged Americans ever more loudly to bayonet the Huns and save the hounds. Possibly this was a result of the necessity for experimental surgery in wartime and the attendant publicity. Possibly, though, it was the result of something more deep-seated in the consciousness of the editors and thereby of the magazine, a vague fear that all threats are physical and that political and military defeat would mean, quite literally, pain for the unoffending, loyal, lovable, petted beings, like *Life*, who were being unjustly victimized by overwhelming circumstance.

The ferocity of the vivisectors as described in *Life* was beyond measure. In 1916, the magazine heard a rumor that experiments in vivisection were being carried on among the patients at the Michigan State Asylum in Pontiac. It insisted that this was only an instance of poor security measures, that the frightful conspiracy habitually performed its violence on helpless, insane patients, not to mention the senile, the indigent, or the merely unlucky. In 1897, it reprinted the testimony of an Elliot Preston, who maintained seriously that vivisection made atheists.

> Vivisection is the blackest crime that the law of any land ever let go unpunished.
> The agony it inflicts upon helpless animals is so appalling that the mere knowledge of its atrocity has darkened, forever, with its hideous, leprous shadow, the sunshine in many a generous and noble heart. It has destroyed, in many a breast, the belief in the existence of a just and loving God.[10]

Life gave this its resounding approval, and added some comments of its own about "sport for medical students." It is easy enough to see how medicine and atheism might become connected in *Life*'s mind, since it saw both dosing and dismemberment as clear contravention of God's will;

but the jump to "sport" significantly suggests *Life*'s inability to see its opponents as anything but the most degenerate villains.

One of its chief villains was Dr. George W. Crile, and its treatment of Crile was typical of its eagerness to believe the worst on the flimsiest evidence. After the Spanish-American War, Crile published *An Experimental Research Into Surgical Shock*, and "from accounts received" (no staff member, apparently, had troubled himself to read it) *Life* commented:

> G. W. Crile, M. D., had fun; there is no doubt about that. And what fun he must have had when a boy! He could have great fun with a horse when nobody was looking. And many dogs and cats must have come his way. How lucky for a boy with those instincts that he studied medicine instead of architecture, or law, or divinity; otherwise he could not have mutilated live animals during a summer afternoon without some protest from his neighbors.[11]

In the next war, Crile, who had gained prominence since the beginning of the century, wrote that at the front he had had to revise his ideas and discard many of his preconceptions about surgery. *Life* was enormously amused at this bit of scientific honesty. It proved that Crile had been indulging his secret passions all along, and that he knew nothing and was unlikely to learn anything. It is doubtless to *Life*'s credit that it scorned to go after small fry in its war on vivisection and its related vices, but its attacks on Crile in America, and the likes of Koch and Pasteur in Europe,[12] seem at fifty years' remove among the least defensible of all its foibles. The sanest anti-vivisection comment that appeared was a letter by Mark Twain to the London Anti-Vivisection Society which *Life* reprinted in 1900. Twain's ideas were the ordinary ones. He could see no good to come of knowledge gained by the torment of dumb animals. But his expression was his own, and beyond *Life*'s capabilities. "I could not even see a vivisector vivisected," he wrote, "with anything more than a sort of qualified satisfaction."[13]

Life made less bitter forays against inoculation, quarantine, and all sorts of preventive medicine, particularly when a public health agency was involved. It felt that a grown man who willingly let himself be shot full of horse-serum could take the consequences, but that something should be done to protect the children. Furthermore, it simply did not believe in public health. When, in 1897, the New York City Board of Health decided that there was sufficient evidence of the communicability of tuberculosis to warrant quarantining the city's known cases, *Life* protested via one of Martin's editorials that there were worse things than consumption, and restriction was one of them. When in 1915 the Board of Health outlawed the sale of unpasteurized milk in New York, *Life* protested again. When the army draftees of World War I were subjected to compulsory vaccination, some despite their religious objections or, worse yet from *Life*'s point of view, those of their mothers, a number became seriously ill and even died from the reactions. *Life* roasted the army, the president, and anyone who came within range. When in 1917 it was suggested that schoolchildren undergo regular medical inspection, *Life* enumerated the evils to follow: it would bring on compulsory medicine, it would foster graft, it would encourage the ever-lurking surgeons to perform injurious operations on unsuspecting children, it would interfere with parental and family rights, it would utilize schools for purposes for which schools were never intended, it would be a step toward universal inspection, and if it found anything wrong with a child, its diagnosis would very likely be faulty. The whole thing struck *Life* as a vicious plot against the freedom traditionally enjoyed by Americans. Besides, had not *Life* printed statements from some of the doctors themselves to the effect that "Consumption follows vaccination as effect follows cause;" and "I have seen hundreds of children killed by vaccination;" that vaccination causes cancer and kills mules? Hadn't *Life* pointed out that only the propaganda of the evil doctors was keeping the germ theory alive? Regimentation of American life was terrible enough, to *Life*. Regimentation by lying child-and-mule-murderers was a crime beyond imagining.

One last note on vivisection. Writing of *Dr. Jekyll and Mr. Hyde* in 1887, Bridges suggested that Dr. Jekyll would have been much better off if he had "tried it on a dog."[14] The aptness of the phrase is striking, but one wonders. Stevenson was one of *Life*'s favorites. Would *Life* have thought as well of him if he had, indeed, allowed Jekyll to try it on a dog?

Life's involvement with anti-vivisection had one effect, at least, that was undeniably good. For several years it publicly and vociferously deplored the administrative laxity of the New York Society for the Prevention of Cruelty to Animals, and in 1906 it joined and cheered on the SPCA membership in a successful effort to oust the Society's president, John P. Haines. Haines resigned, and subsequent allusions by *Life* to the SPCA were considerably more friendly than they had been in the past.

Life's extreme class-consciousness, which led it to malign the alien and see the rich and the poor alike as amusing but not to be taken seriously, assumed an unusual impartiality when its own class interests were not at stake. The labor movement, and its allied undercurrents of Socialism and Anarchism, which one might think would cause a magazine conservative by habit and insecure by nature to over react, struck *Life* as a struggle between the robber-barons and the underprivileged; and while its sympathies, whenever engaged, sided with capital, it could see both reason and justice in the other camp. Never, even as a joke, suggesting the total abolition of labor or wages, it occasionally doubted that sort of profit that the more rapacious capitalists extracted from their enterprises. When after the disastrous fire of March, 1911, that killed one hundred and forty-seven workers, the owners of the Triangle Shirtwaist Company were acquitted of responsibility by the courts, *Life* wrote with unusual sarcasm that the industry could not make a profit without sweat-shops, and where there were sweat-shops there would be occasional fires, and where there were fires there would doubtless be a few children burned up. What, it asked, did the critics have against profit? The Triangle owners were, however, Jews, and Jewish profit always to *Life* seemed the worst kind.

Violence upset *Life*, and it had no use for Anarchists who, besides being violent, were aliens. It disapproved of strikers who tried to protect their jobs with force. It suspected that organization was not the right answer to labor's problems. It railed against speakers for labor, although it did not attack them personally. But, it championed the underdog, and when labor seemed to be victimized did not hesitate to take its part. It abominated child labor, taking every opportunity to scourge both the states that allowed it and their Congressional representatives. It considered trusts and the protective tariff as un-American as Anarchists. Here, too, its instinctive impulse to attack men rather than facts is evident. The names Morgan, Carnegie, Rockefeller, and Sage appear repeatedly in *Life* nearly always with satiric intent. Jay Gould's obituary is a case in point. *Life* almost never spoke ill of the dead. Some public figures it least admired, among them President McKinley and Charles Frohman the theatrical entrepreneur, were given their first good notices in *Life* at their deaths. But for Gould, *Life* made an exception. Martin wrote that Gould was a "public enemy, worthy only of public condemnation, whether alive or dead."[15]

Life's earliest notice of labor unrest came with the Chicago Haymarket bombing of 1886 and the ensuing legal complications. This historic trial hinged on a question of law about which *Life*'s mind was long since made up: Can men who advocate a criminal act, later committed by persons unknown, be held responsible for that act? *Life* believed that they could and should. How this applied to its own approval of lynching, it never explained. Seven Chicago anarchists who had been connected with the *Alarm*, a paper that urged in print that the anti-labor police should be dynamited out of existence, were sentenced to hang after a dynamite bomb exploded into a squad of marching policemen in Haymarket Square at a labor rally, killing seven. Governor Oglesby of Illinois later commuted two of the sentences to life imprisonment. *Life* was thoroughly pleased by the verdicts, which seemed a blow for Americanism. Five of the sentenced anarchists were German-born, and some spoke no English. That the justice of hanging one man for another man's crime is suspect did not bother *Life*. The fewer anarchists in the world, the better. Hanged they were on November 11, 1897.[16]

The most notorious labor disturbances of the nineties were the Pullman strike in Chicago and the steel strike at Homestead, Pennsylvania.

Life had little to say about the former. However, it handled the Homestead riots quite differently. The management of the Carnegie Steel Company, beset by a stubborn strike in the summer of 1892, had hired two boatloads of armed Pinkerton strikebreakers from Pittsburgh. As the Pinkertons came up the Monongahela, the strikers met them with flaming oil, cannon-fire, dynamite, and whatever firearms they could muster, and a regular pitched battle ensued, in which fourteen were killed or wounded. Public opinion turned against the company. But a few days later, a heavily armed man named Alexander Berkman, who had no known connection with the strike or the union, entered the Pittsburgh office of Henry Clay Frick, the company president, and shot him with a pistol twice at close range, wounding him seriously. Frick, a rock-hard industrial baron who in another day might have looked Francis Drake in the eye, got out of his chair, wrestled away Berkman's gun, called for a doctor, and went on working.17 The murderous attack on Frick outraged the press all over the country. The war on the town by the Pinkertons was obscured.

Life, however, did not forget it. It deplored the lawlessness of the strikers and the attempt to kill Frick. But the Homesteaders were Americans, not aliens. It was perfectly apparent to *Life* that an alien anarchist was ripe for hanging, while an American striker could only be misled. It saw the strikers' side, at least enough to call for a "better way to deal with riotous strikers" than turning the dregs of neighboring towns into "special officers" to shoot at them. It suggested the regular army or the militia, a proposal which from the strikers' point of view was hardly charitable, but which at least would have taken away from management the privilege of raising a private army. *Life* placed the blame for the whole incident squarely on the strike leaders. "The truest friend to whatever is valuable in the organization of labor," Martin wrote, "is the man who stamps most effectually upon its lawlessness and tyranny (of the labor leaders)."18

This was no new idea to *Life*. Nearly two years before it had protested that the labor leaders were America's new kings. In 1916 there were strikes against food processors, which threatened to cause a food shortage. *Life* ran a cartoon which pictured strikers, a "strike-promoter," and the food trusts sitting with their feet up on a table groaning with beautiful food, while a wee, shrunken waiter labeled "Public" crept humbly up to serve them. The inclusion of the Trusts in the 1916 cartoon shows that they were in *Life*'s bad graces, but this meant no change of opinion. Magnates were no more members of *Life*'s favored class than were union bosses. Between 1890 and 1916 the magazine stuck to its idea that no matter how just labor's complaint might be, the strike was an evil weapon and the labor boss an evil influence.

Capital took its share of *Life*'s anger, too. In 1908, a commentator on Jack London wrote in Life:

> Possibly Mr. London feels that because fire and sword have been used in the
> past by Christians to show their devotion to God, that [sic] these two relics
> may still be used by socialists to show their devotion to their fellow men. This
> does not seem unreasonable.[19]

The trusts were in full flower, and *Life* found capital-gone-bad far more formidable than labor at its most riotous. Violent overthrow of the great corporations actually seemed to *Life* a conceivable, if regrettable, way to restore the American Way. Possibly the most telling remarks by *Life* about a leftist were its comments on the parents of Emma Goldman. The Goldmans had told an interviewer that their daughter's radical notions did not come from them, that they were only "business people." There, *Life* pointed out triumphantly, was the rub. Parents who are business people *and nothing else* had better expect their children to be corrupted. Gentility, not commerce, was *Life*'s ideal. A communist was a person who saw only the bad side of business, and who was more likely to see it than the children of purblind business people? *Life* identified communism with socialism. Its sympathies with the socialists were more unconscious than conscious, and only the nefarious activities of the trusts brought them to the surface, from where they subsided again as soon as *Life* found its own interests involved; but *Life*'s vision of a perfect America was far nearer to that of a socialist than to that of most business people. *Life*'s nostalgia for the dear old farm, its generous impulses toward the helpless, its exaltation of leisure, all sound more nearly socialistic than commercial.

Once *Life* got its signals crossed on labor vs. capital. A poem by S. E. Kiser, presumably passed on by Masson, appeared in the April 11, 1918, issue. The poem suggested rather peevishly that organized labor and the rich could do what they pleased about the war effort, but the plain citizen had to give up his life if he was asked to. Ill-natured humor was standard *Life* fare by 1918, and the poem was unremarkable for anything else. But a few weeks afterward, Martin editorialized at length on a poem that had appeared "in a national magazine" and had libeled the rich. He did not mention that labor had been included in the libel, although the poem is too evidently the same one. Mitchell, at this time, was ill, and was soon to suffer his fatal stroke. With the captain disabled, the officers were beginning to quarrel among themselves.

By far the brightest chapter in *Life*'s history is the story of the charities it sponsored, most notably *Life*'s Farm, the most important functioning organ of *Life*'s Fresh Air Fund, the *Life*-sponsored, reader-supported annual drive to send New York slum children to the country each summer.

Life's main contributions to the fund were its prestige and its circulation. It reached thousands more potential contributors than a publicly operated charity could have reached, at no cost to the charity. It began simply by asking for contributions which would be passed along to the proper persons, but the response soon became so great, and *Life*'s own enthusiasm so high, that it took over the entire operation and administered the fund, besides collecting it, free of charge.

On the eleventh of August, 1887, *Life* printed its first request for Fresh Air Fund contributions. It called the fund "that most noble and practical charity." It suggested that contributions be in the sum of three dollars or more, since three dollars would pay for two weeks' country board for one child. It made it clear, however, that it was grateful for all contributions, however small.

Within six weeks, readers had contributed $800. The season was by then all but over, and the appeals stopped, but the next year *Life* threw itself into the Fund collections. Writing in 1908, Mitchell insisted that 1887 was the year in which Rev. Willard Parsons suggested *Life*'s Farm to him, but the 1887 collection campaign had been entirely impersonal.[20] This year it was *Our* Fresh Air Fund, and the implication is that the month's response of the previous summer had suggested to *Life* that there were advantages in changing from a mere agency to a self-operating charity. The 1888 campaign was kicked off with the announcement that "more than 320" children had been helped the year before, which suggests that well over $900 was collected before that campaign closed. *Life* began to illustrate its weekly pleas with a malnourished, grimy waif titled "Before" and a chubby, healthy child labeled "After."

During the first week of July, *Life* ran a full page cartoon by Gibson: "Our cartoon this week tells an unvarnished tale," he wrote. "Its object is to assist our readers in realizing the good their subscriptions are doing." On the left (Before), two slum children stand vacantly in a gutter, pencil-thin, staring at nothing. A mournful, scrawny cat accompanies them. In the background, a policeman leads away a drunken trollop. But on the right (After), the same two children and the cat, swelled up to pillowlike contours, pursue a butterfly through breezy meadows while a farmhand in the background sharpens a scythe under the eye of a pert milkmaid. This is not exactly unvarnished, but *Life* never ceased to boast of the pounds gained by children at the Farm, and it printed letters and photographs, later on, to demonstrate that Before and After were true pictures. The Farm's menu offered, among other things, all the fresh milk the children could drink. Many of them had to have milk explained to them before they would drink it.

In 1888, the first full season of the *Life* Fund, the collections amounted to $6,042.83. In 1889, *Life* announced that it now needed $4.00 contribution per child per two weeks. Then in July of 1889, *Life* had a windfall, acquiring a "deserted village" an hour and a half from New York with nine acres of land with seventeen slate-roof cottages.

Life quickly took advantage of the acquisition. Within two weeks after the lease was announced, it had ten of the cottages renovated and filled with children, seven or eight per cottage, with a matron. *Life* told its readers happily that the cottages would hold ten or eleven children, later on, with no crowding. Within a month, the village was filled. *Life*, as it had done for two years, sent the overflow to its regular cooperating farms.

The magazine had a splendid time that summer with its new toy. Never again, not even when they moved from this little village to a larger and better situated farm in Connecticut, was *Life* so excited about its pet charity, so full of news about its "little guests" and what was being done for them. Every time a new baseball turned up at the farm, *Life* reported it as excitedly as though it were a carload. Besides money, readers sent dolls, sandpails, baskets of fruit, croquet sets, candy, wagons, and more toys, to hear *Life* tell it, than ten times 170 children could use at once.

The village at Eatontown remained *Life*'s pride and joy for just two years. In 1891 *Life* obtained from Mr. Edwin Gilbert a two-year lease at Branchville, Connecticut, on "Fourteen acres with a large barn and out-buildings, all in excellent repair." The new Farm had an orchard, a running brook, and room for two hundred children.[21] Branchville remained *Life*'s Farm until 1934.[22]

Every summer the call for support went out, and every summer pictures of appealing urchins swimming, eating, sleeping, or playing games appeared regularly in *Life* so that contributors could see how much fun their money was buying. Contributions ran between five and six thousand dollars annually, and the Farm entertained each year from 1000 to 1200 children while *Life* sent another thousand to private farms. In 1912 the magazine reported that it had collected $133,340.25 and provided country vacations for 33,737 children in the twenty-five years since the Fund's beginning. The children, naturally, loved it. Two boys walked from New York to the Farm in 1907, fifty-four miles in two days, so that they could enjoy an outing there. In 1914 the Farm's director, the Rev. U. O. Mohr, asked publicly that Farm "alumni" try to understand why their children were sometimes turned away—there just was not room for everybody.

In 1917 *Life* began to rally public support for a legal battle which had dragged on for more than a year. Mr. Edwin Gilbert, of Reading, Connecticut, the owner of the Gilbert & Bennett Mfg. Co., and the original donor of the farm, had died in 1906, and had willed a trust fund with the stipulation that after his wife's death all income and dividends from 300 shares of Gilbert & Bennett Mfg. Co. stock be "used for the maintenance of the work carried on at *Life*'s Farm." Mrs. Gilbert had died in 1910, but the three trustees of this fund who were known as the Branchville Fresh Air Association and whose names and addresses *Life* supplied, refused to release any of the money entrusted to them for the Farm. *Life* maintained that the accumulated fund by 1917 amounted to rather more than $10,000, but complained that under the existing laws of Connecticut, there was no way to force the trustees to give up the money.

Mitchell himself was a trustee of the fund, and the men named were his personal friends and neighbors at Ridgefield, Connecticut, adjacent to Branchville, where Mitchell owned an estate and spent his summers. The other trustees were slow to part with the accumulated money, but they were by no means unwilling to do so, for in 1925 they gave *Life* $15,000 for specific building improvements.[23] It was just that they believed that *they*, not *Life*, had been entrusted with the money, and that they had neither a legal nor a moral right to allow *Life* to dictate to them its disposition. The courts agreed with them when the case was brought to trial. Mitchell's unnecessarily bitter quarrel here with his friends, like his war hysteria, shows that his temper grew quarrelsome toward the end of his life.

In 1919, *Life* announced that two hundred dollars worth of Liberty Loan bonds or Victory notes would be accepted from any contributor as a Fresh Air Fund endowment, which would pay for one child every year in perpetuity. The editors and employees contributed one such endowment in the name of John Ames Mitchell while the artists contributed five. The money was still in art. The Farm had been Mitchell's pet, but the new editors carried it on until the magazine could support it no longer. It closed in 1934, to be re-opened four years later under the auspices of the New York *Herald-Tribune*, which functioned as *Life* had functioned, sending children to the Farm and paying for insurance and upkeep.[24]

A sort of corollary to the Fresh Air Fund began in 1916 and ended three years later, having collected more than $350,000, well over the entire collections for thirty-three years of the Farm Fund—a drive to collect support money for French war orphans. The War Orphans' Fund was another idea of Mitchell's, and a natural one, because he had spent years in France and had an enormous affection for the country. *Life* campaigned for this fund more intensely than it had (except in the first years of the Farm) for the Fresh Air Fund, printing photos of the orphans who were to be the beneficiaries of the readers' charity and their letters of thanks in *a la carte* English. The readers responded generously.

Before concluding, this survey of *Life*'s history must include a handful of names which refuse to fall into any particular category but which were prominent butts for *Life*'s shafts during Mitchell's years as editor. *Life*'s fascination with personality at the expense of fact often led it to express a violent dislike for some public figure without reference to the realities of that person's career. Also, since *Life* was unlikely to change its opinions except in the greatest extremity, it sometimes turned viciously, after such a change, on its former heroes who had not recognized the extremity that converted *Life*. The best examples of this are the cases of

Henry Ford and Robert LaFollette. Early in 1915, *Life* was strongly isolationist, and Martin spoke in an editorial of Ford as a fine example of what one deserving man could make of himself in America. In 1912 it had defended LaFollette as a good and able man. But Ford and LaFollette remained pacifists after *Life* had turned into the most bloodthirsty of belligerents. By 1916, Ford was *Life*'s living symbol of American dishonor; by 1917, it branded LaFollette a traitor. Three other individuals deserve mention as victims of *Life*'s "persecution," some of it good-natured, but some definitely deserving of the name: John L. Sullivan the prizefighter, Queen Victoria of England, and Josephus Daniels, Woodrow Wilson's secretary of the Navy.

Sullivan appeared prominently in *Life* during the early years. At the time, *Life* in its capacity of champion of New York City was sniping at Boston whenever it ran out of better subjects. It sneered at the older city's intellectual claims, and Sullivan was heaven-sent as an example of Boston mentality whenever Boston became too extravagantly highbrow for *Life*. *Life* was sure that Sullivan's name had only to be mentioned to be amusing. Victoria's case was similar, but somehow more bitter. *Life* used Sullivan, who never claimed to be anything more than a prizefighter, to exemplify the rival center of culture; it used the English Queen, as an expensive adjunct to an outmoded system, to exemplify all of England. As an adherent of republican government, it found the very idea of a queen distasteful. As an opponent of solemnity, it found Victoria's character distasteful. As a representative of middle-class America, it found the Anglomania of the rich distasteful. It typified the Englishman as a penniless snob whose whole concentration was on the main chance, and it considered the Queen the boss snob. It deplored and satirized everything English, from dropped r's to foreign policy, and it managed to connect Victoria to all of them. All this notwithstanding, Martin wrote an eulogy for the Queen's diamond jubilee.

During America's furious preparations for the World War, *Life* looked for somebody to take the blame for everything that was wrong with the Wilson administration. It found him in Daniels, an intelligent and able executive whose probity, at least, *Life* very likely would have admired at an earlier, less hysterical period. Daniels had pushed an anti-alcoholic drive in the navy, and *Life* added blue-nosed prohibitionism to his calendar of sins. He became *Life*'s symbol for a government more interested in nonsensical trivia than in the nation's security, and as such, throughout the months immediately before and after America's entry into the war, he was a weekly target for vituperative squibs and insulting cartoons.

Thus the personality of *Life* and its personal relations with society. It was opinionated, conservative, insecure, naughty, moralistic, honest, vengeful, light-hearted, and charitable, and all at once. It spoke to the genteel middle-class citizen of New York, and by extension to his counterpart in any American city. It admired Harvard—it was a standard office joke that no one who was not a Harvard graduate with a name beginning with M could get a job with *Life*. It detested things it considered to be fads bicycles, automobiles, spirit-rapping, anaesthetics and Prohibition. It believed in culture, as anyone with genteel pretensions should. It mistrusted intellectuals, as all defenders of the middle class must. Its greatest pride was its integrity, then its charity, and after that its self-proclaimed good sense, and only then its sense of humor. And it had the estimable advantage of being run by a man who understood its personality and was able to cope with it.

NOTES

1*Life*, XXXI, 1898, p. 317.

2See Martin's remarks on Lewis, *Life*, LXIII, 1914, p. 176.

3"Police Court Dramas," *Life*, XVII, 1891, pp. 60, 72, 96, 136.

4*Life*, XIX, 1892, p. 315.   5*Life*, LIX, 1912, p. 155.

6*Life*, XX, 1892, Special Christmas Number, pp. 10-16.

7In 1897, Volume XXIX, page 136, *Life* advertised for three young men to join an exploration. This enigmatic ad was never repeated, nor is there any record of any exploration. *Life* might have been having its fun with Bennett or it might have had a momentary notion of competing with him. It might have actually backed some sort of expedition. This is the most troublesome note to *Life*'s history.

8*Life*, LII, 1908, p. 442.   9*Life*, LXVI, 1915, p. 330.

10*Life*, XXIX, 1897, p. 157.   11*Life*, XXXIV, 1899, p. 267.

12*Life*, XIX, 1892, p. 188.   13*Life*, XXXV, 1900, p. 420.

14*Life*, X, 1887, p. 164.   15*Life*, XX, 1892, p. 346.

16Bernard R. Kogan (ed.), *The Chicago Haymarket Riots* (Boston: D. C. Heath & Co., 1959).

17Stewart H. Holbrook, *Dreamers of the American Dream* (Garden City, N. Y.: Doubleday & Co., 1957), pp. 279-288.

18*Life*, XX, 1892, p. 116.

19Probably Mitchell, whose 1906 novel, *The Silent War*, had toyed with the idea of revolution. *Life*, XLVII, 1906, p. 464.

20*Life*, LI, 1908, p. 571.   21*Life*, XVII, 1891, p. 350.

22Personal interview with Mr. Francis D. Martin, Ridgefield, Conn., and Minutes of the Branchville Fresh Air Association.

23Minutes of the Branchville Fresh Air Association.

24Personal interview with Mr. Francis D. Martin. Ridgefield, Connecticut.

JOHN AMES MITCHELL
Founder and Editor of LIFE

CHAPTER III

THE STAFF OF *LIFE*

John Ames Mitchell

John Ames Mitchell was born in New York City on January 17, 1845, son of Asa Mitchell and Harriet Ames Mitchell, the eighth and youngest child of Oliver Ames of North Easton, Massachusetts, the manufacturer of the famous Ames shovels.1   Two of her brothers were Oakes Ames and Oliver Ames, the financiers of the Union Pacific Railroad. Oakes Ames was also the president of the Credit Mobilier, and the scandal which resulted from the exposure of that company's political activities, in 1872, helps to explain John Mitchell's heroic attachment to his mother and his resolute dedication to her comfort. The last decade of her life could not have been happy. Mitchell never publicly claimed relationship with the Ameses of the Union Pacific. Mitchell's attachment to his mother, throughout her lifetime, was heroic. He dropped one career—painting— for her sake, and the decision to do so was one of the more important steps leading to *Life*'s founding.

Mitchell attended school at Phillips Exeter Academy, Exeter, New Hampshire, and went on to Lawrence Scientific School at Harvard. After graduation, he went to Paris to study architecture at the Ecole de Beaux Arts from 1867 to 1870. He returned to practice and study at Boston from 1871 to 1876. He decided then that painting, not architecture, was his real life's work, and he returned to Paris in 1876 to study at the Atelier Julien, where his teacher was Albert Maignan, who had been in his turn a pupil of Noel and Lumminais.2 Mitchell's training, and later on his taste, was uncompromisingly academic. His second homecoming, this time at his mother's wish, was in 1880.3

Young John Mitchell was a talented and promising artist, both as architect and painter-draftsman. An anecdote which its author admitted to be of doubtful authenticity was included in Mitchell's *Harvard Graduate's Magazine* obituary. According to this story, Mitchell, while he was practicing architecture in Boston, submitted a design for a church at Springfield, Massachusetts. Among the other competing architects was Henry Hobson Richardson, later the designer of Trinity Church and one of

America's foremost architects. Mitchell's and Richardson's designs were the final survivors of the competition, and Mitchell seemed to have the edge. But when both men appeared before the church's governing board, Richardson proved to be the superior salesman, and his design was accepted.[4]

At the same period, Mitchell was attached to the Boston office of William Robert Ware, who was to found the school of architecture at Columbia University. But his forté actually was drawing. According to Henry Holt, Ware told a story of Mitchell's uncanny skill at freehand drawing.

> Johnnie came in one morning and went to the blackboard and drew a picture of Napoleon dancing. Then he drew a woman in sabots dancing with one hand in Napoleon's, then a man with a hand in hers, and so on. He continued with figures of queens, soldiers, peasants, and what not, until he had completed a circle of a dozen figures, all beautifully proportioned and in true perspective, and the last woman's hand dropped into Napoleon's other hand as naturally as if they had all been alive. Ware said it was the greatest *tour de force* he ever saw, and Mitchell was only playing with a piece of chalk.[5]

Holt also tells of Mitchell's early successes in painting. He received honorable mention at the Atelier Julien salon, and his etching of the Place de l'Opera "had been selected as a premium by *L'Art*, then the world's leading artistic periodical."[6]

Mitchell's final achievement as an artist seems to have been something of a question even among his well-wishers. None of them had any doubt that he could draw superbly, and many hailed him as one of the great artists of his time. However, all had different favorites among his drawings. Holt admired one called, "A Diplomatic Marriage," calling it a "really remarkable, perhaps really great, picture," with "one of the most majestic figures ever put upon canvas."[7] But "A Diplomatic Marriage" does not appear in the list of Mitchell's "best drawings" that was included in his obituary in the *New York Times*.[8] Perhaps it is as well to follow today's fashion and let Mitchell's reputation as an artist alone. His editorial talents were enough to secure his election to the National Institute of Arts and Letters.

His work as editor of *Life* also made him an art critic of some eminence. He was one of five contributors to a book of artists' impressions of the Columbian Exposition in Chicago. He wrote of the behavior of the spectators, and was pleased at the taste displayed by the public:

> Those galleries containing the finest works are invariably the most crowded. And this is the greatest compliment we can pay ourselves. If, on the other hand, enthusiastic groups collected around the impressionists, and took pleasure in the purple and yellow "effects" that are sprinkled around the French and American sections, there would be cause for anxiety. But such is not the case. That the impressionists still count their warmest admirers among themselves, their wives, sisters and aunts is a hopeful sign. As a people, we take many things less seriously than some of our contemporaries, but in matters of art we

like it with a purpose. Too little clothing still strikes us as frivolous and improper. Blood, violence, and all unpleasantness are sometimes historically instructive, but, as a rule, we are fond of comfortable subjects. We still like a taste of sugar in our art.[9]

Mitchell was consistent, in or out of *Life*. His magazine too was purposeful and decorous, and it tasted of sugar.

Mitchell's pictures show him as a stocky man with a high forehead, a fringe of hair, and steel-rimmed glasses. He wore a bristly mustache and beard, which gave his upper lip the appearance of being unusually long and made his mouth look drawn down at the corners after the manner of one who is waiting for somebody to get the point of a joke. His eyes look sly. His picture is that of a man who has put ginger into your pie and is waiting for you to take a bite.[10]

His personal life seems to have been remarkable only for regularity. In June of 1885 he married Mary Hodges Mott, who survived him by fourteen years.[11] The Mitchells had no children, a circumstance deplored by those who knew Mitchell's capacity for affection where children were concerned. But if he felt a lack in his life, he filled it with his charity toward the children on *Life*'s Farm and the French orphans. His story is that of a man quiet beyond reproach, married for more than thirty years to the same woman, lunching for twenty years in the same chair.

But while Mitchell's private life appears uneventful, his professional personality has been openly attacked. The evidence suggests that the attack is unjust.

In a study of Charles Dana Gibson titled *Portrait of an Era*, Fairfax Downey has published the only relatively recent assessment of John Mitchell's personality and talent. Downey admits that Mitchell was a tactful and gentle rejector of unwanted drawings.[12] Elsewhere he insists that Mitchell's relations with his staff were strained. He calls him "the autocratic Mitchell," and suggests that he sought notoriety through hostility by adding, "They used to say on *Life*, 'We need a good hate.' "[13] He also says that Mitchell's staff called him "The General."[14]

But Downey concentrates on a single, brief period between the outbreak of World War I and Mitchell's death. We have Martin's own testimony that Mitchell reversed *Life*'s policy toward the war when Germany invaded his beloved France.[15] There is no evidence that Mitchell interested himself in military matters up to that time. It would seem likely that the nickname "The General" was irreverently bestowed by staff members on their editor-in-chief because of his sudden attack of militarism. Other accounts of his personality, written both before and after his death, show him as anything but a martinet.

We have Thomas Masson's word that Mitchell could occasionally be out of temper. In 1912 Masson wrote that he had seen Mitchell angry three times. The first was when a printer put three exclamation points instead of one on a caption. The second was when a paragraph written by himself was omitted from the magazine. The third was when Masson asked him if he had read Schopenhauer. Mitchell replied that he supposes he was a fool, but it made him so mad to read a book that was so badly written that he could not see.[16] The three instances show that the mechanical perfection of his magazine, his personal control over it, and rigid standards of clarity and simplicity were all close to Mitchell's heart. Children and dogs made him emotional, and so did *Life* and style.

But however jealous he may have been of his personal stake in *Life* he proudly denied any interference with his staff. He told the story of a woman whose contributions had been regularly rejected by Masson. This lady wrote Mitchell a personal letter, enclosing another offering. Mitchell destroyed the letter unread, but handed the contribution to Masson, who accepted it. Mitchell thought it quite a joke that the lady probably still believed her letter to the editor-in-chief brought her success.[17]

Those of Mitchell's friends who admitted that he had faults were uniformly eager to forgive them. Henry Holt called him impulsive. Martin wrote of him:

> He was incurably a child, and troops of children swarm through the paper that he made.[18]

But Martin's epithet, "child," is seven-eighths a compliment. He appreciated his colleague's warmth while he gently chided his inclination to over-enthusiastic sympathies.

Mitchell apparently cared little for the financial rewards of his work. He left an estate of $953,000,[19] a sum that must be gratifying to anyone. But surely every man who succeeds beyond his expectations in one field suspects that he might have succeeded even more grandly in another. The editor in Mitchell must have had moments of self-reproach when he accused himself of holding down the artist. Such moments did not dampen his affection for his work, though, nor embitter his placid temperament. He was by no means unhappy with his fortune and his executive position.

His friends testify that it was Mitchell who carried on *Life*'s crusade against inoculation and vivisection. His leadership in the national anti-vivisection movement was acknowledged. The *New York Times* interviewed him a few months before his death, and all his talk was of the evils of vivisection.[20] For his other enthusiasms and antipathies we must turn to his writings. These show that John Mitchell loved not only children and dogs but art, the romantic side of science, the civilized charms of Europe, the underdog, and above all his country.

Mitchell's fiction was his avocation, almost entirely separated from his daily editorial work. Three of his fourteen published books appeared first in the pages of *Life*: *The Last American* in 1889, *Life's Fairy Tales* in 1892, and *That First Affair* in 1896. None of these, even with illustrations, is long enough to cover a dozen pages in *Life*. Of his other books, three are collections of drawings: *Croquis de L'Exposition*, published in Paris some time between 1877 and 1880; *The Summer School of Philosophy at Mt. Desert*, published by Holt in 1881; and *The Romance of The Moon*, published by Holt in 1886. The other eight are novels. Selections from *The Summer School* appeared in early issues of *Life*, but all of the novels were born and grew quite independently of the magazine.

Mitchell never took his writing seriously. He never told anyone what he was working on until it was published. At the same time, Thomas Masson wrote that Mitchell believed a writer should first get an idea, then work it out painfully and slowly. The combined picture is exactly that of the home craftsman turning table-legs in his basement shop, unsure of his product until he suddenly recognizes it as finished. The contrast between this attitude and the professional aplomb with which Mitchell ran *Life* points up the separation of the two activities.

But he was a successful amateur novelist, both financially and critically. Sinclair Lewis compared *Amos Judd*, Mitchell's most popular work,[21] to Hawthorne. In justice to Lewis it should be pointed out that he was at the time no successful novelist himself, but a twenty-six-year-old journalist. Mitchell's other novels were well received. All of them seem to have made money for their author, who as president of the Life Publishing Company was also the publisher of four of them.

The novels and stories fall into three classes. In all three there is a mixture of social protest and fantasy, but fantasy dominates *Amos Judd*, *Drowsy*, and *The Villa Claudia*, whereas protest carries the day in *Life's Fairy Tales*, *The Silent War*, and *Pandora's Box*. In *That First Affair*, *The Pines of Lory*, and *Gloria Victis*—later rewritten as *Dr. Thorne's Idea*—the protest takes a specifically religious form. In *The Last American*, a tale of the year 2159, social and religious ideas combine with fantasy in an almost dreamlike projection of what Mitchell most feared for America. The book is unclassifiable.[22]

Mitchell's books' least attractive feature is their genteel romanticism. His fictional world was one where delicacy reigned supreme. His characters were occasionally introduced as sinful, but never discovered in sin. Sometimes this works to his advantage. In *The Silent War* the representatives of Labor are assassins and those of Capital are tyrants. But both sides speak soberly and rationally of their aims and purposes. The result is that the conflict appears genuine and dramatic. In *The Pines of Lory*, on the other hand, Mitchell casts away hero and heroine on a wilderness peninsula which they believe to be an island. After several weeks the young man forgets himself so far as to steal a kiss from the sleeping lady. Her subsequent tantrum drives him into the woods, and the next hint of any such urge comes at the end of the story, when the two are joyfully reunited in the lucky presence of an ordained cleric. The result is painfully contrived, and the characters appear less genteel than abnormal.

The whole story line in Mitchell's novels is in fact the ritual of court-ship. The ritual as prescribed by his class and time was indeed genteel, distant, punctilious, and asexual. To it Mitchell added romantic hyperbole, so that in his novels Indian princes, scientific geniuses, financial wizards and bohemian artists perform the sterile rites with daughters of earls or anarchists. The prissy courtship of the romantically unattainable female by the romantically excluded male is the substance of Mitchell's plots.

His plots, however, are of minor interest. The ideas which cluster around the plots are those of the man who was *Life*'s guide, and whose ideas become *Life*'s ideas.

His religious ideas, on the positive side, were genteel-Christian. In *That First Affair* he retells the story of the Fall, concluding that Adam and Eve were well rid of Eden because they found love outside it. The same idea can be touching when it comes from a vocal anti-Christian like Mark Twain in "Adam's Diary." In *That First Affair* the implications of this preference for romantic love over holy love are ignored. The impression it leaves is that Mitchell believes romance to have brought Adam and Eve closer to God as well as to each other.

Gloria Victis, which later became *Dr. Thorne's Idea*, is a nearly per-fect prevision of "Hollywood religion." Dr. Thorne's idea is that Christ has come to earth not once but many times. In fact, He is always available in time of crisis to lend a hand to the virtuous. Dr. Thorne proves to be correct, for when the heroine dies in the last chapter a gentle stranger enters from the street, brings her to life again in time for the wedding, and silently steals away. The fact that Mitchell reworked this idea so exten-sively as to publish it under two titles testifies to his own attachment to it and to its public acceptance.[23] Martin was the optimistic partner in *Life* insofar as public utterance was concerned. But Mitchell's "pessimism" always included the eventual triumph of spiritual beauty, which he equated with romance.

On the negative side, Mitchell's ideas are clearer and their reflection in *Life* is more readily recognizable. Mitchell was violently anti-Catholic. While his own convictions took less from Calvin than from E. P. Roe, he at least rejected firmly everything offered by Rome. *The Pines of Lory* is half anti-Catholic tract, half sentimental tale. Its point is that nature will triumph over unnatural self-denial. The point would be better taken if Nature were not brutally emasculated and thoroughly sentimentalized. However, the reader is never allowed to forget the alleged unnaturalness of the sort of self-denial recommended by Catholicism.

This conversation from *The Pines of Lory* follows the hero's obvious question upon seeing the heroine for the first time—"Who is she?" He is told that she is an heiress who is planning to give her fortune to the Roman Church:

"Too bad! She doesn't look so unintelligent."

"No: and she's not. Her mother and sister, all that remained of her family, were both drowned in the same accident, and the shock upset her for a time."

"And it was then the Church got in its work? That explains the Holy Roman Cherub who seems to be along."

"Yes; that's Father Burke. He is part of the comedy."

"Comedy! It's a blood-curdling drama! Hasn't she a brother or some relative to reach out a hand and save her?"

"She doesn't care to be saved. She is one of those women with a conscience. A big one: the sort that becomes a disease unless taken in time."

"I know. She feels guilty if she's happy. But she doesn't look all that. She seems a trifle earnest, perhaps, but very human, and with real blood in her veins."

Mr. Townsend sighed—a long, deep sigh that seemed to come from below his waist. "Yes, she was mighty good company and rather jolly before the vultures closed in on her."

"Is she really in the coils of the anaconda?"

"I am afraid so. She won't talk about it herself,—at least, not with Protestants,—but some of her friends say she thinks of going into a convent."

"Well," said Patrick Boyd, with a sudden warmth, as they turned to go below, "all I can say is, that the institution, sacred or secular, that tries to lure such a girl into a convent ought to be hustled into space."

"Amen to that."

Later, on board ship, the girl laughs in the priest's presence:

Heretofore he had known her as a thoughtful, serious-minded woman, with a leaning to melancholy; and this unexpected and evidently enjoyable flight—or plunge—into pure nonsense, caused him a distinct uneasiness. The girl was brightening up, even becoming merry; a state of mind that never leads to a nunnery.

Again, the hero admonishes the girl when they are alone on the island:

"But the Roman Enterprise has two enemies that are thorns in the flesh, the bath-tub and the printing-press. Whenever they march in, she marches out. The three can't live together."[24]

All of the anti-Catholic ideas in *The Pines of Lory* appear also in *Life*. Catholicism and the Irish were to *Life* identical, and *Life* inevitably showed the Irish as ignorant, dirty, and spineless, ready to obey the slightest whim of priest or Tammany ward boss.

The element of fantasy in *The Pines of Lory* and *Gloria Victis* would seem huge, but it was not large enough for Mitchell. In *Amos Judd* the title character is an exiled Indian prince with second sight. In *Drowsy* the title character is the son of an American physician and a Hungarian opera star and is gifted with telepathic powers. He invents a means of propulsion by electricity, builds it into a birdman suit, flies to the moon, and collects diamonds bigger than apples. In *Villa Claudia* a jug of wine tasted by Horace has survived two millenia, and it has the power to bestow "a lifetime's pleasure compressed into a single night."

It would be easy enough to see these as erotic fantasies with just enough hidden to keep the dreamer from recognizing them. It is not necessary, though, to go so far. All are dreams of freedom—flight, telepathy, visions, fabulous wealth, instant hedonism. Possibly the indulgence in such dreams had a therapeutic function for Mitchell. Surrounded by and participating wholly in a society so restraining that these children's fantasies could be sold as adult entertainment, Mitchell might have found a release in his avocation. It allowed him to be, for a little while and in a perfectly safe way, the self that his whole environment had denied.

Life offered just such an escape to its readers. Mitchell, of course, could not be a mere reader, and he sought to indulge his fantasies and dreams elsewhere. But the readers of *Life* were provided with fantasies and dreams equally comforting. They were told that they were the most virile men and most beautiful women on earth, that they were superior by birth and training to the snobs of Society and the lower classes alike, and that as Americans they were the hope and salvation of the earth. Surely there was a common basis for the freedom with which Mitchell's books indulged his taste for heroic fantasy and the freedom with which *Life* indulged its readers' tastes for heroic fantasies.

Mitchell's tales of social protest came from another level in his mind, even though they too were occasionally overlaid with the fantastic. *The Villa Claudia* is in part the story that Henry James and Mark Twain told so often: coltish America pitted against depraved but fascinating Europe. Mitchell embodies America in a young man named Morris Lane, who venerates classical Europe but is abashed by its modern descendants. *He* is a model of ambition and the self-sacrifice that goes with it. His European rival is a pleasure-seeker. Thus the situation of *The Pines of Lory* has been neatly reversed. Good is now American Puritanism: Lane is eventually a partner in a Massachusetts cotton mill. Evil is now European, specifically Italian, self-indulgence. The Italian "villain" gets the Horatian wine and the American gets the girl, thus demonstrating that the transitory pleasures of the world are bitter in the mouth when compared to the lasting, sentimental ones.

Pandora's Box has a comparable theme, only this time the villain is not Italian decadence but British snobbery. A humble American architect, distinguished for his wit and his fondness for his mother, fascinates the heiress to a British manor house. He gets girl and manor house both, while Mitchell speculates about inherited memories. The identification of the young American, Ethan Lovejoy, with his creator is too evident. The bold self-possession of Lovejoy is Mitchell's idea of the way he would have liked Europeans to see him.

This certainty of American superiority to Europe was typical of *Life*, too. Mitchell evidently liked Europe, and had reservations about American behavior there. But he turned them into compliments. When in Europe we Americans may seem crude, he said in effect, but really we're only bursting with vitality. We may seem ignorant, but really we are preoccupied with greater enterprises. We may seem sycophantic, but really we are only trying to humor those relics who have come to expect sycophancy. *Life*, whenever the subject came up, said exactly the same thing.

Mitchell's *Fairy Tales* are mere anecdotes, and although most of them have sharp points they are diffuse and unconnected, the result no doubt of their serial publication. Their satire is aimed at hypocrisy and humbug. A stuffy Episcopal clergyman is found to be a cosmic error, having been intended for a coachman. A pious confidence man congratulates himself on having "sold experience" to a bilked widow, experience being a priceless commodity. In all of them, someone's picture of himself is contrasted to the reality magically revealed. The book suggests that Mitchell knew when he was deluding himself, although subsequent books suggest as strongly that the knowledge did him little good.

The Silent War is the best of his novels. It is satiric enough to be classed with the *Fairy Tales*, and its protest is vigorous enough to have some bite. It is also fantastic, however, and its fantasies are revealing. Mitchell wrote to support Labor's cause; but he was, after all, an executive and a capitalist, and his personal fears are as much in evidence as his impersonal sympathies.

The story of *The Silent War* makes no apologies for its author's socialistic sympathies. The hero is Billy Chapman, a young man of unbelievable wealth by virtue of inheritance and acumen, but generous and unspoiled. One evening, on an impulse, he simply gives away nearly five hundred dollars to a destitute ex-convict and his little daughter, solely because he believes the man deserves help.

The story breaks, and takes up again nineteen years later. Billy Chapman and his fellow tycoons are now made aware of the People's League, an organization dedicated to exterminating tycoons. They also hear of the Committee of Seven, the organ of the League that extorts huge sums from tycoons by threatening their lives. Most are willing to give in to the threats. Chapman and a few others are not. One by one the unwilling ones are assassinated. The reader learns that the chairman of the Committee of Seven is the man whom Chapman helped years before. The daughter, now riper, works as a nurse for Chapman's aged aunt. She and Chapman fall in love. The Committee meets. Should they kill Chapman or not? The argument goes: Chapman is a good man. There are few enough good men in the world. We would do our own cause more harm than good if we killed him. The opposition replies: We have committed ourselves. We cannot turn back, or all our work will be destroyed.

Then, at the last moment, the daughter learns that Chapman and the mysterious benefactor of years before are one and the same. She sends a message to her father, and he casts his tie-breaking vote in Chapman's favor.

While all this is going on, Mitchell introduces such ideas as: Christ was a socialist; money buys politicians, and this leads to tariffs, tax inequalities, and usurpation of public domain; the rich are conspicuous consumers, mere drones; child labor and adulterated food are crimes incomprehensible to sane men; a dozen or a hundred wealthy men quietly assassinated is better than a revolution, and revolution is exactly what America is headed for. Mitchell's Committee of Seven is shown to be genuinely trying to avert a blood bath. The People's League which they represent is shown as vast, dark, patient, and American. It is also invincible and inescapable.

The paranoidal idea of a conspiracy so wide-ranging that only one man stands against it is too evidently Mitchell's basic idea for the novel. When the same idea appears in Sax Rohmer's *Fu Manchu* books it is deliberately sensational and meant only to amuse. In *The Silent War* it is more than half serious. Mitchell believed in the possibility of such a conspiracy. He meant *The Silent War* as a warning.

The Americanism of the conspirators is Mitchell's real contribution to the conspiracy novel. The idea that Americans were capable of such a thing became a recurrent theme in the novel.

> For these men . . . were not enemies of order from beyond the sea; they were not ignorant foreigners with an inborn hostility toward all more prosperous than themselves. In no sense were they Nihilists or Anarchists. They were industrious, thoughtful, representative Americans. Yet, not only was their resentment, their hostility avowed, but they were discussing calmly, in Anglo-Saxon fashion, revolt—and assassination. That a gigantic conspiracy in one shape or another was well under way he no longer doubted.
>
> They are Americans this time, not peasants. They consider their republic in danger when they become servants of corporations that own the industries of the country and control the whole machinery of government. It is not merely a question of wages—of food, clothes and shelter. And even if it were, our country is the richest in the world, and incredibly prosperous. The American workman has awakened to all this, and demands a share in its prosperity. He doesn't get it, however hard he toils. That is his grievance.
>
> "Even an unskilled laborer likes to keep his family alive, but he has been so infernally meek, under the tariff, and with all this free immigration taking the bread out of his mouth, that I had begun to lose sympathy for him."[25]

An ironic sidelight to Mitchell's plea for genuine Americanism in *The Silent War* is his use of a quotation from Kaiser Wilhelm of Germany as a chapter epigraph.

> "You in America may do what you please, but I will not suffer capitalists in Germany to suck the life out of the working men, and then fling them aside like squeezed orange-skins into the gutter."[26]

The Kaiser was to become Mitchell's bugbear at the end of his life. When it happened, *Life* became less a vehicle for humor than one for hate and vindictiveness. The man whose social idea Mitchell admired in 1906 so enraged him in 1916 that Mitchell seriously undermined his own life's work hoping to spite him.

Life never adopted a view as violently anti-capitalistic as Mitchell's of *The Silent War*. Nevertheless, it never forgot that American workmen had rights, as Americans if not as workmen. It also fought against corrupt politics, conspicuous consumption, impure food, and child labor.

The Last American is the work that contains the essential Mitchell. It is fantasy, set in a ruined, forgotten America of a far-off future time. It is sentimental, for the last American, degenerate and repulsive though he is, dies bravely at the foot of George Washington's statue trying to defend his beautiful mate from an insulting boor. It is anti-Catholic: the Persian explorers who rediscover America find in the rubble a coin bearing the likeness of Dennis, last of the Hy-Burnyan dictators. It is satiric: Mitchell suspected that archaeology was largely humbug, and the speculations of nineteenth century archaeologists are satirized when the explorers find a cigar-store Indian and the piers of the Brooklyn Bridge. Above all it is American, in the sense in which Mitchell and *Life* used the word. The American of the title chews tobacco and has enormous feet, but he is proudly Anglo-Saxon and overflows with the milk of human kindness. His savagery as compared to the Persians' barbarism is approximately Morris Lane's impulsive good-heartedness compared to his Italian rival's mannered confidence. Mitchell's American is untutored. But he is intelligent, pure, generous, and far braver and stronger than anyone suspects.

Mitchell's view of America's future in this brief story is not cheerful. America will decline under the Hy-Burnyan dictators, he predicts, and because of climatic changes the population will die off. The pitiful survivors will inherit only the unshakeable moral qualities of the great race that sired them. Physically, they will decay. The men will, anyway. Mitchell refused to imagine an American woman who was other than beautiful, chaste, and refined. But even at its death, Americanism will be a great moral lesson to those who see its end.

Americanus sum, read *Life*'s motto. Its editor chose the motto, and its editor defined its Americanism.

So far we have investigated only *what* Mitchell wrote. A word remains to be said on *how* he wrote it. As might be expected of a man who was first of all a draftsman, Mitchell was a poser of characters and a setter of scenes. The plot of *Amos Judd* hinges on a "scene" envisioned by Amos as a future certainty. The hero of *Pandora's Box* is an architect, and architectural descriptions take up large sections of that novel as well as of *The Villa Claudia*, *The Last American*, and even *The Pines of Lory*, in which a comfortable house has been built in the woods by a recluse. A portrait comes to life in one of the *Fairy Tales*. Mitchell's exoticism seldom became admiration for splendor, but in *Drowsy* the scenes of the ruined, jewel-encrusted moon cities are certainly pictorial, if not exactly typical. A passage from *Amos Judd* demonstrates his use of form and color to provide a background for a very ordinary conversation.

> One afternoon in August, when there were visitors at neither house, Amos and Molly climbed over a wall into a pasture, for a shorter cut toward home. The pasture was extensive, and their course lay diagonally across a long hill, beyond whose brow they could see nothing. A crimson sunshade and white dress were in dazzling contrast to the dull greens of the pasture, whose prevailing colors were from rocks and withered grass. Patches of wild bushes where the huckleberries were in overwhelming majority necessitated wide detours or careful navigating among thorns and briars. Her companion seemed indifferent to the painful fact that knickerbockers are no protection against these enemies. But pricks in the leg at the present moment were too trivial for notice. He was speaking with unusual earnestness, keeping close at her side, and now and then looking anxiously into her face. It may have been the heat and the exercise that drove the color to her cheeks, and there were also signs of annoyance as if she desired to escape him; but the ground was uneven, and the stones and bushes rendered haste impossible.[27]

Ever the architect, Mitchell believed that a man's character is shown by the house in which he chooses to live. The foursquare New England homes of Amos Judd and of Cyrus Alton, hero of *Drowsy*, are the real indices to their characters. The romantic circumstances that surround them are fortuitous. The ruin in which the last American dwells reflects his inner state. The Villa Claudia is ancient and mysterious and beautiful, but its most important occupant would prefer sunnier and more enlivening surroundings. She chooses to give up the villa for the textile works.

Sinclair Lewis did not explain why *Amos Judd* reminded him of Hawthorne's works. The setting is New England and the trappings are fantastic. The comparison goes no further. Unlike Hawthorne's, Mitchell's pace is pell-mell. He introduces characters elaborately and then drops them completely in his eagerness to get his story told. Unlike Hawthorne, Mitchell is a crude manipulator of symbols. His characters can occasionally be said to embody ideas, but he doesn't even suspect the existence of deeper levels of symbolic connection. Symbolic representation meant for Mitchell just what artistic representation meant for him—uncompromising literalness. Unlike Hawthorne, Mitchell always is certain who the good persons are and who the bad persons are, and how to tell them apart. And so are his readers.

Mitchell died of a stroke on June 29, 1918, at his summer home in Ridgefield, Connecticut. His health had been poor in his later years, and his eyesight had grown so bad that he had to wear glasses described by one who knew him as "so thick you wouldn't believe it."[28] He is buried at Ridgefield.

Edward Sandford Martin

Edward Sandford Martin, the co-founder of *Life* and its leader writer throughout nearly all of Mitchell's editorship, was born on January 2, 1856, at Owasco Lake, New York, the son of E. T. Throop Martin and Cornelia Williams Martin. A paternal great-uncle was Enos T. Throop, a former governor of New York. Martin attended Phillips-Andover academy as a boy and entered Harvard in the fall of 1873.

His college career was remarkable for extra-curricular activity. He was elected to the Porcellian Club, the most exclusive of Harvard's undergraduate clubs, and in 1876 he founded *The Lampoon*, Harvard's still-surviving magazine of humor. He was graduated in 1877, and went to Auburn, New York, to study law. After a year there, he joined the State Department and moved to Washington, D. C. He contributed verse to various journals. Charles Dana of the New York *Sun* offered him a newspaper job. He accepted, but in 1882, almost at the same time his first book of verse was published, his health failed. He took a voyage around Cape Horn to re-invigorate himself, and it seemed to effect the intended cure. His book, *Slye Ballades in Harvard China*, was being noticed both in America and abroad.29   Among those who noticed it was John Mitchell. When Martin returned,30 Mitchell proposed that he take over the managing editorship of the proposed new *Life*. Martin had believed for some time that the *Lampoon* idea had commercial possibilities. He accepted.

But he was not done with roaming yet. In the summer of 1883, having struggled through *Life*'s first six months, he suffered an attack of recurrent malaria. He left *Life* and went to Rochester, where he began to study law. He was admitted to the New York bar in 1884, and practiced briefly. Then in 1885 he joined the Rochester *Union and Advertiser*, a semi-weekly paper, as associate editor, a position which he held until 1892. In 1886, he married Julia Whitney of Rochester, and the Martins eventually had three children. In 1887, Martin began to write *Life*'s editorial page, and he continued to do so until 1928. At the same time he reappropriated *Life*'s editorial page, he began to contribute to *Harper's Weekly* and other New York magazines. From 1893, after he had resigned from the *Union and Advertiser*, until 1913, when *Harper's Weekly* was sold, he did a regular column, "This Busy World," for that magazine. He wrote another regular column, "The Point of View," for *Scribner's Magazine* in the nineties. In 1896 he moved back to New York City.31

His editorials for *Life* made his earlier reputation, but in 1920 he took over *Harper's* "Editor's Easy Chair," left vacant by the death of Howells. For eight years he wrote for both *Life* and *Harper's Monthly*, and his later reputation has rested largely on his performance in *Harper's* from 1920 to 1935. His "Editor's Easy Chair" pieces were very much like the editorials he had done and continued to do for *Life*. If there was a difference, it was that his writings for *Life*, being shorter, were more concrete. For example, in December of 1921 he was interested in the disarmament conference being held in Washington. He wrote it up in both magazines, leading off two of *Life*'s editorial pages with remarks about it. In *Life*, he mused over the problems faced by the conference—the conflicting interests of former allies, the questions of which countries should disarm and which weapons should go first. He wished the delegates well in their Herculean undertaking.[32] In contrast with this, his "Editor's Easy Chair" offering did not mention the specific problems to be solved, although it was a much longer essay. It concentrated on expressing the hope that religious persons all over the world would unite to find some way out of the present unhappy world situation.[33] This is typical of his handling of similar ideas in the two magazines. Any advantage gained from the comparison seems to fall to *Life*, and yet biographical sketches of Martin are capable of concentrating on *Harper's* and his work there and nearly excluding *Life*, as though it were a youthful indiscretion. The difference to the commentators is that *Harper's* was a reasonably serious magazine, while *Life* was not.

Martin's opinions had mellowed somewhat with age, and coming to the "Editor's Easy Chair" as he did at nearly sixty-five years of age, he ran that department so that it seldom aroused controversy. He was a libertarian with a deep conviction that things would balance out if left to themselves. The following is taken from the "Editor's Easy Chair" for April, 1924, and its subject is advertising; but it could as well have been taken from a concurrent issue of *Life*, and its subject could be anything on earth. The ideas are universally applicable:

> There is a connection between the power of advertising and of the revenues that are derived from it and the current propensity of newspapers and periodicals to be concentrated in the control of strong hands. When the papers, whose main purpose is the circulation of ideas and the advocacy of social or political policies, come into competition with the papers whose chief concern is the diffusion of goods and the acquirement of the resulting revenues, the papers which deal in ideas are apt to go to the wall. The others are too strong for them. They can buy away both their contributors and their supporters. They can vastly out-advertise them.
>
> But these are temporary conditions. Advertising is in the condition of the rabbit in Australia before the Australians woke up to appreciation of what was going on, and so is the linking up of newspapers and the cutting of the throats of those whose existence is not so profitable to some buyer as that of other papers whose ideas suit him better and whose prosperity he wishes to promote.
>
> After all, this world as it is is a grand "catch-as-catch-can" world, proceeding rapidly through space. Who is for slowing it up?[34]

Martin was never for slowing up the world, but only because he believed that the world was heading inexorably toward the balance that it had held in the good old days, before the pressure of unusual circumstances rocked it.

In 1935 he retired from *Harper's*, and on June 13, 1939, after an illness of three months duration, he died in New York's Orthopedic Hospital. He was eighty-three.

Martin's contribution to *Life's* store of opinions is inestimable. Mitchell wrote in 1913 that the readers thought "the editorials may have been the best things in the paper" for the previous thirty years. Martin's editorials for *Life* on the subjects of women's suffrage and neutrality were collected and published as books, and are discussed in Chapter IV. He was *Life's* official spokesman on those two questions. He did not echo Mitchell's opinions, but their differences were of degree rather than kind. Martin was less sympathetic to labor than was Mitchell. Martin saw the greatest threat to America in Jews, Negroes, Chinese and other "unassimilable aliens," whereas Mitchell saw it in the Roman Church. But these differences are important only because *Life* leaned farther toward Martin's side than toward Mitchell's. The editorial writer spoke for the paper more loudly than did the editor-in-chief. He was also a copious commentator on literary matters. His important ideas about literature were almost exactly those of Bridges: both believed that American fiction should combine the point-of-view of a man of breeding with the "virile purity" of American life. (These ideas are investigated at length in Chapters V and VI.)

Martin's hallmarks when he wrote for *Life* were geniality and good sense. While still in his twenties he adopted the tone of a Dutch uncle when addressing the public, and he kept it throughout his life. The temptation to task him for intellectual vanity is strong. He reminds one irresistibly of Melville's Mr. Hautboy, in "The Fiddler," who is thus described by a splenetic observer:

> His wonderful cheerfulness, I suppose, originates not less in a felicitous fortune than in a felicitous temper. His great good sense may exist without sublime endowments. Nay, I take it, in certain cases, that good sense is simply owing to the absence of those. Much more, cheerfulness. Unpossessed of genius, Hautboy is eternally blessed.[35]

Melville's Hautboy is later seen to be a man who has come to terms with disaster, and perhaps Martin's physical disabilities, which included deafness and malaria, would have been disastrous enough to crush a lesser man. Nevertheless, his dogged cheerfulness, geniality, and assumption of intellectual superiority are surfeiting.

One of his favorite poses demands a specific objection; he pretended to a literacy which he did not possess. This is important because he was *Life's* spokesman on so many literary matters, and he never hesitated to tell a Howells or a Henry James exactly what that author ought to do to improve his work. Yet one searches in vain through Martin's published writings for literary references or evidence of literary knowledge. In a collection of Martin's "Editor's Easy Chair" pieces called *What's Ahead*

and Meanwhile, the index contains two names recognizable as literary—
William James and Matthew Arnold.   Martin quotes Arnold once, indirectly, from a current newspaper article which quoted him.   Martin
repeats James's words eight times, but only twice directly.   Both times he
uses the same quotation.[36]

Martin's literary hero was William Makepeace Thackeray, but Martin
did not honor even Thackeray with frequent quotations.   When he wrote
on literature for *Life*, Martin was fond of comparing characters in American novels to characters in novels by Thackeray, particularly to those in
The Newcomes, *Pendennis*, and *Henry Esmond*; but although he left no
doubt of his admiration for the British satirist he gave no real evidence of
either a deep or a wide knowledge of his works.   The level of society at
which *Life's* sympathies were pitched resembled in many ways the one
with which Thackeray habitually worked—in the former case, an upper-
middle class viewing an upstart plutocracy with both contempt and envy;
in the latter case, the lowest rungs of aristocracy's ladder, where vulgar
climbers and decaying aristocrats elbowed and sneered at one another.
Life's social jokes were frequently those to which Thackeray was addicted.
Both found amusement in the problems of henpecked husbands, undow-
ered or homely daughters, worthless sons, and the pretensions of every
sort of person who entered their social milieus.   But Thackeray, in *The
Book of Snobs*—written originally for the British magazine *Punch* and
very near to the vein of *Life*—calls *Punch* "the universal railer."   *Life* did
not rail at snobs.   Its satire was milder, more forgiving.   By the same token,
Martin was more forgiving than Thackeray of the sins of the upper classes.
The two men differed too widely on specifics for Martin to model himself
after his hero.   Only rarely did Martin show specific Thackerayan influence, as for example his consistent reference to the House of Hanover
as "the Guelph family" after Thackeray's *The Four Georges*.

However, there was a more basic affinity between the personalities
of Martin and Thackeray than any fondness of quotation would have revealed.   Martin was not really a literary man at all.   Thackeray's anti-
literary side was strong.   Martin, too, mixed stern common sense with
moralistic prudery which can be attributed easily, if not certainly, to a
fear of being thought soft and unmanly.   "Virility" was a fetish with him
even more than it had been with Thackeray.   His common sense always
stopped short of approving anything that threatened his "manliness."

Martin's "common sense" was indeed uncommon.   His reliance on it
for the answers to all possible questions is to be suspected, though.   Perhaps in the mid-twentieth century we put too much emphasis on the expert, but Martin was inexpert by any century's standards.   It is difficult to
understand how a man who boasted of being expert at nothing could become a spokesman for any large group.   Yet we have Mitchell's word that
Life's editorials appealed to its readers beyond any of its other features.[37]

Martin's obituary in the *New York Times* called him "an enlightened optimist."[38] His optimism was the result of his common sense. Common sense told him that extravagance was doomed, that things would balance out in time, that equilibrium was the natural state of the world, that things-as-they-were were better than things-as-they-are, and that things will return to normal in time. That is the substance of Martin's whole thought.

Martin's geniality was born of his optimism and conservatism. He lived in a leisurely mental world, and could well afford to do without enemies. He believed that balance would be restored in time; why then should he condemn or attack the unbalanced? He was willing to wait. Occasionally, of course, his patience ran short. When that happened, he sought causes for the lack of balance. And because he was dedicated to things-as-they-were, or rather to things as he conceived them to have been, he inevitably found the causes among new public figures or new ideas: aliens, suffragettes, William Jennings Bryan, Mark Hanna, prohibition.

This is not to say that Martin fought everything new. He threw whatever weight the "Editor's Easy Chair" carried into arguments for the League of Nations, although he insisted that America would never join. He saw the League as an aid to restoring the balance so dangerously upset by the war.[39]

In his optimism and trust in a non-existent golden past, Martin was easily tolerant as only the thoroughly secure can be. He was even daring enough to advocate upsetting the balance in various small ways:

> Our poets are somewhat too apt to be spruce gentlemen in patent-leather shoes, who make verses in such odd hours as they can spare from the serious concerns of life. And one cause of their being so is the reiterated suggestion of a stiff-necked generation, that a sincere poet who believes in his office and lives up to it is a more or less absurd creature, who owes us all an apology for not doing something more lucrative and really useful. We have talked that way about poets so long that it looks a little as though ours had finally come to believe us, and put their best energies into other work. It might be better for them, and for us too, if they would shut their eyes to our quirks and giggles, and pattern a little more after Tennyson, who chose to be a poet, and was that and nothing else, all his life, without evasion, apology, or remorse.[40]

Here he is in top form. He patronizes the whole clan of poets, and in the next breath he admits, with an almost visible genial smile, that *his* ideas and those of his readers *might* not be the last word on poets. Then he calls for stronger poets who will not give in to the smothering pressures of the world's Martins. He has managed to work in two separate insults to poets and an enormous compliment to his prosaic readers, and the whole thing is perfectly easy-going and entirely sensible.

Another characteristic of Martin's essays and particularly of his editorials for *Life* is his inclination to see all issues as moral issues. This is,

I suspect, a cause of his conservatism rather than a result of it. It is a habit so deeply ingrained that his common sense never questions it. It shows most in his political writings, but it also shows in his comments on literature. No doubt his common sense needed an ethical basis on which to operate. Martin's ethics, however, were sentimental ones. He believed that motherhood was surpassingly noble and that America was singled out by God to perform His will on earth. Mitchell supported him on both counts.

Martin's stylistic strong point was the aphorism. He was really an adept at the art of generalization. He attacked all kinds of questions, but he preferred questions of the deepest concern, like religion, history, or politics. Chapter titles in *What's Ahead and Meanwhile* include "The Pith of Religion," "Current Civilization," "What the Colleges Must Teach," and "Immortality as a World Cure." His remarks on these subjects are by no means unintelligent, although Martin, like anyone else whose publications are voluminous, said unintelligent things from time to time. His presumption and taste are in question, not his intelligence. He honestly believed that by knowing as little as possible and applying common sense to the situation at hand he could reach satisfactory conclusions.

Some examples from the first pages of *What's Ahead and Meanwhile* will help show that Martin's prose, properly gleaned, yields a lexicon of conservative cliches, all neatly phrased:

> The great factor in history that is constant is the fallibility of man.[41] We hate to think; we hate exertion; we hate discipline and self-denial; we hate innovation.[42] What made the war? Vanity and fear; love of riches and love of power. What has delayed the peacemakers? The same—vanity and fear; love of riches and power. . . . The cure of them is not political nor economic. . . . It is spiritual.[43] When the mass has produced a great leader, the thing is to get something valuable out of him while he is still good, because leaders spoil so fast.[44]

Martin's common sense, while it led him in circles at times, acted on *Life* as a counter-force to Mitchell's enthusiasm. The moralist in Martin felt strongly about more things than did Mitchell, but the optimist in him never felt *as* strongly about things. Mitchell's wars with the doctors and the trusts occasionally threatened to overwhelm *Life*, and his war with the Kaiser did just that. Martin pleaded always for sanity.

Besides Martin's first book of verse he published two more, *A Little Brother of The Rich* and *Pirated Poems,* both in 1890. After that he brought out eleven books of essays and a biography of Joseph H. Choate.[45] He was a knight of the Legion of Honor and was elected to the National Institute of Arts and Letters in 1908. He held an honorary degree of A. M. from Harvard, granted in 1916, an honorary degree of Litt. D. from Rochester University, granted in 1917, and an honorary degree of LL. D. from Lafayette College, granted in 1924.[46] He was the close personal friend of a number of eminent men, including Choate,

Colonel Edward House, and Brander Matthews.[47]

In *What's Ahead and Meanwhile* Martin outlined a portrait of an admirable man. It does not seem to be intended as a self-portrait, but it is near enough to deserve citation:

> I knew Cousin James about fifty years and he always had in him these senti- ments and these preferences that I have tried to describe. He never was ex- emplary according to the prevailing standards, never particularly acquisitive nor thrifty, nor ever pleased with prohibition, but the basis of his thoughts was always religion, this old church religion that he seemed to have been born to. His main occupation in life was reading, but he liked music and architecture and painting. He could play old-fashioned whist and did play it. He was interested in his family, very fond indeed of his friends, self-depreciative and over- appreciative of others if he liked them, and quite caustic and amusing in his remarks about the people who offended his prejudices. Indeed, he was de- lightfully amusing on most subjects. He had not much will power for action, but a great deal for inaction. His ideas and sentiments, deeply founded and pondered, were very little affected by what happened to be going on. He dis- believed in a great deal that most other men valued and he believed a great deal that other men had let slip. When his mother died he adorned the chapel of a church.[48]
>
> He had only a limited confidence in democracy. He wanted the best people to rule, and he did not think democracy was getting them, nor see how it was ever going to sort them out and give them the necessary power. He was not sure of the destiny of the United States, though he hoped for the best about it, and in his heart was a true patriot.
>
> He hated change. He did not care for money-making and disapproved of people who did.[49]

Miller, Metcalfe, Masson, Bangs,
Bridges, Kerfoot

The third founder of *Life*, Andrew Miller, was *Life*'s treasurer and business manager from the day when Martin introduced him to Mitchell until Mitchell's death. Then for a year he shared the editorship with James Metcalfe. He died of heart disease on December 31, 1919. Miller's con- tribution to *Life* was entirely on the business side. Miller saved *Life* in its infancy and made it prosper. Miller and Mitchell both reaped fortunes from their magazine. Miller invested in race horses and became rather better known in racing circles than journalistic ones. He was a steward of the Jockey Club.[50] He never interfered with the editorial side of *Life* nor was he ever mentioned there.

James Stetson Metcalfe was *Life*'s dramatic editor from 1889 to 1920 and from 1890 to 1895 was its literary editor. After Mitchell's death he was the art editor for a little over a year. Metcalfe's most important contribution to *Life* was his combativeness. He was a good enough dramatic critic to be hired by *Judge* and *The Wall Street Journal* after he left *Life*, but controversy, not criticism, was his strongest point.

His sharp criticisms caused some victims to question his acumen. Booth
Tarkington wrote to Kenneth Roberts after Metcalfe had reviewed a new
play by Tarkington:

> Your Mr. Metcalfe of *Life* was the only New York critic who did what I was
> sure they'd all do to *Clarence*. His English is as faulty as usual and altogether
> he's up to the customary snuff.[51]

But it was his persistent attacks on theater managers, scalpers, newspaper reviewers, and even the audience, that made *Life*'s dramatic column
its most frequently sued and—for a time, at least—most avidly read feature.
Metcalfe abominated vulgarity onstage and off. He accused the New York
theater managers, particularly the Theatrical Syndicate, of calculated
vulgarity inspired by greed and of abetting the activities of the ticket
scalpers, activities which he described as downright brutal. He felt the
newspaper reviewers were venal and implied that the managers black-
mailed the papers by threatening to withhold advertising. He thought
the audience had vulgar taste in plays and in hats.

His outspokenness led *Life* into several lawsuits. The most important
of these, the see-saw legal battle with the Theatrical Syndicate, occasionally threatened to spill out of the courts and into the street. Metcalfe was
first threatened with bodily injury, then barred from the Syndicate's
theaters by what the managers maintained was the independent individual
action of each manager. He insisted on seeking admission nightly, and it
became a local amusement in New York to watch him being thrown out
of his chosen theater each evening. The full story of this fight is told in
Chapter VII.

Metcalfe's gentlemanly distaste for vulgarity was matched by his
gentlemanly contempt for intellectuality. He disapproved of all theatrical
experimentation, usually on moral grounds. He admitted that Ibsen and
Strindberg and their imitators in English were not motivated by the same
urges that created vulgar and tawdry reviews, but he could see little difference in their effects on their audiences. He believed that the audience
of the legitimate theater expected and deserved something better. This
attitude, too, is examined in Chapter VII.

Like Mitchell and Martin, Metcalfe claimed a long American heritage.
Like them, too, he feared for the future of an America which was being
increasingly populated by persons whose heritage was vastly different from
his own. His attitudes derive largely from his pride in his ancestry and
education. His fifth of six published books is a genealogy of his family,
The Metcalf Family, published in 1912.[52]

Metcalfe was born in Buffalo in 1865. He earned an A. B. and an
A. M. degree from Yale in 1889 and 1891, respectively. He was married
twice. Like Martin, he held positions on various publications while working for *Life*. He was managing editor of *Cosmopolitan* in 1895. He died
on May 26, 1927.

Thomas Lansing Masson was, next to Mitchell himself, the member of *Life*'s staff most dedicated to the magazine. Masson thought of himself, in his capacity as literary and managing editor, as a joke writer and an overseer of joke writers. Masson was born in Essex, Connecticut, on July 21, 1866, and was the "baby" of *Life*'s "Sanctum" during Mitchell's editorship. He was a traveling salesman when he sold his first jokes to Metcalfe, and he joined the staff as managing editor in 1893. Masson revered Mitchell. He left *Life* to take over an associate editorship of the *Saturday Evening Post* in 1922 when it became evident to him that the new *Life* and the old were incompatible.

Masson decided what would or would not appear in *Life*'s joke columns, which made up the bulk of the magazine's content after pictures. He was in agreement with Martin for the most part about what sort of person *Life* should speak to and how its remarks should be cast:

> You must have principles to be a humorist. Then from the standpoint of your principle, you are struck by the absurdity, by the incongruity, by the positive injustice of a certain thing. Being a gentleman, being inured to the inevitable, being under control, you do not lose your temper over this thing. You do not rant at it like a Bolshevist; you take it up gently and begin to poke discreet fun at it.[53]

Masson believed that he knew what sort of person would succeed as a humorist:

> I think it is true that the best wit and humor among amateurs comes out of the colleges and the college papers. The reason for this, I take it, is that the boys who go to college have had the advantage of good homes, they have acquired manners, and manners are immensely important. The moving picture people tell me that the hardest thing is to get someone to take the part of a gentleman. Manner is acquired only under certain conditions, and humor is born of a critical instinct, plus sympathy. You must be mentally at ease—more or less confident of yourself, yet tolerant.[54]

When material ran thin, Masson was always able to fill in the gaps himself. He wrote, he said, an average of fifty jokes a week for twenty years, and sold seventy percent of them. This cost him two hours weekly effort. It was just as well for *Life* that Masson was able to create so mechanically. Masson insisted that he had read every manuscript contributed to *Life*. He explained that a few names reappeared in the magazine repeatedly because only a few writers were funny enough to print. He so seldom received anything good, he said, that his greatest worry was the possible public reaction to the mediocre contributions with which he sometimes had to fill the columns.[55]

Masson's mechanical, factory-production-line output of jokes called for the method, not of a weaver operating a handloom meticulously to create the effect he wants, but of a textile mill turning out yards on yards of fustian, characterless and indistinguishable from all the other products of the mill except by its little flaws. He cheerfully admitted this. A joke, he said, is almost always a dialogue, and it needs two things to be success-ful—an idea worth joking about, and two characters to speak it. The best method for a joke-writer, he said, is to keep a store of situations and characters handy. Know what ideas are the proper material for jokes that season. Know what characters appeal to the public's sense of humor. Keep your tools sharp, and with practice you can manufacture a saleable joke in a little more than two minutes.[56]

It is apparent that the joke-maker who works as Masson describes himself as working is not the free-wheeling critic conjured up by the name "American humorist." The use of such material implies a toadying to public taste that is hardly thinkable in an "American humorist." It is in fact—and Masson was humorist enough to see it—funny to think of the commercial hack described by Masson solemnly trotting out his file cards, carefully selecting his situation and characters, and methodically building a joke around them. Masson averaged $1,700 dollars per year from his two-hour weekly stint,[57] and proper Americans are likely to excuse this humorless attack on something that pays so well. Nevertheless, he begins with humor and ends with a joke. A proper American humorist begins with facts and ends with humor.

Masson's humor, then, was absolutely commercial and made no claim to originality. It had the advantage, however, of being ready at all times. Masson was an invaluable asset to a magazine which had to publish a new number each week. He collected some of his best work into hard covers, and at least one anthologist of American humor, Joseph Lewis French, selected the best from one of his collections, *A Corner in Women* (Moffat, Yard and Company, 1905). One example bears out everything Masson said about his own facility and everything which this implies about his originality. It is the end of a sketch called "The Man Who Came Back." A man named Henry Bilkins returns from the dead under the auspices of the Society of Psychical Research. He borrows a hundred dollars from his reluctant son-and-heir. Then he visits some old acquaint-ances. He returns to his son's office after a few hours:

> "Arthur," said Henry Bilkins, at last, "I have made a singular discovery. Nobody wants me back. My old friends have all forgotten me, and while they expressed a certain degree of pleasure in seeing me, it was mostly perfunctory. I couldn't take up the threads again, I left you my money. It would be awkward, even if it were practicable, to give it back to me. The ties by which I was united to you were broken, and have all healed or been united to other interests. Now, Arthur, I am going back—nay, don't protest. We might as well be honest. Be-sides, it's perfectly natural that I should be forgotten. Yes, Arthur, I'm going to return. But there's just one thing, Arthur, before I go—just one thing. I know, of course, your mother's married. I saw it in your face. But I'd like to see her—to press her hand—to say good-day to her, just for old time's sake. Can you arrange this for me, my boy—over the phone?"
>
> Henry Bilkins' voice actually shook. His son got up.
>
> "Father," he said, "I, too, have been thinking this over. You are right. It

isn't because I'm hard-hearted—but this is a practical world. And so, father, I'm ready to agree with you. Yes, you'd better go back. But it wouldn't be advisable for you to see mother."

"Why not? Isn't she happily married?"

"Oh, yes. But, you see, father, mother has married a man—well, he's a nice man, but he needs regulating. And the only way she can succeed in regulating him is to hold you up to him as a model. She keeps your picture on the wall as a constant example. We all help her more or less. Your memory, your virtues, keep him toeing the mark. He has to live up to you. Now, father, you see what would happen if—"

Henry Bilkins got up. He held out his hand.

"I understand," he muttered, "those new cars that pass here go to the cemetery, don't they? Well, good-bye, Arthur, I'm glad to have seen you even for this short time. I'm going back, don't worry," He was gone.

The door closed behind him. There was a moment's pause.

Then Arthur got up and opened it.

"Father," he called.

The old gentleman turned on the landing.

"Excuse me, father," said Arthur, "but you might let me have what's left of that hundred—if you don't mind, father."[58]

Masson died on June 18, 1934, after serving as book reviewer for the *New York Times* and the *Christian Herald*.

John Kendrick Bangs is best known as the editor of *Harper's* "Editor's Drawer" and of *Puck, Life*'s rival. However, he spent four years, from 1883 when he was twenty-one years of age to 1887, as assistant editor of *Life*, taking over when Martin's health forced him to give up the post and go to Rochester. He was studying law at Columbia where he had edited the *Acta Columbiana* when Mitchell approached him.

Bangs was born on May 27, 1862, and died on January 21, 1922.[59] He continued to contribute to *Life* after he resigned from the staff in 1887.

Bangs did not fit into the "atmosphere" of *Life*. For one thing, he believed in the real value of imaginative literature, and while he was assistant editor he used more literary allusions and literary jokes on *Life*'s pages than either Metcalfe or Masson later printed. For another thing, he enjoyed writing about literary matters. He was particularly amused by the Shakespeare-Bacon controversy brought into national prominence by Ignatius Donnelly in 1886. He supplied three or four outrageous "theories" of Baconian authorship. The best was a "cryptogram" which "proved" that on Shakespeare's gravestone, "t/y" really stands for "f/b." Bangs explained that if one uses the alphabet backward, *y* corresponds very easily to *b*, and *t* corresponds to *f* if one follows Kent's advice in *King Lear*, Act II, Scene 2, and omits the "zed! Thou unnecessary letter!" Bangs added that cryptogrammarians of Shakespeare's day frequently used the alphabet backward to conceal their meaning, not having yet learned to do it forward, he said, as did Swinburne and Browning.[60]

A third difference between Bangs and *Life* was that even his occasional contributions were likely to be saltier than the usual run of *Life*'s offerings. He read Howells' poems and wrote to admonish him:

'Twere best, we think, that you should sing
Your songs, dear sir, in prose,
For then a grand and swelling hymn
Your work harmonious flows.

But when on Pegasus you ride,
You score him deep with rowels:
Your songs degenerate from hymns
To most unpleasant Howells![61]

When it was reported that a fund had been gathered to build a memorial to Brigham Young, the Mormon leader, Bangs managed the sort of mild snigger that *Life* ordinarily avoided in its urgency to protect the young person. These are the first ten lines of Bangs' versified comment:

To The Father of His Country

Let his praises loud be sung!
Raise a shaft to Brigham Young.
Let it pierce the spreading blue,
Rising high and pointing true,
Heralding the virtues of
Him who was so full of love
He'd enough and some to spare
For the old maid everywhere.
Mortal who could faithful be
Not to one but sixty-three.[62]

Robert Bridges, known as "Droch," was *Life*'s literary critic from 1883 to 1900. Born on July 13, 1858, in Shippensburg, Pennsylvania, Bridges held degrees of A. B. (1879) and A. M. (1882) from Princeton, and had worked for the New York *Evening Post* before coming to *Life*.[63] Bridges' ideas and his contribution to the magazine are discussed at length in Chapters V and VI. He was an exceptionally well-informed man in his field. He did not share Martin's belief that good sense was all anyone needed to achieve greatness. But his ideas and Martin's harmonized so closely that his column, "Bookishness," was for many years as eloquent a spokesman for *Life* as were Martin's editorials. He fought Realism and Aestheticism in American literature, he hated Boston, and he praised and patronized "the American Girl." He shared Martin's passions for Thackeray, the gentlemanly life, and American virility. (All of this is expanded in Chapters V and VI.)

He left the magazine under a cloud. The exact cause of his resignation cannot be determined, but it appears to have been a personal quarrel with Mitchell. Mitchell announced publicly the chagrin and pain that he felt when Bridges severed connections with *Life*.

Bridges continued to work for the *Evening Post* as assistant news editor while he wrote criticism for *Life*. In 1887 he moved to *Scribner's Magazine*, where he became assistant editor. In 1914, he took over as editor-in-chief of *Scribner's*, and held the post until 1930. During his editorship, *Scribner's* printed stories by Sherwood Anderson, Ernest Hemingway, and William Faulkner. Afterward, until 1939, he was literary adviser to Charles Scribner's Sons. He never married. He died on September 2, 1941.[64]

John Barrett Kerfoot served as *Life's* book reviewer and literary editor from 1900 to 1918. Born in Chicago on November 18, 1865, Kerfoot was a graduate of Columbia University, class of 1887. His curiosity ranged over a wider field than that of most of *Life's* staff members; his three published books are *Broadway*, 1910, a journalistic profile of the street; *How to Read*, 1916, a collection of essays; and *American Pewter*, 1923, a self-explanatory title. Well known as an antiquarian, after leaving *Life* he operated an antique shop at Freehold, New Jersey. He was also a devotee of photography and was associate editor of *Camera Work* magazine from 1905 until his death, April 17, 1927, in London, England.

Kerfoot's literary judgments were sound, but he had none of Bridges' love of controversy. He preferred not to judge at all, if he could help it. Rather quickly after Kerfoot took over the literary column, *Life's* interest in literature flickered and expired. Kerfoot often reviewed non-fiction, with a leaning to antiquarian subjects.

In the reviews he accurately gauged new and relatively difficult work. He praised Carl Sandburg, calling the *Chicago Poems* "the new wine of today's vision poured into bottles made to hold it; and there are both beauty and inspiration in them."[65] He called James Joyce's *Portrait of the Artist as a Young Man* "a work that no understanding student of the influence that modern psychology is having on literary art can afford to miss."[66] He wrote of the Irish Renaissance that while it was too early to make final judgments, "two more or less enduring pieces of literature seem likely to be credited to it: Synge's plays and (George Moore's) Hail and Farewell."[67] He defended the right of H. G. Wells to write a novel of "mind action" rather than physical action.[68] He called Edgar Lee Masters' *Spoon River Anthology* "the most basic thing done, fictionally, in America in the present century."[69] He wrote of Theodore Dreiser's *The Titan* and of its predecessor *The Financier* that "when we look back upon the dual work it is not Cowperwood himself, nor the mass of secondary characters clustered round him, nor even the ruthless unromanticism of the author's philosophy of human motives, that stands out clearest and most significant in the retrospect of our realization; it is a spiritual synthesis that we see; the soul of America—seeking."[70] He did not like Edith Wharton's *The House of Mirth*, but he admitted its "pathos and tragedy" when others attacked it as immoral.[71] He wrote that Sherwood Anderson's first novel, *Windy McPherson's Son*, had "tremendous possibilities."[72] And he imitated Oscar Wilde. The difference between his outlook and *Life*'s is nowhere better shown than in his attitude toward Wilde. Kerfoot was a practicing aphorist,[73] and he venerated Wilde as a master of the craft. But Martin and Metcalfe found Wilde loathesome. Martin and Bridges, also, had expressed very strong opinions against the aesthetic movement in literature. Kerfoot's mind and *Life*'s were irrevocably separated by Kerfoot's admiration for an aesthetician who had been publicly disgraced and had lost his claim to both respectability and manhood.

When he took over *Life*'s literary column in 1900, Kerfoot was thirty-four years old. Though a generation younger than Mitchell he was not significantly younger than the other members of the Sanctum. It is therefore to his credit that he understood and appreciated the ideas of the new century, since none of the others did. He was particularly interested in the psychological approach to literary criticism. This is another contrast to Bridges and Martin, whose approach to literature was entirely through its social utility. In 1917 Kerfoot wrote:

> Nothing would seem more certain than that the next twenty years will see laid the firm foundations of a new literary criticism; not superficially based, as heretofore, on the more or less naive dogmatizings of individual "tastes," but constructively organized from accumulating investigations into the fundamental needs of the imagination, the true function of fiction with regard thereto, and the interoperative psychology of reading on the one hand and of creative writing on the other.[74]

Contributors

The ephemeral nature of *Life*'s letterpress makes comment difficult on its contributors who were not staff members. Jokes, paragraphs, and light verse were *Life*'s stock in trade. Some of the regular contributors were writers of good reputation. The majority of practicing American humorists of the time were occasional contributors. But assessment of their work is nearly impossible. When they wrote for *Life*, they wrote what *Life* wanted, and *Life* wanted gentility, good sense, and brevity. Contributions to *Life* might make up an appreciable part of the enormous output of a man like John Kendrick Bangs, but they would be a relatively bland part. Even writers whose work appeared almost weekly for years must be disposed of simply by saying that their paragraphs or verses in *Life* were like the other paragraphs and verses in *Life*.

A case in point is Agnes Repplier. She contributed copiously to *Life*, and it is even possible that a thoroughgoing review of her contributions might reveal something worthwhile about her habits of thought or her ideas of humor. For example, among her contributions for 1902 is an exposition of what she called "Repplier's Theorem." She said that the looting of China after the Boxer Rebellion would benefit the American and British public, because according to Repplier's Theorem today's thieves are tomorrow's philanthropists, and stolen goods inevitably end in museums as public property. Her work for *Life* was by no means always so original or so thoughtful, though, because *Life* did not expect it to be.

But although *Life* did not use the finest work of its contributors, it was often perceptive enough to use the earliest. More than one reputation was made through contributions to *Life*, and more than one writer sold first to *Life* and then, encouraged by his first commercial success, went on to more ambitious work.

Carolyn Wells was among the latter. Her lifetime output of books included more than one hundred and seventy titles, but her first periodical publication was a piece on theater hats in *Life* in 1897. After *Life* accepted her work, she began to contribute to *Puck* and other magazines. In 1912, *Life* reported that she had fifty-odd books to her credit and twenty-two publishers. Besides humor, she wrote juveniles and mystery stories. She was also a notable anthologist.

Booth Tarkington, too, collected his first check from *Life*. He sold *Life* a joke, and followed it with a drawing and text. He received thirteen dollars for the drawing and seven for the text, and made up his mind that art was to be his life's work.[75] Subsequent return of thirty-one of his drawings from *Life*, however, resulted in his return to fiction.[76]

A regular *Life* contributor to whose career *Life* gave first impetus was Nancy Mann Waddel Woodrow, who as Mrs. Wilson Woodrow wrote a round dozen novels and abundant periodical literature. She and her husband, a cousin to Woodrow Wilson, moved from Chillicothe, Ohio, to New York City in 1900, whereupon she sold her first story to *Life*, and shortly afterward became one of its most dependable contributors. Her novels, now unread, are boy-meets-girl entertainment. Her work for *Life*, however, was among the best humor the magazine published in the relatively dull period between 1900 and 1912. Her specialty was parody. The following example is not parody, but it is a fair specimen of her work. It is irreproachably ladylike, but it reaches further for its subject than Masson's humor and it approaches the hyperbolic fantasies of the best American humorists. A diarist has been noting the delightful picture postcards sent to her by her vacationing friends. And noting them— and noting them—and noting them:

> Heaven forgive me, but these picture postal cards are worse than the plagues of Egypt. They still continue to come in by the hundreds. After the arrival of the last batch today I had some kind of an attack. The doctor who was summoned thought it serious and insisted on a consultation of physicians. They have diagnosed the disease as postcardophobia. Whenever I see a picture card, I

bark and foam at the mouth. They hope, however, to save me. A clever young surgeon in Vienna has discovered that by boiling down the most virulently colored cards, a serum can be obtained, which if injected into the veins in time, has the most beneficial results. If this fails—.[77]

Kenneth R. Roberts, later the author of popular historical novels, gained his first national recognition through *Life*. As a prominent novelist, he earned a reputation for iron-clad conservatism. This suggests that his ideas and those of *Life*'s "Sanctum" were in excellent *rapport*. He conducted a humorous column for the Boston *Post* when he began to contribute to *Life*. He found the extra income gratifying, and in 1917 his name appeared in *Life* three times as often as that of any other contributor.[78] Roberts' humor was ponderous and his satire brutal, but in 1917 that was precisely what *Life* was looking for. A verse and an excerpt from a sketch will do for examples:

> "I am fighting for freedom," said Private Brown,
>   As he thrust out his square-hewn jaw.
> "I have come here to shoot at the Prussian brute
>   As lover of order and law!"
>
> But into the ranks burst the sweet Babette
>   With eyes that were filled with mist,
> And ere Private Brown had a chance to frown,
>   He was thoroughly hugged and kissed.
>
> "What a pickle I'm in!" remarked Private Brown:
>   "It was Freedom I came to get,
> But I plainly see I shall always be
>   A slave to the sweet Babette!"[79]

In the sketch, Lt. von Zwiebach of the German Army suggests to his superior that a military acquaintance be named governor of Belgium:

"Yes," declared Lieutenant von Zwiebach enthusiastically, "and he would install the good old custom of shooting a score of Belgians at sunrise each day." General von Schnitzel rose from his chair and kissed Lieutenant von Zwiebach on the brow. "My boy," said he, "you have the true military genius. Some day I hope to see you made governor of the United States, and to rejoice in the firmness with which you turn the machine guns on the Yankee swine and their painted women." Overjoyed at these words of praise, Lieutenant von Zwiebach rushed from the room and expressed his delight by trampling to death a kitten belonging to the little daughter of the janitor of the town hall.[80]

Late in 1917, Roberts became an army officer, and army regulations at the time forbade officers to publish anything. Roberts conspired with Masson to circumvent this rule, and in 1918 a contributor named Laurence Kane was credited with as many paragraphs and jokes as Kenneth Roberts had written the year before. Kane was Roberts.[81] Out of the army, Roberts gave up humor to become first a *Saturday Evening Post* correspondent and later a novelist.

Kate Masterson and Ramsey Benson, both novelists in their own right, contributed heavily to *Life*. Miss Masterson, born in 1870 at Newburgh, New York, was a New York City resident and a contributor to *Puck* and *Judge* as well as to *Life*. She worked for both the New York *Mirror* and the New York *American* and covered the Spanish-American War in Cuba for the latter paper. Benson, nearly all of whose contributions to *Life* were unsigned, was a Minnesotan. Born in 1866 at Anoka, Minnesota, he was a graduate of the University of Minnesota and his vocation, at least in 1911, was potato farming. His novels—*A Lord of Lands*, 1908; *Melchidesec*, 1909—are concerned with simple, almost primitive men and their struggle to maintain a simplistic ethical code against the corruption of the city or the brutalization of the country.

Guy Wetmore Carryl, although he did not contribute copiously to *Life*, supplied some of the best humorous verse the magazine printed. Carryl was born March 4, 1873. His father was Charles Edward Carryl, also a writer. Carryl was graduated from Columbia University in 1895. One of his teachers was Harry Thurston Peck, and it was in Peck's class that Carryl made the remark that has passed into folklore, "It takes two to make one seduction."[82]

Carryl began to contribute to journals while still an undergraduate. He wrote for *Munsey's*, *Collier's*, and *Outing* as well as for *Life*. Early in 1904, Carryl contracted "rheumatic grip" while fighting a fire that had broken out at his home. Blood poisoning followed, and he died April 1, at the age of thirty-one.

Carryl's verse depends heavily on models, and he achieved his best effects in burlesque or travesty. His books of light verse are *Fables for The Frivolous (With Apologies to LaFontaine)*, 1898; *Mother Goose for Grown-Ups*, 1900; and *Grimm Tales Made Gay*, 1902. Despite this delight in derivation, however, Carryl remains among America's finest composers of humorous verse, and the only one among them who contributed to *Life*. Carryl's early death was a painful blow to American humor. He was also the author of a book of serious verse, a book of short stories, and three novels.

Two of the funniest of *Life*'s regular contributors were Joseph Smith and Carlyle Smith. Joseph Smith was a Dubliner, born in 1853. He lived in America from about 1873, and began to contribute to *Life* in 1897. During the Spanish-American War and the McKinley era in general, Smith was *Life*'s best satirist of America's new imperial pretensions. About Carlyle Smith nothing is known, not even whether or not "Carlyle Smith" was his real name. Nevertheless, he was one of *Life*'s earliest contributors, and one of its funniest. During the 1880's, and particularly during the 1884 Cleveland-Blaine campaign, Carlyle Smith's buoyant political satire enlivened *Life*, which was normally apathetic where politics were concerned.

In the late years of Mitchell's editorship, Ellis O. Jones contributed many paragraphs and an occasional longer piece in the editorial vein. Jones was born in Columbus, Ohio, and was a Yale graduate. He had done newspaper work in Columbus and held an editorial post on Edward Bok's *Ladies' Home Journal.*

Wallace Irwin, best known for his "Letters of a Japanese Schoolboy," contributed regularly to *Life.* He was born in Oneida, New York in 1876, and began to sell to *Life* in 1904. Like most humorists of the day he was prolific, and once provided a poem a day for a year to the New York *Globe.* The "Japanese Schoolboy," named Hashimura Togo, is usually identified with *Collier's* rather than *Life,* but *Life* printed a number of the letters. Their humor derives mainly from the wide-eyed naiveté of the "schoolboy" and the strict logic with which he tries to explain America to his Oriental kin. The garbled English of the letters was also a humorous device, and Irwin maintained that he had imitated real letters sent to him while he was in college by a Japanese friend. Irwin, too, sold his first verse to *Life.*

William Trowbridge Larned and Arthur Guiterman were regularly featured in *Life* as book reviewers. Larned wrote "The Literary Zoo" column from 1907 to 1911 and Guiterman did "Rhymed Reviews" beginning a few years later. Both of these columns eventually took over better positions in the magazine than Kerfoot's regular book review, but neither one compares to Kerfoot's work in quality.

Larned was born in St. Louis and led a fascinatingly peripatetic life, working as a government clerk, cowboy, farmer, reporter, and eventually dramatic editor for the St. Louis *Post-Dispatch.*[83] He was something of a linguist and among his published books are translations from French fairy tales and Hungarian drama.

Guiterman was born in Vienna, of American parents. He held editorial jobs on the *Woman's Home Companion* and the *Literary Digest.* He was a graduate of the College of the City of New York, and while a student there he won a medal "for greatest proficiency in literary composition."[84] It was that proficiency that found him room on *Life.* His "Rhymed Reviews" are plot synopses in doggerel, often more than a hundred lines long. They did not appear weekly, but more than once Guiterman turned out one a week for several weeks without a break. The "Rhymed Reviews" were neither penetrating nor clever, but they were amazing virtuoso performances.

These were the important regular contributors to *Life.* A list of occasional contributors would contain some impressive and unexpected names—Gertrude Stein even sent in a half-column, once[85]—but it would be nothing more than a list.

He: SHALL WE TALK OR DANCE?
"I'M SO TIRED. LET'S DANCE."

LIFE

1904

NEW YEARS

The Artists

The artists who worked for *Life* may in the long run be more important than its writers. Mitchell himself contributed far less than one would expect, after the first year. Nearly every pen and ink artist in America who achieved any sort of prominence between 1883 and 1918 was represented in *Life* sooner or later. Possibly *Life*'s artists will provide the future with more knowledge of the late nineteenth and early twentieth centuries than its writers ever could. An exhaustive list of *Life*'s contributing artists for the period 1883-1916 appeared in *Life*, LXIX, 1917, p. 27.

Charles Dana Gibson deservedly has had a booklength biography of his own.[86] He was born in Flushing, New York in 1867. Mitchell's opinion of Gibson was exalted, but the public's was higher still. Gibson sold his first drawing, of a dog baying at the moon, to *Life* in 1886 for four dollars. He came to be identified with *Life* in spite of his brilliant work for *Collier's* and other publications. In 1889, Mitchell believed that Gibson was the best artist in pen and ink practicing in America.

The exact origin of the term "Gibson Girl" is uncertain, but the Gibson Girl and the 1890's are inseparable ideas. The Girl, however, was not *Life*'s favorite among Gibson's contributions. In 1898 and 1899 *Life* ran a series of Gibson's drawings titled "The Education of Mr. Pipp," which was collected between covers in 1899. Mr. Pipp was an undersized, apprehensive husband and father, continually browbeaten by his wife and cajoled by his beautiful daughters. He was wealthy, but not wealthy enough to keep up with his family's extravagances. He preferred to stay at home with his pipe and slippers, and they towed him to the ends of the earth while they pursued "culture." But he was not all pipsqueak. His women trampled him into the mud, but no man could presume to do the same. Mr. Pipp, in short, was *Life*'s idea of the comic American male, and his situation was that which *Life* found typical of American men of the class to which it catered. Mr. Pipp was forceful enough and even successful among "his own kind." But he crumbled into sentimental fragments when faced by women. In 1912, *Life* wondered aloud whether it had ever printed anything else as good as Mr. Pipp.

Gibson was not only an illustrator. According to Downey, a campaign waged by *Life* to discredit, through satire, the practice of marrying American heiresses to penniless European noblemen was Gibson's idea. Gibson's cartoons provided the bulk of the ammunition. When the European war broke out, Gibson caricatured the Kaiser as a hoggish, power-mad imbecile.

For much of the period between 1883 and 1918, Gibson worked exclusively for *Life*, and he headed the syndicate which purchased the magazine in 1920. The elegant Gibson Girl and the elegance for which she stood were integral to *Life*'s view of the world. Gibson's art fitted *Life*'s personality perfectly.

In 1899, Mitchell discussed several other artists who drew for *Life*, among them Francis Gilbert Attwood:

> Mr. F. G. Attwood, of Boston, is a brilliant apostle of what I have alluded to as the intellectual side of art; that is, his drawings appeal more to the intellect than to the artistic sense. Before his pencil touches the paper he has a distinct and clearly defined conception of what he intends to convey, and he regards his art simply as a means of expressing that idea. The art is always there, however, for without it his story could never be told with the force and delicacy and the exquisite humor with which his work abounds.[87]

Attwood was a Harvard man and a *Lampoon* veteran.[88] He died April 30, 1900, at Jamaica Plain, Massachusetts.[89] He had been one of *Life*'s first and most trusted contributors. He was also, along with F. T. Richards, one of only two practicing political cartoonists who worked for *Life*.

Another contributor to *Life* from its first issue forward was William Allen Rogers. In the article quoted above, Mitchell wrote:

> Mr. W. A. Rogers had already a reputation . . . Himself a man of strong individuality and positive convictions, he is able to stamp his work with a character of his own, direct, clean-cut, and always conscientious, / emphasized by a manner of drawing at once forcible and refined. His drawings are true to nature—or, at least, they have that effect, a vastly more desirable quality—and they are full of light. The man who can produce in pen and ink a composition that is both strong and refined, with no sign of indecision, and that also is fresh and brilliant in effect, is a master of his art. This can be said of Mr. Rogers.

Rogers was born at Springfield, Ohio, May 23, 1854, studied at Worcester Polytechnic Institute but did not graduate, and died on October 20, 1931.[90]

The third "original" contributor to *Life*'s portfolio of art was Edward Windsor Kemble. Kemble's favorite subjects were ragged and clownish men and women. He achieved his greatest popularity with "The Thompson Street Poker Club," drawings of comic Negroes which were provided with a running commentary. Mitchell wrote of Kemble that he possessed "a fund of humor, with an unusual facility of hand; and . . . a spirit and expression that are far too rare." Of the Thompson Streeters, Mitchell wrote, "These sable gamblers are full of character and are irresistibly funny."[91] Kemble is perhaps best remembered as the illustrator of the first edition of *Huckleberry Finn*. He was born on January 18, 1861, at Sacramento, California, attended the New York public schools, and died on September 19, 1933.

S. W. Van Schaick's hallmark as an artist for *Life* was the absence from his drawings of large areas of black. He used innumerable fine lines to create shadow effects, and his drawings had a lighter tone than those of most of *Life*'s artists. Van Schaick was a prominent illustrator. One book he supplied drawings for was Bangs's first book, *The Lorgnette*, 1886.

Michael Angelo Woolf specialized, in *Life*, in drawings of round-eyed and pinch-cheeked urchins. He was not the only regular contributor who drew poor people—Kemble was famous for it—but he was the only one who drew poor people who genuinely looked poor. Woolf was born in London in 1837 and died in the United States in 1899.

Palmer Cox, of "Brownies" fame, was an early and regular contributor to *Life*. Cox was a master of several styles, but his "Brownie" books are better known than his humorous drawings for *Life*. They are among the first American children's books to combine artistic composition on the page with the text. Cox was born in Granby, Canada, on April 28, 1840, of immigrant Scots parents. He was graduated from the Granby Academy but had no further artistic training. He died July 24, 1924.

One of *Life*'s contributing artists who abandoned realistic drawing in favor of stylization was "Chip," Frank P. W. Bellew, the son of Frank H. T. Bellew, also an artist. "Chip's" drawings edged away from realism gradually, but toward the end of his career he was drawing in the style of Egyptian mural painting. "Chip" was born in 1862 and died in 1894, another of several contributors to *Life* whose lives were cut short.

Oliver Herford was writer as well as artist, but in Mitchell's opinion, his drawings were his most important contribution to *Life*. Herford came to *Life* early and stayed late, and might well claim the title as *Life*'s longest-standing contributor, at least after Martin. Herford's drawings are barren by *Life*'s standards; in some cases they are nearly as simplified as modern cartoons. In fact, Herford soared to the top of the list of *Life*'s artists only after Mitchell's death, when the new styles came into vogue. Herford was born on December 1, 1863 at Sheffield, England. In 1875 his family moved to America. He studied at Antioch College, at the Slade School in London, and at Julien's in Paris. After a long and varied career, he died at the age of seventy-one in New York City, July 5, 1935.

The contributors to *Life* who "drew like Gibson" were legion. Two of the most important were Henry W. MacVickar, who preceded Gibson as a *Life* mainstay, and Henry Hutt, who did many of the center two-page drawings during those years after the turn of the century when Gibson was abroad or working elsewhere. MacVickar was a disciple of George DuMaurier, as was Mitchell, and presumably Gibson himself. MacVickar was superseded by Gibson. Hutt tried to take Gibson's place. He was not entirely unsuccessful, but Gibson's reputation was too great to be seriously challenged by an artist who simply did the same thing almost as well. Hutt used wash rather than pen and ink, and his drawings are darker and deeper than Gibson's. Many of his aristocratic women look as though they were in mourning. Hutt was born in Chicago in 1875. He sold his first picture to *Life* when he was sixteen. I have been unable to find a record of his death, or of MacVickar's.

Frederick Thompson Richards was unquestionably the finest satirical cartoonist in *Life*'s history. He specialized in politics, but his satire could be aimed in any direction he chose. Almost uniquely among *Life*'s important artists, Richards favored outdoor scenes, with plenty of depth in the background. His figures are characteristically angular, and he did caricatures of thin men and women better than he did stout ones. His sense of humor went unerringly to the point in his satirical cartoons; and whereas every Gibson Girl wore the same expression, Richards' figures were capable of a gamut of facial expressions which has been equalled only by those of Walt Disney. Richards was born May 27, 1864, in Philadelphia. He studied for a year at the Pennsylvania Academy of Fine Arts, and came to New York in 1890. At different times, he was the daily cartoonist for the New York *Herald*, the Philadelphia *Press*, and the *New York Times*. His drawings were exhibited in the American show at the Paris exhibition in 1890. *Life* was particularly proud that a drawing by Richards had caused *Life*'s banishment from Turkey during the Turkish-Armenian fighting. It showed a befezzed and fiercely mustachioed gladiator about to hack a cowering and helpless woman labeled "Armenia" while from the emperor's box Uncle Sam, John Bull, France, Germany, and Russia looked on approvingly. Mitchell was so pleased by the ban that he ran the same cartoon in 1900, only this time the Turk sat in the box while a fat Mr. Bull held his sword over South Africa.92 Richards died in Philadelphia in 1921.93

Otho Cushing was a conspicuous contributor to *Life* for many years. He was also very much in demand for advertising art. His figures were delicately drawn, but they fairly burst with muscles. He maintained that he copied Praxiteles. So long as he concentrated on Greek statuary and athletes, which were his specialties, the style was in harmony with the subject. But on those occasions when he drew women—particularly women with clothes on—the sight of a pair of Cushing-style shoulders bulging out of a long gown could be ludicrous. Wisely, he usually confined his drawing of women to those who dressed for warm weather, like Eve and Cleopatra. Cushing was born on an Army post, the son of an officer. He studied at the Boston Art Museum and at the Academie Julien in Paris. I have discovered no record of his birth or death.

Another curious stylist who contributed in quantity to *Life* was T. S. Sullivant. Sullivant was a master of grotesquerie. His figures, whether human or animal, were likely to be distorted so that the important feature was exaggerated enormously out of proportion to the rest of the drawing. He liked to draw monstrous animals with little, round, inquisitive eyes. His figures look as though they know how strange-looking they are. Sullivant was born in Ohio. He spent his early life in Germany, and did not begin to draw seriously until he was thirty-two. He studied at the Philadelphia Academy. Along with Gibson, Herford, and Hutt, he is the fourth artist for *Life* whom a serious historian of American Art considered worthy of mention in 1931.

The list of *Life*'s contributing artists could be prolonged endlessly. There was Arthur Crawford, who did not draw but ran a cartoon syndicate, providing ideas and selling drawings. There was Forbell, Crawford's most frequent collaborator, who drew tiny scurrying people in massive surroundings, and contributed a drawing to *Life*, titled "That Second Cocktail," that is one of the most amazing *tours de force* of perspective drawing that I have ever seen.[94] There was Gray-Parker, who drew beautiful horses, nearly all of which faced the left of the page. There was Harrison Cady, who drew crowded rural scenes where the frogs and caterpillars looked wise and the people looked bland. And there were many, many more. I have tried to include those who were early, those who were significant, and those who were idiosyncratic enough to make their work stand out. I have chosen my "important artists" largely for their humor. *Life*'s record is open, and its artistic history is unwritten.

NOTES

[1]National Cyclopedia of American Biography (New York: James T. White & Company, 1910) Vol. XIV, p. 201.

[2]*Men and Women of America*, 1910 (New York: L. R. Hamersly & Co., 1910), p. 1178.

[3]*New York Times*, June 30, 1918, p. 19.

[4]Edward Sandford Martin, "John Ames Mitchell: 1845-1918," *Harvard Graduates' Magazine*, XXVII (September, 1918), p. 27.

[5]Holt, *Garrulities of An Octogenarian Editor*, p. 239.

[6]*Ibid.*, p. 239.   [7]*Ibid.*, p. 240.

[8]*New York Times*, June 30, 1918, p. 19.

[9]John Ames Mitchell *et al.*, *Some Artists at The Fair*, no pub., ca. 1893, p. 50.

[10]*Life*, LXXII, 1918, p. 88, (portrait).

[11]*New York Times*, March 26, 1932, p. 11.

[12]Fairfax Downey, *Portrait of an Era* (New York & London: Charles Scribner's Sons, 1936), p. 50.

[13]*Ibid.*, p. 356.   [14]*Ibid.*, p. 54.

[15]Martin, *Harvard Graduates' Magazine*, *op. cit.*, p. 30.

[16]John Ames Mitchell, with Thomas Masson, James S. Metcalfe, and Sinclair Lewis, "John Ames Mitchell, The Man Who Is Responsible for *Life*," (New York: Frederick A. Stokes, n.d.), p. 7. This is a pamphlet, reprinted from *The Book News Monthly* for March, 1912.

[17]*Ibid.*, p. 9.

[18]Martin, *Harvard Graduates' Magazine*, p. 29.

[19]*New York Times*, March 21, 1920, p. 6.

[20]*New York Times*, January 20, 1918, Section 5, p. 4.

[21]*The Library of Congress Catalog of Printed Cards, First Supplement*, Vol. XXV, p. 135, lists a *fifteenth* edition of *Amos Judd*.

[22]*The Last American, The Silent War*, and *That First Affair* have been reprinted in library editions, 1969-70.

[23]It was reprinted in pocket size by the George H. Doran Co. in 1910.

[24]John Ames Mitchell, *The Pines of Lory* (New York: The Life Publishing Co., 1901), pp. 18, 34, 44.

[25]John Ames Mitchell, *The Silent War* (New York: Life Publishing Co., 1906), pp. 80, 122, 159.

[26]*Ibid.*, p. 70.

[27]John Ames Mitchell, *Amos Judd* (New York: Charles Scribner's Sons, 1895), p. 172.

[28]Personal interview with Mr. Francis D. Martin, Ridgefield, Connecticut.

[29]*New York Times*, June 14, 1939, p. 23.

[30]I have been unable to pin down exactly what Martin was doing when Mitchell first approached him. The version here, from his obituary in the New York *Times*, is repeated in the *Dictionary of American Biography*. But Martin wrote in 1936 that he was "working in the office of a paper mill in Portland" at the time. (*Life*, CIII, 1936, November, p. 28).

[31]*DAB*, XXII, p. 434.

[32]*Life*, LXXVIII, No. 2040, p. 14 and No. 2041, p. 14.

[33]Edward Sandford Martin, *What's Ahead and Meanwhile* (New York & London: Harper & Bros., 1927), p. 105.

[34]Martin, *What's Ahead and Meanwhile*, p. 158.

[35]*Selected Writings of Herman Melville* (New York: The Modern LIbrary, 1952), p. 236.

[36]Martin, *What's Ahead and Meanwhile*, p. 55 and p. 280.

[37]*Life*, LXI, 1913, p. 14.

[38]*New York Times*, June 14, 1939, p. 23.

[39]Martin, *What's Ahead and Meanwhile*, pp. 7-16.

[40]Edward Sandford Martin, *Windfalls of Observation* (New York: Charles Scribner's Sons, 1895), p. 255.

[41]Martin, *What's Ahead and Meanwhile*, p. 1.

[42]*Ibid.*, p. 2.   [43]*Ibid.*, p. 4.

[44]*Ibid.*, p. 4.

[45]Martin's last book was published in 1933, fifty-one years after his first.

[46]*New York Times*, June 14, 1939, p. 23.

[47]*DAB*, XXII, pp. 434-435.

[48]Martin, *What's Ahead and Meanwhile*, p. 44.

[49]*Ibid.*, p. 43.

[50]*New York Times*, January 1, 1920, p. 15.

[51]Kenneth L. Roberts, *I Wanted to Write* (Garden City, N. Y.: Doubleday & Co., Inc., 1949), p. 131.

[52]*Who Was Who in America*, Vol. I, p. 835.

[53]Thomas Lansing Masson, *Well, Why Not?* (Garden City, N. Y. & Toronto: Doubleday, Page & Co., 1921), p. 127.

[54]Masson, *Well, Why Not?* p. 125.   [55]Masson, *Well, Why Not?* p. 126.

[56]Thomas Lansing Masson, *Our American Humorists* (New York: Moffat, Yard and Co., 1922), p. 434.

[57]*Ibid.*, p. 432.

[58]Joseph Lewis French, ed., *The Best of American Humor* (Garden City, New York: Garden City Publishing Co., 1941), pp. 155-56.

[59]*DAB*, I, pp. 573-574.   [60]*Life*, X, 1887, p. 234.

[61]*Life*, VII, 1886, p. 32.   [62]*Life*, XLVII, 1906, p. 21.

[63]*Who Was Who in America*, Vol. I, p. 137.

[64]*New York Times*, September 3, 1941, p. 24; September 4, 1941, pp. 20 and 21.

[65]*Life*, LXVIII, 1916, p. 293.   [66]*Life*, LXIX, 1917, p. 742.

[67]*Life*, LXIII, 1914, p. 1075.   [68]*Life*, LXIII, 1914, p. 360.

[69]*Life*, LXVI, 1915, p. 204.   [70]*Life*, LXIV, 1914, p. 268.

[71]*Life*, XLVIII, 1906, p. 318.   [72]*Life*, LXVIII, 1916, p. 825.

[73]Sample aphorisms from Kerfoot's columns: A cynic is excellent company when things are going your way. (*Life*, XLVIII, 1906, p. 210.)

Melodrama is reality with its ugly skeleton of cause and effect removed, and the cavities filled in with poetic justice. (*Life*, LXIII, 1914, p. 112.)

Most of us have to die to go to heaven. Elijah, however, was translated. And it is pretty much that way with foreign literature. Most of it has to die and be buried, locally, before it gets into English. But occasionally one gets translated while it is still alive. (*Life*, LXIV, 1914, p. 228.)

To boys throwing rocks from the top of a ninety-foot cliff, the water two-hundred feet away looks easy to hit, and they can't understand why their missiles fall short. Some supercultured novelists are like that. (*Life*, LXIII, 1914, p. 730.)

[74]*Life*, LXX, 1917, p. 720.   [75]Roberts, *I Wanted To Write*, p. 367.

[76]*Life*, XCI, 1928, p. 47.   [77]*Life*, LVI, 1910, p. 354.

[78]Roberts, *I Wanted To Write*, p. 68.

[79]*Life*, LXX, 1917, p. 302.

[80]*Life*, LXX, 1917, p. 820.

[81]Roberts, *I Wanted To Write*, p. 77.

[82]*DAB*, III, p. 530.

[83]*Life*, LVI, 1910, p. 1160.

[84]*Life*, LVII, 1911, p. 556.

[85]*Life*, LXX, 1917, p. 1076.

[86]Fairfax Downey, *Portrait of an Era* (New York & London: Charles Scribner's Sons, 1936).

[87]John Ames Mitchell, "Contemporary American Caricature," *Scribner's Magazine*, Vol. CI, No. 1 (January, 1937), p. 39, reprinted from *Scribner's Magazine* for December, 1889.

[88]*DAB*, XIII, p. 53.

[89]*Life*, XXXV, 1900, p. 416.

[90]*Who Was Who in America*, Vol. I, p. 1053.

[91]Mitchell, *Scribner's Magazine*, p. 37.

[92]*Life*, XXXIII, 1899, p. 552.

[93]Daniel Trowbridge Mallett (ed.), *Mallett's Index of Artists* (New York: Peter Smith, 1948), p. 368.

[94]*Life*, LXVII, 1916, p. 621.

CHAPTER IV

A SKEPTIC ALONE IN TIME

Life's politics were Martin's politics. Mitchell kept his eye on social problems, but his political ideas were those of *The Silent War*—that politics are no substitute for action. Over the years scores of contributors had their satiric say about political matters. From all these no homogeneous viewpoint can be expected. Martin, as chief editorialist, did for *Life*'s politics what Mitchell did for the magazine at large. He set the prevailing tone when matters seemed to deserve serious treatment. Martin usually insisted on the essential morality of every question, literary, social, artistic, or religious. But in politics he was flexible and willing to accept facts for what they were worth, so long as they were not at variance with *Life*'s cherished mythology. Martin's single boast, that he was a thoughtful and sensible man, is nowhere more nearly proved true than in politics. Once his mind was made up he did not easily unmake it. His greatest political battle, against women's suffrage, seems ill-advised at a distance of fifty years. But even there he had ample good sense on his side, and his opposition to the suffragettes was an argued opposition rather than an emotional one. The mildness of *Life*'s political views has its roots in Mitchell's first idea of what his new magazine should be. Both *Puck* and *Judge*, the established humorous papers against which *Life* was to compete, were bitter political partisans.

This is not to say that Martin and *Life* had no political principles. These were neither so narrow nor so rigid as their aesthetic or nationalistic principles, but they were real enough. Their first principle was an optimistic faith in the pragmatic triumph of good sense over whatever error chance might produce. Concerning national affairs this became, in practical terms, a sour resignation to fate when the two great parties offered nothing more to *Life*'s taste than a Bryan and a McKinley. But it was alleviated by the assurance that America could survive even this. Internationally it became a thankful isolationism. America had both ability and time to learn from European errors of statesmanship. *Life* had a genuine sense of history, but that sense said that history was a continuing upward spiral propelled by men of intelligence and good will. There had always been enough of such men to nullify the forces of destruction. It took time to work things out, and time, to the America of 1883 to 1918, was a drug on the market.

This comfortable idea of time allowed *Life* to survey politics with good humor and without agitation. The magazine demonstrated some strong likes and dislikes in these thirty-five years, but only in one case was it injudicious—during the Great War itself, in the end, when time ran out. Politically, *Life* lived up to its claim to be a magazine of humor.

But there were forces at work against *Life*'s political humor. The best-willed reader will find *Life* repetitious. There are perfectly simple explanations for this, the first one being that topical satire is harder to write when one's mind is not made up. Also, national politics during this period were not notably experimental, and what was true during one administration was likely to be true during the next. The most obvious exceptions to this were Civil Service reform and Theodore Roosevelt's Bull Moose Party, but the first occurred before *Life* was in full stride, and the second died in the bud. *Life* never took free silver or its exponents seriously, and when government intruded into business via Roosevelt's trust-busting, the justification for it all seemed to *Life* so obvious that the magazine treated it as a simple extension of government's obligation to keep the peace rather than as a politically revolutionary step. Tammany held New York politics in a mighty grip that loosened only relatively as men of differing shades of independence held the offices of mayor or governor. Every four years, a national election was held, but the campaigns were all nearly alike and the candidates, with the sole exception of Grover Cleveland, were just not *Life*'s type.

Despite *Life*'s habitual preference for men over issues its choices of national political candidates were seldom different from those of the country at large. It opposed James G. Blaine because it questioned his honesty, and it supported Cleveland because his was beyond question. It supported Roosevelt and (once) Taft, although it thought of Roosevelt as one who took responsibility far too lightly and of Taft as an unknown quantity; but Roosevelt was running against Alton Parker, whom *Life* did not even consider. Later on, it was to support Wilson against Hughes for the same reason. Taft, of course, was running against Bryan, and *Life* would have supported a Chinese laundryman against Bryan, although it could never bring itself to support William McKinley. McKinley was the single great point of division between *Life* and the American voters. *Life* did not like him, nor support him, nor even, by *Life*'s standards, mourn him. McKinley's expansionist policy was too much for *Life*. *Life* saw it as willful abandonment of the beautiful isolation that had made America what she was; McKinley was reversing everything the country had stood for so long. *Life* did not exactly think of him as a radical. But it protested that American policy before McKinley had the sanction of good sense, that expansion brought good neither to the expander nor his object, and that America, with South Africa before her, ought to know better than to emulate England's example. *Life* advised its readers to forget the candidate and vote for the gold standard.

This near-perfect tally of *Life*'s opinions and the voters' record led to a curious smugness in *Life* when it was called upon for political predictions. Possibly the smugness was justifiable. Every time the magazine predicted that its candidate had the election as good as won, that candidate really did win. In the case of the 1916 election, though, *Life*'s withering scorn for the Republican candidate was not quite borne out by the election results. Hughes nearly won, and *Life* seemed a bit abashed by it. It had been certain that Wilson would win in a walk. However, *Life* was not to be kept down for long. It did not like Wilson very much, anyway. Until then, whenever *Life* finally made its decision between two candidates, it invariably began to treat the election as though it were over and *Life*'s choice had won.

The combination of repetitive situations and lack of strong preferences makes a humorist's job stultifying at best. *Life*'s contributors tended to stand clear of larger issues and concentrate on Roosevelt's teeth or the *New York Tribune*'s unusual fervor for Blaine. Having reached its conclusions by sensible means, *Life* had to believe that all contrary conclusions were nonsense, and for *Life* to dignify nonsense with opposition was impossible. Therefore it chose to condemn rather than attack. It is difficult to find in *Life*, for example, any really humorous hits at Bryan. *Life* barely acknowledged the existence of such a creature, even though he ran three times against two different Republicans. *Life*'s optimism nullified those things that *Life* disliked, and its good sense told it to ignore them. Doubtless this fits well with the theory of the continuing natural improvement of civilization that *Life* held, but it is poison in the well for satire.

The presidential campaign of 1884 was the first major political issue to confront the infant *Life*. In its first year—indeed, for many of its early years—it gave less attention to national politics than to municipal corruption in New York and Boston. "We believe in the Republican party," said its editorialist, very likely Mitchell,[1] but evidence indicates that it did not believe in Chester Arthur, nor James Garfield, nor Rutherford Hayes, nor any issue the Republicans tried to boom in 1884. *Life* thought Arthur was a mistake, elected by that Civil Service reformer, Charles Guiteau. It found Hayes politically beneath notice. Among the Democrats, it saw Samuel Tilden waiting hopefully for a nomination even while senility waited for him. But all these people were ciphers, and, excepting Tilden, who was singled out for other reasons, *Life* ignored them and concentrated its batteries on two candidates it considered utterly unfit to hold any office whatever—General Benjamin Butler of Massachusetts, the Anti-Monopolist (a Democratic splinter) candidate and the man to whom we owe the nearly national celebration of Memorial Day, and James G. Blaine of Maine, the Republican nominee.

Life represented Butler as a hysterical demagogue. Unwashed, unkempt, dressed in a leopard-skin chemise like a strong-man in a freak show, he appeared over and over in cartoons, usually stuck off in a corner of a picture devoted to lampooning somebody else. But the editors saw little real threat in Butler, though he assiduously wooed the labor vote, the very existence of which disturbed *Life*'s conservative mind. He made promises which *Life* thought absurd. He did battle with the monster Monopoly in drawing after drawing, and Monopoly seemed to survive all the same. He did not really have a chance. He was only Abou Ben Butler, who loved just everybody and wanted his name at the head of all lists. He would run, *Life* reported him as saying, with equal energy for President, governor, or "the Salt River Boat. It's a cold day when I don't run for something."2

Blaine, as a candidate of a major party, was the satiric mark of *Life*'s 1884 political humor, and cruel humor it was. "During this campaign the satirical cartoon attained a power and effectiveness difficult to realize now that it has become an ordinary feature of journalism, equally available for any school of opinion,"3 wrote the historian Henry Jones Ford thirty-five years afterward; and whatever their effectiveness, *Life*'s anti-Blaine cartoons were undoubtedly powerful. He chose to be known as the Plumed Knight, and so *Life* depicted him. But *Life*'s Knight's name was Sir Jingo, and his motto was *Rex Vestibuli*, King of the Lobby. His running mate, General John Logan of Illinois, brooded on his shoulder in the likeness of a crow; and he dragged with him by a string a marvellously frowsy poodle representing Whitelaw Reid of the New York *Tribune*, conveniently renamed the *Tryblaine*. This combination of Knight, crow, and poodle took up several double pages of *Life* between June and November, 1884. In print, *Life* accused Blaine of egotism, venality, and sympathy with Irish Republicans and Suffragettes. It opposed his nomination ("The delegates arose en masse, and assassinated the party to which they owed allegiance"),4 opposed his election, and congratulated "About Ninety Million Americans" on his defeat, when it came.5

Life had its reasons. Blaine's record as Speaker of the House was spotted with suspicious-looking friendships toward suddenly successful pressure groups, and it appeared to Democratic observers that his income and style of living were somewhat too opulent for a man with a Congressman's salary. In 1869, Speaker Blaine had saved a land grant for the Little Rock and Fort Smith Railroad. Blaine had been rewarded with a franchise to sell Railroad bonds at an unspecified margin of profit. His profit, however, was considerable, and his political enemies viewed the whole transaction as sale of public lands for private enrichment. The "Mulligan Letters," which Blaine had, he claimed would have exonerated him. But he refused to make them public.

Then there were the tendencies that had earned him the sobriquet "Sir Jingo." Carlyle Smith wrote regularly in *Life* of the candidates and the campaign. He "interviewed Blaine" in March, and the words he put into the Knight's mouth reflected *Life*'s views of his policies, foreign and domestic:

> "Well, if I were compelled to accept the position, I would take the first year to get my hand in, and would hardly move from the line of my predecessor. In the second year I'd monkey with the Interior Department, and would give those poor Indians, for whom my heart bleeds, more whiskey and guns, so as to give 'em a better chance to fight their oppressors; I'd hang every Mexican who got caught in Texas, and let every Texan who got caught in Mexico go the way of all flesh. We must be equitable with the Mexicans . . .
>
> By the time I'd got to my third year my vigorous foreign policy would be ready to work . . . so that by my fourth year every known nation in the world would be at my feet, armed to the teeth, and ready to remove the United States from the face of the earth."
>
> "Yes, but what would become of the country in the fifth year after your election?"
>
> "To Texas with the country in the fifth year. *I wouldn't be President* then."[6]

Life's real quarrel was not with Blaine's judgment but with his ethics. "Every Patriot who votes for Mr. Blaine," wrote Mitchell, "will feel that there will lie no dollar in the United States Treasury so humble that Mr. Blaine will not look after it."[7] And the parodists turned out:

> I'm a most intense old man,
> Both sides of the fence old man,
>   Take all I can gettery,
>   Mulligan lettery,
> Solid for Blaine old man.[8]

followed by:

> I come from Fable Mountain
> And my name is Lootful James.[9]

Blaine had the temerity to publish a book just before the party conventions. Its title, unassuming enough, was *Twenty Years in Congress*, and *Life* made capital of the suspicion that it was ghosted by Gail Hamilton (Mary Abigail Dodge), a popular satiric novelist and essayist, Blaine's biographer, and his wife's cousin. *Life* reviewed the book quietly and fairly in the June 5th number, calling it "methodical" and "accurate," and its author "a good historian." However, Carlyle Smith had already given the work considerable advance publicity by "quoting the author" as "interviewed."

> "Young men in politics will find the chapter I'm writing on how to go to Congress without a cent, get a salary of $5,000 per annum, spend $15,000 per annum, and retire with several millions of dollars in hard cash, not to mention Fort Smith and Little Rock Railroad bonds and other insecurities to a large amount, very interesting indeed."

"Who will you take for a model, Mr. Blaine?"

"Modesty, sir, forbids me to go further."[10]

Possibly *Life*'s strongest evidence for its contention that Blaine was less than scrupulous was a piece of unimpassioned research published anonymously immediately after the Republicans had closed their convention and left Chicago.

> One by one are the idols of our youth shattered. The last straw comes, utterly breaking our faith in that man who has ever been identified in our hearts as the type of all that was good, honorable, and just.

The words of James G. Blaine, in his letter of acceptance, 1884.	The words of ex-president George Washington, in his farewell address, 1794.
"The name of American, which belongs to us in our national capacity, must exalt the just pride of patriotism."	"The name of American, which belongs to you in your national capacity, must always exalt the just pride of patriotism more than any appelation derived from local discriminations."

George Washington a plagiarist!![11]

During the campaign, *Life* was so busy trying to defeat Blaine that it seldom found time to mention his Democratic opponent. Mitchell stated the magazine's editorial choice shortly after the Democratic convention.

> If Mr. Cleveland could be separated from Mr. Hendricks, we would drop the latter. (Hendricks, *Life* discovered later, played the accordion, and thereby disqualified himself as a serious candidate.)
>
> Unfortunately, this is impossible, and being of the opinion that a ticket composed of common sense and an honest head combined with a copperhead in a position where the copperheadism is harmless, is preferable to a front of brass with a tail fit only to be wagged, we support Cleveland and Hendricks rather than Blaine and Logan.[12]

The chief humorous issues of the new administration's inaugural months were what to do with the new Washington's Monument, which *Life* piously hoped would not be blamed by posterity on Washington, and the agitation by some Congressmen to restore "Republican simplicity" to the Democratic party. We are not inclined, today, to think of Chester A. Arthur as an American Nero, but the shade of Jefferson was invoked to lead the White House out of the sybaritic swamps in which it floundered. *Life* noted that Jefferson's wine bill during his period in office had been $10,855.90, and suggested that even such was the austerity that most appealed to the reformers. Along with the Washington's monument controversy, *Life* considered the more localized question of Bartholdi's giant bronze, which still languished for want of a pedestal on "Bedlam's Island."

Three years later, and four years after that, *Life* still supported

Cleveland, although without the fire it displayed during the first campaign. The reason for the mildness was that Benjamin Harrison was less vulnerable to satire than Blaine had been. At least the editors found him less objectionable. The 1888 campaign was conducted practically without *Life*'s help.

Life backed the President on the tariff. It believed that regulations that excluded statuary and literature and welcomed sugar, lumber, iron, and immigrants, which is to say Tammany votes, were due to be changed. In October, it urged Cleveland's reelection, but as the closeness of the contest became more and more apparent it seemed bemused. When Harrison won, *Life* did not even find a joke in the fact that its candidate had received a greater popular vote. A cartoon by Gibson a week after the election called for national unity, but *Life*'s treatment of the campaign had hardly indicated that national unity was threatened.

By 1892 the Tammany beast had swelled until it blotted out the view of Washington almost entirely. David Bennett Hill, Tammany's Senator from and former governor of New York, who had inherited the governorship when Cleveland went to the White House, appeared early in the year to be gathering strength in a move to storm the Democratic convention. *Life* editorialized much and joked little about Hill's candidacy. It adopted the sobering viewpoint that "practical politics," Hill's avowed single principle, was defensible so long as it was unblemished by corruption, but that it was hardly what the Democratic party claimed to stand for. When Hill took the New York delegation to Chicago in July and limped home again, his political aspirations all but obliterated by the Cleveland avalanche, *Life* felt a little more chipper, and crowed some over the remains. "Mr. Hill was the representative of about all that was vicious in American politics," wrote Martin, and all subsequent references to Hill in the election year were contemptuous. Subsequent references to non-Tammany candidates, though, were scanty and furtive, almost embarrassed. *Life* backed Cleveland, but even more languidly than it had four years previously. The Republican opposition was a sick elephant in an occasional cartoon.

In order, perhaps, to satisfy its jaded appetite for a candidate to satirize, *Life* proposed its own slate in 1892; for President, Ward McAllister, social arbiter; for Vice-President, Albert Wettin, Prince of Wales. It had fun at its nominees' expense, making particular capital out of the Prince's fondness for cards and McAllister's *ex cathedra* pronouncements. The objection that the proposed Vice-President was not an American citizen, said *Life*, "need not be considered, as *Life* has paid a Tammany judge five dollars to naturalize him." The slate was unsuccessful.

Life proposed a ticket in 1896, too. Its platform was free coinage of leather money.[13] Its Presidential choice was John W. Goff, New York's assistant district attorney who had not long before put several election officials from both parties behind bars.   Anthony Comstock, the moral overseer, one of the really outlandish aberrations that America has promoted to public eminence, was to be Vice-President.[14] Goff's record was allowed to speak for itself, but *Life* told Comstock, "Tony, when we want to see how big an ass someone else is, all we have to do is to place him alongside of you."[15] It could not have picked a better standard of asininity.   Since his elevation to the presidency of the New York Society for the Suppression of Vice in 1873, Comstock had, or so he boasted, caused more than fifty suicides, and once had come down on *Life* for publishing that horrid obscenity, the naked little cherub who was its personification. But *Life*'s interest in its ticket pined away. Perhaps *Life*'s candidates meant too little to the country beyond the Hudson. Anyway, the real campaign was lively enough, this time, to make the most enervated political commentator bestir himself.

Bryan vs. McKinley, silver vs. gold, West vs. East, demagogue vs. oligarch, with some side remarks on tariff and soldiers' pensions—these were the issues of the 1896 Presidential campaign. *Life*, like the majority of the electorate, understood only a few and disliked them all. Bimetallism had been the big front wheel of the political bicycle for a long time. *Life* was adamantly against it.   It even questioned the Republicans', especially McKinley's, piety on the subject, and with some reason. *Life* had appraised the major from Canton as a man who would willingly tootle both ends of the fife at once, if he could get away with it. Before there was a Republican platform, before the Republicans convened in St. Louis in June, *Life* had editorialized on McKinley's qualifications:

> A man whose availability as a candidate consists in his ability to disguise or conceal his sentiments is not the sort of person to whom an opinion can be trusted to adhere, even though it should be forced on him.[16]
>
> Where, oh where does he stand and what does he stand for? We hear him chanting from Canton, "I'm sitting on the stile, Marie, where we sat side by side."[17]

It had set its doggerel loose upon him:

> When Whitcomb Riley did declare
> That "June wants me and I'm to spare,"
> He dreamed not of the present day
> When Bill McKinley feels that way.[18]

And finally it had "wrung a statement of Mr. McKinley's intentions from him:"

> I always have been, now am, and intend to remain whatever I consider for the best good and future welfare of
>
> Yours very truly,
> William McKinley[19]

If before the campaign McKinley was characterized by *Life* as a selfseeker, William Jennings Bryan of Nebraska was scorned as an irresponsible and somehow pitiful puppet manipulated by easy money radicals, Populists, and probably dynamiters, but not really to be blamed for his words or his actions. "Why do they always call me 'the boy orator'?" Bryan was made to ask *Life*; and *Life* replied, "To distinguish you from a man orator." "But they say I'm a menace," Bryan "protested." "Calm yourself, Willie," said *Life*, "I can assure you that you are absolutely harmless."20 The curious thing was not that *Life* should oppose Bryan, who was Western, demagogic, and for free silver, nor even that it should dismiss him so offhandedly. In the serene depths of its political conservatism such dismissals were the rule by which *Life* strictly adhered when dealing with politically unpleasant persons. If *Life* really distrusted a man, *Life* believed that that man did not have a chance. But it was quaint that *Life* should accuse Bryan of slavish obedience to some unnamed and unseeable master, when it had been assured (but by Hearst's papers, which it trusted no further than the weather reports) that McKinley scarcely dared to stretch without consulting Marcus A. Hanna, of Cleveland, first.

Hanna was the second of the newly arrived major figures. His biographer, Thomas Beer, has argued that he became a kingmaker not through lust for power, but from an idealistic and quite fervent conviction that the gold standard could not be tampered with without totally ruining American credit abroad. His choice of McKinley as a candidate and his manipulations at the St. Louis convention, Beer writes, were dictated by the convictions that gold *had* to win, that no Easterner could be elected, and that McKinley was popular and handy.21 To *Life*, Hanna's directing hand was evident in the Republicans' campaign from the time "Mr. Hanna's convention" in St. Louis named McKinley until after the election when *Life* assured Hanna that although the responsibility for running a government was great, Major McKinley would be a great help. Yet *Life* questioned neither Hanna's actions nor his motives. This was before *Life* and the Trusts quarrelled seriously. The nearest thing to a tilt at Hanna that *Life* printed in 1896 was a rueful concession to his meteoric rise in public attention. Certain celebrities, said *Life*, are sulking because suddenly all the testimonials for patent soap and malt extract are being written by Mark Hanna.

The cartoonists enjoyed the campaign as they had enjoyed no other since 1884. The image of himself that Bryan has passed along to posterity is that of a stout, bald, bleating old man; but *Life*'s artists saw him in '96 as a gangling, wild-eyed, wavy-haired youth in a Buster Brown-ish collar, striking innumerable poses and eternally waving both fists above his head for punctuation. The silver issue appeared in the cartoons, too, one notable double page drawing showing a *grande dame* riding beside her coachman while a footman worked a spigot to drain off the interior of the coach, which was full of silver coins.22 Posters in store windows indicated that prices had risen about ten thousand fold. Then a drawing by F. T. Richards, titled "The Rival Ferryman," appeared just before the election. The rival ferrymen were, of course, Bryan and McKinley, and their rivalry was for the patronage of a perplexed-looking Uncle Sam, whom they wished to transport to the capitol building across the river. Each ferryman's barge tried to be more decrepit, more patched, more jerry-built than his rival's. Bryan's was loaded to the scuppers with silver—coins, jewelry, assorted junk—and on top of this heap a moth-eaten jackass stood and glared sullenly at McKinley's craft. That poor scow was about to founder under the weight of a placidly idiotic elephant which squatted in the stern nearly buried by an enormous load of bundles labeled MONOPOLY, TARIFF, and TRUSTS. While Bryan exhorted from the bow of his boat, McKinley stood arms akimbo on his, considerably over-balanced by the elephant, scowling as magnificently as possible at nothing in particular, striking a Napoleonic pose and wearing a Napoleonic hat. The Napoleon joke was *Life*'s own favorite for McKinley that year; it fitted his stature, his habitual expression, and *Life*'s opinion of his opinion of himself. "Everybody says I look like Napoleon," *Life* made him say, "but I think that Napoleon looks like me."[23] The cartoon by Richards summed up *Life*'s ideas on the campaign. According to *Life*, Bryan was a windbag, his most important plank was his worst liability, and his party was in ruins. McKinley was a figurehead, too small for his party, and almost sublimely unaware of the complacency and favoritism that threatened, from within that party, to swamp him.

Possibly the funniest political cartoon that *Life* ran in 1896 was another drawing by Richards of a meticulously detailed chameleon with McKinley's head and Bonaparte's hat, crouching on a huge gold dollar. From its neck depended a tag reading, "McKinley, Chameleo Vulgaris."

All this notwithstanding, *Life* wrote in November, "The victory that has been won is not a partisan success. It was a victory of the American people for the American republic."[24] This was to say, Bryan lost.

Bryan lost again in 1900, and to the same combination of McKinley and Hanna which had beaten him before. This time *Life* was no longer so sure of the existence of the American republic. The Spanish-American war and the Philippine incident had intervened, and the magazine, staunchly anti-imperialist, was horrified at the Republican administration's policies. It all but believed that McKinley planned to go into active and immediate competition with the European powers for sovereignty over every unclaimed area on earth. It was equally shocked at the notion of empire-building like the Victorian England it loathed and at the possibility that Sulu savages would be admitted to the American electorate. On the other hand, "16 to 1" was a more frightful idea still. It believed that McKinley was a threat to the American system, but that Bryan and silver would destroy the nation utterly.

Happily, Colonel Roosevelt was available for comic relief.

Life's shifting ideas about Commissioner-Secretary-Governor-Vice President-President-Citizen Roosevelt cover nearly all the thirty five years of this history. Roosevelt was amenable to caricature: a New Yorker with society connections and a home in Oyster Bay, a flamboyant soldier, a phrasemaker, and a publicity seeker of mighty accomplishments. His teeth and pince-nez adorned the faces of dogs, horses, buildings, walnuts, and the moon, in *Life*'s cartoons, at one time or another during his career. *Life* had noticed him first during the Blaine campaign. It had hoped that Roosevelt would bring a new honesty to New York politics, but his support of Blaine made it reconsider.

Roosevelt at the time hoped for the next Republican gubernatorial nomination. It did not come, and by the next year he had entered a New York mayoralty election that included, in a crowded field, Henry George. Despite his nearly unique qualifications as the object of political humor, Roosevelt had either the genius or the good fortune almost invariably to share the spotlight with someone *Life* thought was even funnier. So it was with George, whose land reform ideas *Life* preferred to envision as Tammanyesque spoiling raised to sublime heights. It offered its support to George in return for "the block propinquitous to this office, one end of which is occupied by Mr. Delmonico's restaurant." Later, *Life* claimed that George's campaigners "Won't permit us to shout for him because we don't happen to be laboring men. We are nothing but capitalists who publish a weekly journal." *Life* persisted, however ("Go stuff thy pockets, Oh tramp, go gorge, On lunch that's free, Hooray for George."),25 and claimed to be sorry when Abram S. Hewitt, the Tammany candidate, won as expected. At least, it said, this would put an end to talk of class politics in America. Hewitt, by the way, was a good mayor and did not shrink from facing down the Tammany Tiger when he thought it necessary. Two years later, during the next campaign, Martin compared him to Carlyle, an accolade he bestowed on few men and practically no politicians. Hewitt lost.

Life followed Roosevelt closely in his political rise, praising him extravagantly when his literary or anti-machine sides were prominent, and deploring him when it thought his ambition outran his abilities. *Life* saw that as governor of New York, Roosevelt was a thorn in the side of both Tammany and Senator Tom Platt, the Republican boss, who had some ambitions for himself.

In 1900 *Life* fought Roosevelt's nomination for the Vice-Presidency. Throughout the election year *Life* turned to Roosevelt whenever its choler, raised by the other candidates, threatened to choke it. Martin contributed a poem about Roosevelt that is, if not the best thing he ever did for the magazine, undoubtedly a strong candidate for the funniest. The poem celebrates the strenuous Col. Roosevelt's personality, and includes the lines—

> About one strenuous man to every thousand
> folks if right,
> Five hundred lean and vigilant to keep him
> aye in sight;
> Five hundred fat to sit on him hard when he
> happens to want to fight.[26]

The Broncobuster, the Strenuous Life, and a dozen Rooseveltian dreams of glory pre-empted space that one would have assumed to belong to the Presidential candidates.

Of those gentlemen and all their works, *Life* was contemptuous. "*Life*'s Guide to Voters" was reprinted four times between the party conventions and the election:

For War, Teddy, Taxation and Trusts, vote for William McKinley.

For the Constitution, Peace, Panic, and Populism, vote for W. J. Bryan.

Life was not quite so badly off, though, as the voters who were "casting about trying to make up their minds whether their distrust of Colonel Bryan or Major McKinley is the more acute and irrepressible." It preferred good money even in other people's pockets to bad. The Democrats, it opined, held to the notion that sixteen grains of silver should be as good as a grain of gold with the excruciating adhesiveness of a mustard plaster—and with a mustard plaster's perspicacity and foresight.

The Democratic candidate was the same Bryan who had been thoroughly whacked the last time. He was growing stouter and developing in caricature that square jaw and tight mouth that gave him an obstinate, old-womanish look in later years; but he was still playing the same note on his silvery tongue, still representing on the one hand Western radicals like J. P. Altgeld of Illinois and on the other hand *Life*'s favorite political demon, Tammany. *Life* preferred to ignore him during the campaign, and afterwards, when it was rumored that the defeated candidate might enter the Presbyterian ministry, applauded the idea and suggested that he take the new Vice-President along with him.

Not ignoring President McKinley, however, in January *Life* portrayed him in verse and drawings rejecting grandpa's old Phrygian cap and donning an imperial crown to escort Victoria to the "Nations' Ball." In April it pictured Columbia rejecting him violently, along with her other suitor, Bryan. In April there was a brief movement to push Admiral George Dewey, of Manila Bay, into the Republican nomination. Dewey refused, but the fact that *Life* was enthusiastic about it indicates the tenor of its politics. Mark Hanna, compared to Dewey, was a liberal. In June, over the signature of McCready Sykes, appeared the following:

Heroic Symphony: The President
of the United States

He standeth firm, a rock of strength,
    A fortress fast and strong;
Nor heeds the wind that sweeps his foot,
    Nor storms that crash along.

Serene, self-poised, immovable,
    No raging mob doth swerve him;
Nor all the howlings of the crowd
    Nor shouting, doth unnerve him.

He trims no sail to passing breeze—
    Our pilot bold and true—
By Truth and Right he holds his course,
    And guides the mazes through.

His pledge is true as Heaven's truth;
    His promise, Honor's token;
And steadfast as the eternal hills,
    His solemn word unbroken.

Oh, happy nation, blessed in thy
    God-like Chief Magistrate—
A Lincoln come again to earth
    To guide the ship of state!

Postscript—A murrain and a blight
    And fiendish tortures drastic,
On him who dares to intimate
    That this is writ sarcastic.[27]

In August, Joseph Smith began a series called "Zoological Politics," whose characters were the Jelly Fish (McKinley), the Octopus (Hanna), the Bronco (Roosevelt), the Horse Leech (the trusts), the Serpent (Bryan), and the Ass (the public). The Ass was said to be fed up with the whole menagerie, and "in for a kicking matinee." When McKinley won, *Life* was glad silver had lost.

Much of the satire aimed at McKinley in 1900 had little to do with the Presidential race. *Life* was genuinely angry about the "imperialist" war, and lost no opportunity to link it to the British campaign of expansion in South Africa, or to liken Hanna or McKinley unfavorably to the Queen of England, perhaps *Life*'s least favorite personality, saving Charles Frohman. The epithets "Jelly Fish" and "Octopus" fairly represent *Life*'s assessment of the President and his Ohio crony, and a cartoon by William Bengough, "Fun For the Boys," shows the shade of Washington musing over a riotously laughing McKinley and Roosevelt who are in turn watching a smug Hanna unroll the following scroll:

Declaration of Dependence

We bought the Filipinos for $20,000,000. Therefore we hold these lies to be self-evident. That all brown men are created unequal; that they are endowed by their buyers with certain unalienable wrongs; that among these are death, captivity and pursuit.

That to secure these wrongs governments are instituted among Filipinos, deriving their just powers from the consent of the undersigned.

Old Daddy Washington is a has-been. We're it.

Me, Mac, and Teddy[28]

The war with Spain had soured *Life* on the McKinley administration, whatever small virtue it had been able to see in the man who won for gold. *Life* never understood how America got into the war, nor what any American could gain from shooting at Spaniards or, later, Filipinos. *Life* had seen the possibility of American intervention in South America as early as 1896, when America's involvement in the Venezuela-British Guiana border dispute suggested to Martin that America should join an alliance and smash England. When that war was averted, *Life* saw no reason to fight with anybody except England, and as events in Cuba were given greater and greater coverage in the New York papers, *Life* deprecated their importance. Martin wrote that the preservation of America's forests, another question concurrently before Congress, was far more important to the country than anything that might happen in Cuba. Even when the *Maine* was sunk and the country lathered itself into war frenzy *Life* gave equal editorial and art coverage to Emile Zola's trial following his lone campaign to obtain justice for Dreyfus.[29] Earlier, it had "warned" the boy-king Alfonso of Spain that if his country won a war against ours, he would have to take McKinley, Hanna, Congress, and the yellow papers. *Life* thought the war, when it began, was waged for the profit of a few; it was certain that the peace afterward was run exactly for that.

In verse, prose, and cartoon, *Life* deplored McKinley's policy of expansion that followed the war. Its isolationism, its distrust of Britain, its sympathies for the underdog, its suspicion of all new public enterprises, and its belief in the present perfection of American life all combined to turn it against expansion. It believed that McKinley was abandoning America's principles and stood to gain only Britain's hateful reputation as a conqueror. It offered a prize for the best essay defending isolation against imperialism. An 1899 cartoon by Broughton showed Liberty with a bloody sword, flanked on the one side by Hessian troops shooting down American rebels and on the other by American troops executing a Filipino.[30] Another of the same year showed, successively, a vulture attacking a lamb, an eagle driving off the vulture and sweeping the lamb under its wing, and the eagle looking smugly well-fed while the vulture lies dead in the background, the lamb having mysteriously disappeared. Richards did a cover drawing of Uncle Sam magnificently awry in imperial robes. He says, "Say, *Life*, how do I look?" *Life* answers, "You look like a D——d fool."[31] Martin contributed a quiet quatrain:

> The peaceful hours we once enjoyed,
> How calm their memory still!
> But they have left an aching void
> Expansion cannot fill.[32]

And Joseph Smith offered an essay on "The Art of Colonization" that spoke *Life*'s mind and spared nobody. Mark Twain's "Person Sitting in Darkness" would have understood it perfectly, as one paragraph illustrates:

> Colonization is the art of appropriating other people's real estate. The customary rule in acquiring a colony is to select a desirable piece of real estate whose occupants have few sartorial advantages, whose complexions have a different color scheme from ours, and whose views on post-mortem existence are not in accord with those we profess. We then move in and proceed to illumine their intellectual darkness.[33]

The 1900 presidential election already interested *Life* in 1899. It could not believe that Bryan would be renominated, and it was hopeful that McKinley would not. It suggested a ticket of Dewey and Roosevelt. When the "Embalmed Beef" scandal broke out, and Secretary of War Alger, along with ranking generals of the Cuban campaign, was accused by a Congressional committee of conspiracy to defraud the government, not to mention complicity in poisoning several regiments of American soldiers, *Life* suggested, via a Richards cartoon, that the defendants be pilloried with their noses in a can of the vile stuff: McKinley, who refused to take action against them, was to be pilloried alongside them.

Life tried to treat the assassination of McKinley as a shock, but it could muster little emotion beyond surprise. Certainly, *Life* had been surprised rather more violently than ever before in its history. It had poked very little fun at the Buffalo Fair, possibly having run out of fair jokes nine years before, when it needled Chicago half to death. On August 22, 1901, three weeks before McKinley was shot at Buffalo, *Life* wrote, "Mr. Theodore Roosevelt is writing a book on the future of Vice-Presidents. It consists of a preface, introduction and about four hundred blank pages." So much for foresight; but a worse editorial *faux pas* occurred when *Life* printed a cartoon by Walker showing McKinley as a farmer driving a fat team of one elephant and one horse through a field of money—four days after the assassin's attack.[34]

The explanation—that the edition was already printed—sounded peevish, as though *Life* believed that to apologize for an honest error, when that error insulted the likes of William McKinley, debased it. *Life* did not hesitate, though, to point out that its arch-enemies, the Theatrical Syndicate, refused to close their theaters to honor the dead President.

Life also seemed pleased that the assassin was an anarchist, and A. B. Walker did a double page drawing that appeared in the issue that announced the President's death,[35] and a cover for the next number, both about anarchists. When cooler reflection revealed later that Czolgosz was not an anarchist at all, Martin did the handsome thing on the editorial

·LIFE·

MISSED THE BOAT.

page. That is to say, he chided those who were too quick to see in the poor maniac an international conspiracy, but in the same paragraph he applauded the coming execution.

Once again, *de mortuus nil nisi bonum* guided *Life*'s last words on the President. Martin's McKinley obituary contained, in fact, an abnormal amount of self-recrimination, and some notes on McKinley that could hardly have been recognized by readers familiar with the Napoleonic puppet of the cartoons.

The 1904 campaign looked, early in the year, as though it might produce some colorful candidates besides President Roosevelt. Cleveland was around, and available. Hanna was mentioned as a Republican possibility and William Randolph Hearst seemed to mean business in the Democratic camp; but Hearst's chances bloomed and wilted,[36] and Hanna died before the conventions met and was given a handsome obituary notice by *Life*,[37] and when the Democrats nominated Judge Alton Parker of New York, and accepted the gold standard, *Life* settled down to a campaign that was no more than an occasional pause to remark that while Smith was a good man, Jones was a good man, too. If Parker had not been quite so judicial, one suspects, *Life* might have come out for him. He campaigned in the McKinley fashion, saying as little as could be said and weighing his words at about 16 to 1. *Life* never ceased to mistrust Roosevelt's showboating, but it had to admire the vigor that was inseparable from it.

Roosevelt, during this race, was most often portrayed tending a cradle which held an enormous, hoggish infant labeled "Infant Industries" or "Trusts." Joseph Smith saw the President as a knightly figure out of the middle ages. Parker, it was noted, was a friend and former campaign manager of *Life*'s old enemy, David Bennett Hill, and although *Life* several times proclaimed Parker's innocence of any share of Hill's political ethics, it got what fun it could out of picturing Hill leading Parker, or Parker dragging Hill. It was not surprised when Roosevelt won. It seemed satisfied that he could do the job.

In 1908 Roosevelt turned the job over to William Howard Taft and left for what he hoped would be a four-year vacation. The Republican convention at Chicago docilely nominated the imposing Cincinnatian, whom *Life* cartooned as Roosevelt's dancing bear. "No Democratic nominee can be elected without Bryan's cooperation, and Bryan is for Bryan," *Life* wrote, and inevitably as death the Democrats at Denver returned to Bryan, who began to proclaim himself the "real heir" to Roosevelt's reform administration. They fought in the President's shadow, but the President was planning to battle the African fauna for a while before running for office again, and he kept out of it. The Vice-Presidential candidates were more colorless than their senior partners. James S. Sherman of New York, on the Republican ticket, had a reputation as a friend of money; John W. Kern of Indiana, Bryan's running mate, had whiskers.   Martin remarked that "somehow the Presidential campaign appeals much more than usual to the observer's sense of humor," but the magazine did not bear him out.   It had expended its Bryan jokes too lavishly twelve years before, and its capital was used up.   Taft, while he had comic possibilities, was going to be the next President, and *Life* was willing to give him its serious attention until he demonstrated his unworthiness.   It did turn Otho Cushing to caricaturing him, and since Cushing drew debutantes to look like beer draymen his Taft was a mountainous figure indeed.   It also defended him from those who claimed that he lacked self-confidence.   It pointed out that "Mary Baker Eddy defined obesity as an adipose belief of yourself as a substance."   After that, anyone who questioned Taft's belief in himself simply had no case.   However, most of the fun with Taft was over by convention time.   Even the anomalous position of heir-apparent to a democratic chief of state can be milked for only so many laughs.

Perhaps two bits of verse printed by *Life* during the campaign sum up the magazine's whole attitude toward national politics in 1908.   The verses are cheerful, impersonal, and without malice or insight.   The first is a playlet by Tom Masson:

The Political Extravaganza in Ye Year 1908

SCENE: Two large and variegated platforms, separated by a thin curtain, both being very much alike, and composed by planks that have just been sawed and planed by paid experts.   There is a low murmuring sound, accompanied by slow music, and Taft and Sherman step forward.   Sherman keeps in the background, his long Congressional career making him extremely diffident.

Solo—W. H. Taft.

> I would beg to state
> I'm a candidate
> Quite hale and hearty and ruddy.
> And in spite of all talk—
> Though I walk the chalk—
> I am *not* an understudy

> But the G. O. P. that I represent
> Is for me a matter of sentiment,
> And I beg to repeat, tho' you all may stare,
> I'm *not* tied up to the Teddy Bear.

He gracefully retires with his side partner.   There is a loud braying, and several tom-toms are beaten by Tammany chiefs, filling the air with their peculiar music.   W. J. Bryan, leading his running mate by the whiskers, now steps forward.   He bows gracefully, while Kern fans him vigorously.

Solo—W. J. Bryan.

> Twelve years ago,
> As you doubtless know,
> With a cross of gold I ran.

> I was rude and crude—
> Quite far from a dude—
> But now I'm a proper man.
>
> I have traveled wide,
> And my head applied
> To Culture and Art, you see.
> I've broadened my mind
> And I'm highly refined,
> As a President ought to be.
>
> But the common folks that I represent
> Are still a matter of sentiment,
> And with graceful front, why, I beg to sing
> That *I'm* not tied to a single thing.

He bows neatly, several large bouquets are handed to him and he retires. There is then a loud blare of music and the band plays "The Conquering Heroes Come," as the leading Trusts advance, Uncle Sam meekly following, and the G. O. P. elephant and the Demo's donkey bring up the rear, both with their tails between their legs.

The Trusts all mark time, until the Standard Oil Trust steps out in front.

Solo—Standard Oil.

> Ha! ha! Ho! ho!
> Let the campaign go
> The way that it will. Ha! ha!
> For it doesn't (to us)
> Much matter a cuss—
> *We'll* still all be above par.
>
> For appearance's sake
> We should like to make
> Bill Taft what he wants to be;
> But if Bryan should win
> Why *we* wouldn't get thin,
> For we'd still be just as free!
>
> For the piles of Cash that we represent
> Are with us a matter of sentiment.
> And so we say (While the country's bled)
> Each President's only a figurehead.

As the curtain goes down Uncle Sam is distinctly seen, throwing up his hands.   *Finis.*[38]

The second is by Frank C. Wellman. It has an admirable Alfred Noyes trot to it; one suspects that had Wellman seen fit to probe deeper, he might have made a real contribution to the language's meager fund of good satiric doggerel. Three stanzas will give enough of the drift:

Campaign Cogitations

> The Republican convention has assembled and dispersed;
> The achievements of the party have been vividly rehearsed;
> The standard-bearer stable
> Can display the "union label"

As the logical successor of Theodore the First.
And the Grand Old Party Jumbo, with a record-breaking load,
Comes a-swinging down the turnpike in the middle of the road.

The cohorts of Democracy have marshaled in the West;
The oracles have spoken and delivered their behest;
    And the long-eared, lank and bony
    Little Democratic pony
Comes a-loping down the alley on the Presidential quest;
While the ever Peerless Prophet from the city by the Platte
Sits a-straddle of the saddle where he has so often sat.

And when the struggle's over and the hurly-burly's done,
When the verdict has been rendered and the victory has been won,
    The defeated aggregation
    Will declare for publication
That Democracy's a failure and the country is undone.
And the poor, old, undone country will resume her wonted jogs.
And contentedly continue on her journey to the dogs.[39]

The next National election, in 1912, saw the Bull Moose Party erupt,
spread destruction over the political Pompeiis of several national figures,
Taft and Roosevelt not the least among these, and cool again so quickly
that it became a historical curiosity almost before its violent period was
over. *Life* foresaw the explosiveness of the election as early as the second
paragraph of its first issue of the year. "The task of the greatest traditional
importance is to elect a President," it addressed the incoming year. "We
pity you in this job. Things have got into a terrible muddle and the
Presidential timber is unusually poor." Roosevelt was writing copiously
of politics in the *Outlook*, and apportioning much of that writing to the
shortcomings of Taft's administration. In January a cartoon by Cushing
cast Taft as Desdemona to Roosevelt's Iago. But *Life* had little sympathy
for Taft. It did not like his refusal to stand on tariff or anti-trust
questions; it did not like his speechmaking propensities; it did not like
his golf. Significantly, it editorialized, "While Mr. Taft has made plenty
of political mistakes which were damaging to his reputation as a party
leader, he has made very few which were damaging to the country."
Yet, in all fairness, it could not support Taft for President. It did what
it could, though, to support him against Roosevelt, for not only was the
idea of a third term repugnant to *Life*, but Roosevelt later made a real
bid for the support of the Suffragettes, whose names *Life* recognized as
anathema.

    Life made much of Theodore Roosevelt's public statement, four
years previously, that he would never seek the nomination again; but
Life recognized at the same time that Roosevelt sincerely considered
Roosevelt to be the only man fit to hold the office. The sincerity
bothered it rather more than the turnabout.

    Despite the muddle that *Life* predicted—and found and profited
from—its editors were able to predict with uncommon accuracy the

tortuous zigzag of 1912 politics. To be sure, they said in February that, "Governor Wilson . . . has been an interesting player, but his game does not look just now like the game of a winner." And they said only a few weeks before the convention, "It looks, just now, as though the Democrats would nominate Champ Clark." But they predicted the formation of the Roosevelt party; they predicted that "any competent Democrat" would win over the divided Republicans; they predicted that if Taft were the Republican nominee the Democrats would select the most liberal runner in their stable, and that the obvious choice was Wilson; finally, they predicted that because of Wilson's liberalism and the general rejection of the third term, there would be a great flurry of voters crossing party lines. All these except the last were validated, and the last has the bulk of evidence in its favor. Bryan had earned 176 electoral votes in his best year, 1896; Wilson won with 435. One concludes that although the machinery of presidential politics became ever more complicated, neither *Life* nor its readers were particularly confused by it.

Life's humor, as it applied to the 1912 campaign, was, again, creditable if not inspired. Once more Roosevelt was the First Clown and a piece of unfortunate timing in their Moose baiting brought on what must have been one of the gravest editorial crises in the magazine's existence. There had already been a "Wilson Number."[40] A "Bull Moose Number" was planned for October and it was to be dedicated entirely to lampoons of Roosevelt and his party.

> Eighty-four thousand copies had been printed when the tragic news (that a would-be assassin had shot the ex-President) came from Milwaukee.
>
> Those eighty-four thousand copies of the real Bull Moose Number were destroyed. After the paper had been running on the presses for two days and nights, a new paper was substituted—with the exception of the colored cover, which could not be changed—and the Bull Moose Number, as our readers actually saw it, came out on time! This is a typographical triumph which will be appreciated by all who understand the problems of printing.
>
> As for the things that the original Bull Moose number contained—well, the world will never know what it missed.
>
> We rejoice that Roosevelt is all right again, but alas! things will never be the same with us. That Bull Moose Number of Life was hurt much more than Mr. Roosevelt.[41]

Indeed it was. *Life* must have felt the criticism of its error in reporting the McKinley assassination more than it showed. The Bull Moose Number "as our readers actually saw it" contained nothing that could be construed as an insult to a man who, for all the editors knew, might be in a martyr's grave before the ink was dry. A few things from the original number found their way into subsequent issues, notably the middle two-page drawing by William Walker, titled "Progressional," which showed Roosevelt as a bishop leading a suitably labeled group of Progressive altar boys. The world, as the editors said, will never know how funny

Life might have been on the Bull Moose issue. The funniest Roosevelt cartoon of the year was another drawing by Walker of a coyly delighted Roosevelt as Pharoah's daughter who is discovering a toothy, mustachioed and bespectacled baby Moses in a swamp. The caption is, "Found: A Third Party." Probably the funniest commentary on Roosevelt's candidacy was an accidental offshoot of one of *Life*'s everlasting contests, not necessarily political at all, called "*Life*'s Examination Paper" and consisting of ten questions intended to provoke facetiousness, ranging from "Should a Suffragette marry?" to "How would you spend a million dollars to do the least possible good?"

> You never can tell what a *Life* competition is going to develop . . . The early answers disclose an important concrete political fact. If *Life*'s readers are in any way a representative body, the answers to questions Numbers 2, 5, and 6 show that the Bull Moose candidate for President is regarded not seriously, but as a joke. Here are the questions:
>
>> If Diogenes were searching America for an honest man, where would he be least likely to find him?
>> What is the funniest thing in the world?
>> Give a good example of perpetual motion.
>
> "Oyster Bay" comes to us so frequently as an answer to the first that there is an evident general mistrust in the sincerity of one of Oyster Bay's leading citizens. To the next we get a predominance of such replies as "Theodore Roosevelt," "T. R.'s belief that he is going to get a third term," etc. To an impressive number of contestants perpetual motion is represented by "T. R.," "Teddy's jaw," "Teddy's mouth." One competitor goes so far as to believe that the funniest thing in the world is the statement, "Under no circumstances will I be a candidate for or accept another nomination."[42]

John Bangs added to *Life*'s tradition of political parody of James Whitcomb Riley's poems with something called "Little Orphant Teddy." Either Riley, as a former contributor, was revered by *Life*'s editors, or he is particularly susceptible to travesty with a political bias. Orphant Teddy, "with great big teeth a-flarin', an' they made a scrunchin' sound," cleaned up on Bosses, Magnates, Trusts, and the Ananias Club, and in the last verse:

> Little Orphant Teddy says he's goin' to take the earth
> An' give it a lambastin' jest for all thet he is worth.
> He's goin' to lam his Uncle Sam, an' soon as he is through
> He's goin' to tackle Yurrup, an' the folks in Asia too;
> An' when he's cleaned 'em up he says he's goin' to take the sea
> An' pore it down the black hole where the Devil's said to be;
> An' then he's goin' to Heaven, where he'll tell 'em all about
> The Bull Moose as'll get them
>> Ef they
>>> Don't
>>>> Watch
>>>>> Out![43]

Taft and Wilson were far less amusing when they did their stints in *Life*. The best cartoon on Taft, by Art Young, showed a lordly, lardly Taft posting down the Presidential Course on a rat-tailed, hollow-eyed, sprung-ribbed cadaver of a horse labeled Republican Party; the caption is, simply, "Beautiful!" *Life* also allowed Capital or Plutocracy, when personified in cartoons, to affect Taft's walrus mustaches and *embonpoint*; but this appearance may be entirely accidental. No Plutocrat since time began has looked more bloated than Taft. *Life* demonstrated, too, how much the long Wilsonian countenance and the Democratic donkey's face resembled one another, but its favorite caricature of Wilson was as a very proper little girl who tattled on the two little, fat roughnecks from the other party. Wilson must have seemed unusually sterile ground to humorists who were used to Roosevelt, and it is hard to explain why they chose to publish a special Wilson Number, unless it was simply that, as the middle two-page illustration of that number shows, they expected him to win. The number is not funny.

By the presidential year 1916, there had come about a number of unhappy changes in *Life*. The magazine was fat, now, the jokes were tired, the tone of the controversial articles was querulous or sneering. The staff had scarcely changed, but the best new contributions were tucked into the back pages among the ads for cigarettes, which the editors disliked, automobiles, which they mistrusted, and cosmetics, which they accused of crimes against femininity. The format was formulized: the typical issue had its regular editorial page, on which appeared a political cartoon, and added to this a page or more of Martin's genial essays on What Was Wrong With The World. The hyphenated-Americans, the pacifists, and those public figures who preached or voted against preparedness or entry into the European war were abused again and again in more billingsgate than the worst insults *Life* once hurled at McKinley's cabinet. "There are but two lawful topics of thought this summer for responsible grownup people—war and politics," wrote Martin in July. But neither topic was funny and *Life* was afraid of both, and a frightened satirist is likely to abandon all subtlety and range himself with the Yahoos.

Preparedness was *Life*'s main concern in 1916, and because Woodrow Wilson seemed less avid for it than *Life*, the magazine would have been overjoyed to back almost anyone who promised to reverse Wilson's policies. *Life* proposed its own ticket again, several weeks before the convention: Henry Ford for President, Wilson for Vice-President; Slogan: Peace Without Honor. Uncle Sam was pictured following a donkey in a tiny circle, and casting a hopeful glance at an elephant grazing in the distance. Nevertheless, as the convention dates drew near, *Life* noted Wilson's grip on his party. "To the one who is able to predict who will be nominated on the Democratic ticket for President," it wrote, "*Life* will present the privilege of becoming a regular subscriber, on receipt of course, of the proper amount." After Wilson won the nomination, *Life* pictured him jumping the donkey through a hoop. This recognition of his political shrewdness might have warned readers that eventually *Life* would come out for Wilson.

Life's reaction to the Republican nominee, Charles Evans Hughes, was mixed. Martin tried to sneak past the nomination of Hughes on "ifs" and "maybe's," but Thomas Masson, a week after the nominations were in, begged "Exchughes Me" on the first page of the June 27 issue:

> I refuse
> To vote for Hughes,
> No matter what the hues
> Of his whiskers; blues,
> Pinks, greens, grays, browns,
> Or any other shades or tones
> That might fuse. My muse
> Is lame, halt, and blind, but the news of Hughes
>   would not enthuse
> *Any* muse like mine
> If she were nine
> Or a hundred and nine. I'd choose
> Almost anyone but Hughes—
> Someone addicted to booze,
> Who can cuss and abuse—
> A red-blooded burglar, who could infuse
> Me with respect. But I refuse
> Absolutely and unqualifiedly and irrevocably
> To vote for a pious, respectable, hyphenated,
> Hand-picked, pussy-footed candidate
> Like Hughes!

Masson seldom spoke so strongly, but he spoke for *Life*. The magazine, too, would choose almost anyone but Hughes, but it wished that someone besides Wilson would present himself. It had had enough of peace:

> That strange little bug, my child, is the vacillatus Wilsonatus, or Democratic Administration bug. It feeds on hot air and the green leaves of the federal reserve tree, and its principal method of locomotion is going round and round.[44]

> But the G. O. P. morass yielded a stranger specimen:
> That, my son, is the hirsutishughes, otherwise known as the platitudinous frigidatalis, or common trimmer. It has the strong and pliant backbone of the jellyfish . . . If you call it a highbrow it will ruffle up its whiskers and attack you fiercely with its antennae. Otherwise it does no harm, except to emit sounds that have no meaning.[45]

In August, *Life* remembered that it did not like Wilson. It opined, anonymously, that the day the *Lusitania* sank, "Woodrow Wilson fell." It printed a cartoon by Harry Grant Dart which depicted Wilson, prissily dressed as he was always shown, attempting to fly a kite labeled

"Democratic Ticket 1916," patched with notes and the Mexican policy and weighed down by Josephus Daniels and prohibition. The caption was, "You Can't Do It, Woodrow." Even just before the election, Arthur Guiterman wrote a "Ballade of Regret," with an *envoi* that ran:

> Voter, your Hughes is too austere;
>   Your Wilson will not go a-gunning;
> Your whole campaign is drab and drear,
>   Now don't you wish T. R. was running?[46]

Only a week afterward, in the November 2 issue, *Life* came out for Wilson and predicted a Wilson victory. Two things are significant here. *Life* quoted extensively from Dr. Charles Eliot, formerly of Harvard, when it explained its Presidential choice; and *Life*, having been Harvarded into making a choice, presumed that its choice would be the popular one.

If Hughes had not parted his beard in the middle, *Life*'s cartoonists would have found him impossible to caricature. After the election, *Life* showed commendable restraint by restricting itself to one very small drawing showing Wilson striking it rich in California.

Life's treatment of the country's second war since the magazine's birth was in striking contrast to its pained puzzlement and half-unbelief in the Spanish-American war. In 1899 it had sympathized duly with the Cubans; it saw neither reason nor profit in carrying the war with Spain beyond Cuba. As the European war approached in 1914, *Life*'s sympathies were largely pro-German. It had little regard for the Kaiser; as long ago as 1891 it had seen him as a jittery young man out to prove that he was somebody. But it had a great deal less for England and her works and none at all for Nicholas II of Russia. *Life*'s whole attitude suggests that, had the German army behaved itself less barbarically in Belgium, our entry if any into the hostilities might well have been on the German side. *Life* reflected public opinion fairly well, although not so well as it claimed it did. As late as 1911 *Life* was holding up German-Americans as model citizens whose example it would be well for the Irish-Americans and Hebrew-Americans to copy. By the time America entered the war it was suggesting that all German-Americans who admitted it should be lynched. The hyphen became its mark of Cain.

The Belgian atrocities swung *Life*'s opinion against Germany as the aggressor in the war. The *Lusitania* demonstrated to *Life*'s satisfaction that Germany was America's enemy. As neutrality grew less and less to *Life*'s liking, its pro-war sentiments grew more and more forceful, and by 1917 it retained no trace of the calm appraisal of both sides of the story which it had displayed in 1914, let alone the anti-war sentiments that it proclaimed in 1899. It was positively howling for blood and licking its lips over the proposed destruction of the German army by invincible America.

By February of 1916 *Life* could print, "A neutral is the ignoblest work of God." The process was perhaps a little more gradual than this suggests. While *Life* became increasingly critical of Wilson's shilly-shallying it would not condone Col. Roosevelt's "advocacy of Prussian ideals with which to fight Prussia." Also, even after it had cartooned Uncle Sam as a trembling old man scrawling down "Forget the *Lusitania*" over a dusty but bold "Remember the *Maine*," and suggested via another cartoon that the angels themselves were making shells for the Allies, it could contrast the President and the Colonel after what it conceived to be Gertrude Stein's manner:

Wilson	*Teddy*
May I not may I not may I not? Prunes and persimmons pale and placid, pernickety parsnips in a precious portfolio. Darling dove, what is so difficult as a mauve typewriter? Distrust and dislikeableness, doubtless. May I not? Yes, I may not!	There is a something a something an everything and a tumultousness. I am I am slam bang slametty bang bang boom! Wallop wallop wallop Zowie![47]

Common sense suggested to *Life* that neither extreme was preferable. However, the bulk of the sentiment expressed in 1916 and 1917 by *Life* was undoubtedly Wallop wallop wallop Zowie! Cartoons showed pacifists and pro-Germans tarred and feathered in one indistinguishable heap, and soapbox orators abruptly hanged as a means of quieting their unwelcome oratory. The enemies of the magazine took on the aspect of enemies of the state, and suffragettes were shown to be detracting from the proper efforts of the community to conduct the war. A cartoon in the issue of October 25, 1917, showed three very Semitic slackers railing at a soldier. *Life* apologized for this one, a few weeks later, with the usual lame explanation that they didn't mean *all* Jews, but only the kind that did such things.

Life developed a standard "German" caricature—round-headed, dove-mustached, with a magnificent paunch that made a fine target for the inevitable American bayonet. Its anti-German violence finally reached such heights that a cartoon of September 1918, a particularly frightful example but by no means unique, showed four clean-cut American machine-gunners mowing down orderly rows of unarmed Germans, who had obviously been lined up for the purpose. The width of the gap between *Life*'s usual attitudes and its war hysteria is demonstrable by a squib in the same issue, that gave a real dressing-down to somebody who suggested that over-age horses be slaughtered to conserve food. *Life* insisted in a temper that anybody who would do such a thing to a horse would not hesitate to do the same to anything else old and useless, like his grandfather. The discrepancy between this and the gleeful machine-gunning of unarmed men bothered nobody on the staff. The same sets of ideas continued to move together.

Martin's columns from the last months of 1914 were collected and published as *The War Week By Week*, and the book illustrated very well the essential thoughtfulness of *Life*'s isolationism and by contrast the extent of its panic when its first policies proved insufficient. Martin believed that the war was the result of "Prussian militarism."[48] In contrast, the later war "humor" in the magazine indicated that *all* things German, from dachshunds to kraut, were vicious and hateful. But Martin believed the Germans to be capable of learning from their impending defeat the foolishness of aggression. He began by blaming a Prussian-inspired armament race for the outbreak of the war, on the grounds that an assassinated Archduke would cause few wars between nations not already prepared for war. Within a few weeks, however, he was urging America to follow the advice of Franklin Roosevelt, the Assistant Secretary of the Navy, and arm more quickly. *Life* was as vocal as any American publication in its demands for total mobilization of war effort and its intolerance of individual dissent, when the chips were down.

The story of *Life*'s anti-suffragette crusade is a more cheerful one than that of its war policies. Though the one demonstrates as well as the other that common sense is only as good as its premises, there is no comparable venom in *Life*'s attacks on women and those it made on Germans and German-Americans.

Life's whole set of mind toward women is examined in Chapter V, but it was briefly this. It believed that it spoke for a man's world, but it felt insecure. It believed that women were taking over, somehow. Therefore, it divided its efforts about equally between patronizing feminine inadequacy and pleading with womankind to stick to her distaff. When a writer on marital compatibility in 1886 suggested that marriages could be saved if husbands would abdicate their traditional exercise of domestic tyranny, *Life*'s reviewer wrote,

> Any clear-headed bachelor of average intelligence, on reading here the multitudinous precautions that are necessary to secure married happiness, will unhesitatingly choose single misery to such arduous wedded bliss.
>
> His answer to the conundrum, "How to be happy, though married," will be, "Get a divorce."[49]
>
> The neophyte is presented with this formula for conjugal felicity: "Demonstrative affection and self-sacrifice. . . ." The amount of happiness to be gained by constantly yielding your opinions to a woman's whim must be tremendous. Reducing our author's formula to algebraic terms, it reads: Conjugal felicity = Gush + Mush.[50]

One would suppose that even the most masculine man would see a certain advantage, rather than a liability, in being implored to indulge in "demonstrative affection"—maybe even enough of an advantage to offset the concomitant "self-sacrifice." Not *Life*, however. It saw the slightest concession to women as a loss irredeemable.

All the way back before the turn of the century Martin had his eye on the suffragettes, and the magazine took its cue from him. When Ouida (Louise de la Ramee), about as emancipated a woman as the nineties offered, came out against women's suffrage in the *North American Review* in 1894, *Life* reprinted a long quote.

> Their legislation would be, as that of men is too often, the offspring of panic and prejudice; and she would not put on the drag of common sense as man frequently does in public assemblies. There would be little hope from her humanity, nothing from her liberality; for when she is frightened she is more ferocious than he, and when she has power she is more merciless.[51]

This fit *Life*'s ideas neatly, although possibly the editors wished that the confession had come from a more feminine woman than the cigar-brandishing French novelist. The attitude toward the feminine mind is exactly *Life*'s though. To cite the other end of the chronological scale, a 1916 cartoon showed two girls at their ease under a "Tree of Knowledge." The first was reading trashy sex novels; the second was occupied with Dante, William James, Bergson, and a cigarette. The idea was that both were heading for ruin. But feminine meddling in intellectual affairs was funny to *Life* only up to a point; after that the facts of life took over. *Life* was convinced that women were not intellectual, had no business trying to be, and were cruelly deceived by anyone who suggested that they depart from the decorative and domestic existence that God's will and the increasingly more nearly perfect civilization had decreed to be theirs. Politics had no business to make strangers, as it were, out of bedfellows.

Suffrage was the choice of the women themselves, not of the magazine, to lead women's push for what they called equality and *Life* called perversion. Actually, while *suffrage* got nowhere with *Life*, suffragettes improved their status in the magazine somewhat in the course of the years of suffragette warfare. The earliest references to them are uniformly sneering, but after the first decade of this century *Life* began to treat them more seriously and more politely. It has been pointed out that serious treatment of Martin's editorial column of *Life* was genial. If he insulted, he insulted slyly. The humor columns were often more gross. While this applies to the suffragette's case, the change from *Life*'s treatment of their cause as a contemptible joke to its treatment of it as an idea worth serious dispute was a distinct step forward.

The importance of the anti-suffragette cause to *Life* is difficult to demonstrate by excerpts from the magazine. As it did with most things which it truly disliked, *Life* treated women's suffrage to very scattered, very brusque notice for years. In the later years, when the movement gathered a proper head of steam, the war was uppermost in *Life*'s mind. Another collection of Martin's *Life* editorials, *The Unrest of Women*, was published in 1913, and it contains the germ of the later, more thoughtful opposition by *Life* to the whole business of "feminism," then a brand-new word.

Martin bases his arguments on two broad premises—the first, that women and men are different in many ways besides the obvious; the second, that a vote is a useless thing, anyway. Of these premises, the first is indisputable, although succeeding steps are fraught with the worst sort of logical dangers. The second, while hardly indisputable and by any normal standards downright un-American, has been heard often enough since Martin's day that it merits some consideration. Women's votes, wrote Martin, seem to be much like men's votes:

> When a row of pianos make a concert then the voters will make a millenium. At present it is not the pianos, but the players who play on them, who make the concert; and it is not the voters, but the poets, prophets and statesmen who inspire and enlist them, that secure millenial improvements in legislation and government. It does not seem to matter greatly who votes if only all the social groups are represented fairly.[52]

When H. L. Mencken came out strong for oligarchy in the 20's, he offered no apologies, but no oligarchs either; and while a lot of people were amused, nobody was much impressed. Martin's oligarchic principles are lamely propped with "if only all the social groups are fairly represented." As for suggestions as to just who the piano players are, *Life*'s idea of a poet was Thomas Bailey Aldrich; its idea of a statesman, at this point anyway, was anyone who kept America as far removed from Europe as possible; and its idea of a prophet—well, *Life* itself is *Life*'s idea of a prophet. It cherished a beautiful vision of a lulling and mythical past gently catching up with the world. Still and all, the notion that a voter is a statistic to be manipulated just as a pianist manipulates an instrument, far from dying out in America, has completely captured national politics in the past fifty years. Martin, nurtured in New York politics, knew the "machine" metaphor as well as anyone not actively engaged in machine politics might, and knew how near it came to losing its metaphoric qualities. If he were alive today, Martin might be pleased to note that while poets, statesmen and prophets remain in short supply, the place he claimed for them is being increasingly filled by journalists.

Martin expanded his other premise something like this: men and women have separate functions, biologically and historically. Woman's function is domestic, to bear and rear children. Man cannot do it; woman can and must. This is motherhood, and everyone knows how noble motherhood is. Therefore, other functions, including government, are for men. Besides, men have been the governors, *outside of the home*; no doubt they will continue to be; and if they continue to hold the power, it would be better if they continued to bear the responsibility.

This, like so many of *Life*'s other arguments, breaks down only where myth and fact collide. The ennobling experience of motherhood was an article of faith that Martin accepted absolutely literally. When women, many of them mothers, denied it, he clucked in pity at their delusions. They did not understand. Toward other things connected with the suffrage questions—jobs for women, the dangers of organized unrest of any sort, anti-prostitution legislation—he was affably tolerant even when he found himself in strong disagreement with the women's stand. But on motherhood he was adamant. Motherhood was noble. No mere woman could tell him anything else.

And, naturally enough, every question eventually rested here. Every argument, driven to bay, turned at last and brandished motherhood in the faces of its pursuers. Woman's place was not at the polls. Inez Milholland Boissevain, a feminist who once drew Martin's derision for suggesting that pregnancy is a poor reason for a woman's marrying a man she can't stand,53 died in 1916 from some sort of respiratory infection. Everyone, friend or foe, believed it was brought on by an exhausting stump tour which she refused to give up in the face of a physician's advice. Feminists called her a martyr to the cause, and argued somewhat implausibly that a cause worth dying for was a cause that ought to prevail. *Life* answered this in a superior tone that consorts ill enough with any genuine feeling of grief at the young woman's death:

> The lesson of her death is not that women ought to have the vote or not to have it, but that the strongest young woman is not quite made of iron, and cannot hope to undertake and discharge the duties of a strong young woman and at the same time dare adventures fit only for a strong man. Womanhood has its claims on women, and they will not be denied. To flout them is to suffer; to deny them once too often is to die 54

Cruel as this sounds, it is only an example of *Life*'s and Martin's dictum that "Nature" meant the things their common sense approved of and "Unnatural" referred to the things that pleased them not. In this case, Nature answers for God when a power larger than the argument at hand needs to be invoked if the argument is to be saved. But God is never far from Martin's side, and can be called on whenever a final crusher is wanted. His summation in *The Unrest of Women* leaves no doubt as to what God intends:

> And since in our day the spirit of Christ is the great fountain of justice and liberty, it would be an impertinence for anyone to declare that it is opposed to votes for women. It is enough to say that it is patient, continuous and irresistible like the forces of nature, among which, to be sure, it must be reckoned. If the vote as a token of direct participation in politics is something of which woman has been unjustly deprived, then in the larger development and ampler liberty that are coming to her she will get it. But if it is something that belongs to the man's part in life, an overrated power, offset by powers inalienably conferred upon her, then the demand for votes for women is a mistake, and in the long run will not prevail.55

Life, and Martin in particular, saw masculinity encroached upon on all sides by the debilitating ideas of the new times. Any concession at all to womankind would have been deplorable to him and to *Life*. The concession of political power, since it occurred in the area of *Life*'s lowest concentration of inflexible opinion, was treated in the magazine more gallantly than another sort of concession might have been. Nevertheless, when it counted, women were given short sympathy by the magazine. In its Pro-Suffragette Number in October of 1913, *Life* momentarily turned its attention to the women's side of the controversy. The best thing about the number was the cover, by Orson Lowell, which pictured a very lady-like lady flanked by a greasy and ferocious-looking Italian, a drunken and apelike Irishman, a howling-swell checker-vested Negro, and a chinless, fatuous dude. All of the four types, with the possible exception of the Italian, were common butts in the magazine, and it came as no great surprise that *Life* could consider some women's votes as superior to the votes of such men as these. *Life*'s usual suffragette, though, was a warty-chinned dragon who bullied a flock of abashed young things into parades and onto platforms much against their wills. The business of will was a queer side of *Life*'s anti-suffragette argument. The magazine stoutly maintained that it represented women's opinion—*real* women, as opposed to women who looked like Col. Roosevelt with his mustache shaved—and that it stood for women's freedom. It believed that it defended them from the onerous responsibilities of politics, which some unprincipled folk would add to the already taxing demands of motherhood, woman's true and proper function.

NOTES

[1]*Life*, IV, 1884, p. 88.   [2]*Life*, III, 1884, p. 363.

[3]Henry Jones Ford, *The Cleveland Era* (New Haven: Yale University Press, 1919), p. 51.

[4]*Life*, III, 1884, p. 335.   [5]*Life*, Nov. 27, 1884, Cover.

[6]*Life*, III, 1884, p. 277.   [7]*Life*, III, 1884, p. 338.

[8]*Life*, III, 1884, p. 304.   [9]*Life*, III, 1884, p. 340.

[10]*Life*, III, 1884, p. 277.   [11]*Life*, IV, 1884, p. 60.

[12]*Life*, IV, 1884, p. 88.   [13]*Life*, XXVIII, 1896, p. 217.

[14]*Life*, XXVIII, 1896, p. 97.   [15]*Life*, XXVIII, 1896, p. 473.

[16]*Life*, XXVII, 1896, p. 426.   [17]*Life*, XXVII, 1896, p. 472.

[18]*Life*, XXVII, 1896, p. 460.   [19]*Life*, XXVII, 1896, p. 475.

[20]*Life*, XXVIII, 1896, p. 327.

[21]Thomas Beer, *Hanna* (New York: Alfred A. Knopf, 1919).

[22]*Life*, XXVIII, 1896, p. 638.   [23]*Life*, XXVIII, 1896, p. 160.

[24]*Life*, XXVIII, 1896, p. 354.   [25]*Life*, VIII, 1886, p. 272.

[26]*Life*, XXXV, 1900, p. 253.   [27]*Life*, XXXV, 1900, p. 527.

[28]*Life*, XXXVI, 1900, p. 147.

[29]*Life*, XXXI, 1898, pp. 164, 183, 184. *Life* defended Zola, not Dreyfus. The proceedings of the French courts seemed Tammanyesque to *Life*, and the *Maine* disaster seemed overblown.

[30]*Life*, XXXIII, 1899, p. 319.   [31]*Life*, April 13, 1899, Cover.

[32]*Life*, XXXIII, 1899, p. 24.   [33]*Life*, XXXIII, 1899, p. 326.

[34]*Life*, XXXVIII, 1901, p. 205.   [35]*Life*, XXXVIII, 1901, p. 250.

[36]*Life*, XLIII, 1904, p. 301.   [37]*Life*, XLIII, 1904, p. 206.

[38]*Life*, LII, 1908, p. 189.   [39]*Life*, LII, 1908, p. 407.

[40]*Life*, September 19, 1912.   [41]*Life*, LX, 1912, p. 2093.

[42]*Life*, LX, 1912, p. 2000.   [43]*Life*, LX, 1912, p. 1766.

[44]*Life*, LXVIII, 1916, p. 239.   [45]*Life*, LXVIII, 1916, p. 239.

[46]*Life*, LXVIII, 1916, p. 703.   [47]*Life*, LXX, 1917, p. 47.

[48]Edward Sandford Martin, *The War Week By Week* (New York: E. P. Dutton & Co., 1914), p. 52.

[49]Divorce was one subject on which *Life* and the feminists agreed. The advantages of divorce to both parties impressed *Life*, but the vocal opposition of the Comstock element impressed it more. *Life* was for divorce as much because it annoyed Puritans as because it undid errors.

[50]*Life*, VII, 1886, p. 60.   [51]*Life*, XXIII, 1894, p. 423.

[52]Edward Sandford Martin, *The Unrest of Women* (New York and London: D. Appleton and Co., 1913), p. 20.

[53]Martin, *The Unrest of Women*, p. 119.

[54]*Life*, LXVIII, 1916, p. 1140.

[55]Martin, *The Unrest of Women*, p. 144.

CHAPTER V

"WRITTEN BY GENTLEMEN, FOR GENTLEMEN"

For a publication that advertised literature as one of its particular
interests, *Life* was launched at an unpropitious moment in American
history.   Gilded Age materialism clashed with the literary imagination,
and everywhere was the separation of the artist from society that Emerson
had hoped would never characterize America.   There were literary giants
in America between 1865 and 1916, but they were almost unanimously
at odds with *Life*'s America.   Works of merit were increasingly harder to
find in books.   By 1883, the great men of the pre-war generation were
dead or fading.   Poe, Hawthorne, and Longfellow were gone; Melville had
been forgotten; Lowell was the American ambassador to Victoria's court;
Holmes's hurdy-gurdy continued to grind, but the elvish erudition was
perceptibly turning to garrulous nostalgia, and the piquant wit to sadness;
the reviewers waited in vain for their successors, whom the reviewers expected to be their carbon copies.

Not that there were no successors to *some* pre-war writers.   Mrs.
Sigourney's myriad artistic progeny swarmed in the land.   E. P. Roe had
discovered a way to convert their piety, their journalistic penchant and
their grammar into prose.   The Sweet Singer of Michigan had sold well,
and her deluded imitators across the country laid aside their skillets and
took up their pens.   The vanity presses battened on them, and *Life*,
early in its career, amused itself with appropriately pompous reviews of
their work.   The poems reviewed ranged from this innocent gabble of
Wordsworthian rapture:

> What on this wide earth
>   That is made, or does by nature grow
> Is more homely, yet more beautiful
>   Than the useful Po ta *to*?
>
> On the whole it is a very plain plant,
>   Makes no conspicuous show,
> But the internal appearance is lovely,
>   Of the unostentatious Po ta *to*.[1]

to this, by a widow remarried to a Congressman (a widower), which scans
but is enough to give Dr. Krafft-Ebing the shudders:

> Your place, my darling, still is yours
> And still I wear your ring,
> And hold your image in my heart,
> A sacred, holy thing;
>
> And he, who would so tenderly
> Lift up my broken life,
> Is faithful still in memory
> To *his immortal wife.*[2]

Also, it is to an alert but anonymous contributor to *Life* that the world owes the discovery and immortalization of Mrs. Andrew Lang's classic line, "*Sir Charles Grandison*—the book whose separate numbers were awaited with such impatience by Richardson's endless lady friends."[3] But these strange little weeds, however rank their growth, were beneath even a humorist's serious consideration. Very soon the magazine abandoned its bantering and turned to ponder weightier questions of genuine literature.

This chapter will discuss *Life*'s characteristic attitude toward those literary questions. The attitude was called "Not (that of) a comic paper, but (that of) a gently satirical observer" by Frank L. Mott;[4] but this, while accurate, is too generalized. The attitude, the tone, the *pose* of *Life*, if you will, was that of gentlemanly coolness and detachment. In this chapter let us explore the origins of *Life*'s gentlemanly attitude and the applications of it to books and literary ideas as well as to *Life*'s own choice of contents.

For *Life* was not only *about* literature; it *was* literature. As literature, a humorous magazine might appear to lack many if not most of the attributes which make novels, poems, plays, or short stories worth study. First and worst of all, no amount of critical generalization can discover any unity in it. It contains millions of words written by hundreds of persons on an encyclopedia of subjects. There can be no unity in such an agglomeration. As a byproduct of this disunity, the magazine is habitually self-contradictory. Even individual contributors contradicted themselves over a period of time. In such areas as political satire, for example, a humorist might insist in 1908 that the jackass, a habitually loud and obstreperous beast, was the perfect symbol for Bryan's party. It would be notable if he did *not* forget it and four years later insist with equal vigor that the jackass, a preternaturally solemn beast, was the perfect symbol for Wilson's party. Besides disunity and its accompanying contradictions, *Life* suffered from lack of concentration. An issue that earned editorial comment, full-page cartoons, and a half-dozen jokes in one number was frequently forgotten by presstime the following week. An idea or a theme seldom had a chance to grow to maturity. If it did not bear fruit immediately, *Life* discarded it.

All of these shortcomings are the result, primarily, of *Life*'s weekly publication. Mitchell and his staff would have done heroically had they unified *Life* even issue by issue. Indeed, the dedication of issues to various topics, such as the Suffragette Number, the Irish Number, and the Adam and Eve Number suggests that the staff wanted unity as much as any critic could want it. As for contradiction, *Life*'s best contents were often one-line affairs—cartoon captions, jokes, or quick summations of the news. The contributors could hardly be blamed for forgetting, over a period of years, single lines which they must have written hastily.

Although no careful development of ideas can be found in *Life*, over the years enough different points of view were combined there to delineate a few broad literary convictions. On these the magazine operated. The process of discovering them is a little like studying hash to discover onions, and doubtless the conclusions are open to question. Nevertheless, much can be learned from an investigation of *Life*'s collected stabs at an idea.

Mitchell's name took the place of prominence whenever *Life* spoke authoritatively on what literature was or should be. Whenever the contents of *Life* were sifted and the "best" winnowed from the "ordinary," Mitchell's ideas became the ideas of *Life*.[5] Moreover, several ideas were regularly included in *Life* which represent distinct points of difference between Mitchell and Martin, falling very much inside Mitchell's range of toleration but outside Martin's. Notable among these are the idea that Roman Catholicism, given enough room, would blight the world with its proselyting propaganda and the idea that Socialistic sentiments have a place in imaginative literature.

But despite all this, it was Martin and those who agreed substantially with him who were the literary spokesmen for *Life*. The most important reason for this is that they spoke more frequently than Mitchell did and concentrated their attentions more on literature. During the seventeen years when "Droch" wrote the book column and Martin's editorials played a sharp counterpoint to the literary news, the two men agreed so strongly on two great loves and one powerful fear that they set the literary tone for *Life* that lasted until after World War I, long after Kerfoot, whose ideas were considerably different from theirs, was ostensibly in full charge of the literature column. Their shared passions were William Makepeace Thackeray's novels and the genteel tradition in poetry. Their mutual *bete noir* was their fear that women were in league to wrest from the male his dominant social, political, and economic role.

These three ideas are inextricably interwoven in many areas. Their common social bases are evident. Gentility presupposes a rigid society in which gallantry is feasible, and gallantry is feasible only when women are treated as inferior. Thackeray's novels depict such a society, and the morally admirable men and women in *The Newcomes*, the novel most venerated by "Droch" and Martin, are those who behave according to the prescriptions of gentility. The morally abominable characters in *The*

Newcomes are those whose commitment to gentility is hypocritical, for personal gain only. Then both Thackeray and the genteel tradition agree that the proper role of the woman is decorative. Insofar as she departs from decoration she departs from true womanhood and usurps man's rightful place. As for economics, both Thackeray and the genteel poets cherished the idea of the poor little rich girl to whom true love and therefore true femininity is denied, and *Life* applauded vigorously. And Martin's ideas on women in politics and their self-exile from femininity have been discussed already.

These three dominant ideas of Martin's and Bridges', of course, had their effect on *Life* not only in literary criticism but in all other departments of the magazine. The discussion of Thackeray, gentility, and women, however, properly belongs with the discussion of literary matters, since two of them are literary in origin and the third affected *Life*'s criticism at least as much as it affected Martin's anti-suffrage campaign.

Life's debt to Thackeray was immense, both directly as a literary touchstone against which to test the golden content of all other prose, and indirectly as a source of ideas on all possible subjects. The fable-apology which opens *The Newcomes* might have been *Life*'s own literary manifesto. It states as clearly as any collection of extracts from *Life* the magazine's convictions as to what literature and criticism are and what satire (and *Life*) ought to be. *Life* pushed the idea a step beyond Thackeray and argued that the world's duty was to conform to Thackeray's fables, but its fanaticism is hardly the novelist's fault.

Thackeray's literary lessons are threefold: all tales are moral tales; there are three levels of satire—the satire of outright hypocrisy, the satire of foibles inherent in the proper character of any man, and the satire that upsets the reader's apple cart by reversing its apparent direction and giving him virtue where he has been led to expect vice; these three variations on satire *are the substance of all tale telling.*

Life cherished these lessons in its very heart. It criticised the morality of books and plays and sought moral issues in the events of the world. It satirized hypocrisy and was fighting proud of its own reputation for honesty. It believed so strongly in "inherent character" that it leaned toward stereotype. It awarded sizeable cash prizes to stories whose most evident merit was their deft reversal of apparent virtue and apparent vice. Indeed, Mitchell, when he set out *Life*'s idea of the *barest essentials* of a story, insisted on the indispensability of just such a reversal. While "the substance of all tale-telling" and "the barest essentials of a story" may not be synonymous, they are close.

Thackeray taught that criticism justifies itself, but that the critic would do well to remember that the writer has a reason for his "failings." However, self-justification for a critic on Thackeray's terms places that critic in an uncomfortably parasitic situation. He must criticize because that is the sort of annoying beast he is. His only function is to point to this or that and say "aye" or "no" to it. He is a presumptuous appendage to literature. The critic who feels the discomfort of this role can best soothe himself by not taking himself seriously. When Thackeray insists that everything an author does is intentional, he is extending a terrible temptation to anyone who is as moralistically inclined as was *Life*. He leads such moralists straight to the conclusion that the morality of book and author are inseparable. *Life* insisted that it was no prude and it deplored Anthony Comstock, but when it convicted a book of immorality it automatically convicted the book's author of the same. If bad books are written for bad reasons, *Life* thought, then they must be written by bad men.

One who sets up as a satirist might look for his model in far worse places than the works of Thackeray, of course, but the serious criticism of literature and life does not begin and end between Mayfair and the offices of the *Pall Mall Gazette*. Thackeray understood puffers and strutters as well as any man, and saw what good was in them as well as what ill. But 1855 was not 1883, and London was not New York. In order to adopt Thackeray's precepts *Life*'s literary men had to ignore by far the largest segment of their contemporaries. While their Thackerayan satire struck home neatly when aimed at many particulars, they had also to move against the gathering streams of American and New York life, even while claiming to be close observers of reality. Thackeray's *Pall Mall Gazette* was the original "magazine written by gentlemen, for gentlemen." The attempt to transplant it in time and space from fiction to reality was successful financially, but the transplanted magazine, renamed *Life*, never forgot its old roots in fiction and old times and unreal places.

The genteel tradition struck *Life* as American, optimistic, and forward looking. Martin, *Life*'s prophet of optimism, was likewise its strongest spokesman for the genteel life. He had the highest opinion of gentlemen:

> To study how to be a gentleman is not necessarily the study of etiquette.
> It is broader and nobler than that. Followed out to its legitimate conclusion,
> it would mean the study of manners and morals in their effect upon all man-
> kind, and thus might the world be benefitted and man elevated.[6]

For all this, gentility left its mark on *Life*'s thoughts less directly than did Thackeray. That is to say, when Martin or Bridges quoted a literary authority, he turned to Thackeray in preference to Bayard Taylor or Thomas Bailey Aldrich. But its indirect effect was evident in Bridges' reviews, particularly in his reviews of poetry. He appreciated technical slickness in defiance of intellectual content. The effect is also evident in the choice of verse for publication in *Life*. This verse was selected partly by Metcalfe and partly by Masson, who as successive managing editors were responsible for the choice of jokes and sketches too. *Life* counseled moderation in all literature. It was equally suspicious of life in raw gulps and of art-for-art's-sake. The genteel poets avoided the first by concentrating on delicate perceptions and sentimental reactions, and the second by accepting traditional *forms* without applying themselves too closely to *form*. They knew, that is, how many syllables to include in a villanelle and where the rhyme fell, but they did not care to bind their ideas any more compactly than stress and rhyme demanded. Also, they refused to work with ideas that needed any more careful presentation. This approach to poetry, and by extension to all literature, struck *Life* as nearly perfect.

Since "the genteel tradition" is usually a term applied to a kind of poetry, we may concentrate on poetry in the discussion of *Life*'s gentility. Within the genteel tradition I would include not only those American poets usually so classified, but also their British contemporary sympathizers. I do this in the face of Bridges' unflagging skepticism toward contemporary British poetry, for Bridges disliked the poems of Tennyson and Browning and scoffed at Alfred Austin. Bridges first called Tennyson "Chief Lord of Her Majesty's Rhymesters, Barren Tennyson," but later he decided that the laureate was acceptable despite his unfortunate senility. When *The Princess* arrived in the same mail with a novel by Edgar Fawcett, Bridges chose to review the novel, explaining the choice by pointing out Fawcett's Anglophobia. He devoted just one column to Browning—on the occasion of the poet's death. *Life* had long since decided that Browning was good only to keep unattractive girls from Boston amused while their betters led the german. Bridges' obituary comment was a gruff one and only faintly complimentary. He wrote that if Browning had continued to live he would have written only more hard verse, and that it must be singularly pleasant to die in Venice. Bridges admired Kipling's verse, but he early concluded that Kipling's real talents were for prose. The only British poet to whom he gave unreserved praise was Austin Dobson, a prime example of the British genteel school.

Bridges wrote of Dobson:

> The verses of Austin Dobson are like beautifully decorated china, fragile and light, yet perfect in form and color. To sip tender sentiment and delicate fancy from these dainty cups of song is a most refined pleasure.[7]

While we are unlikely, today, to speak of Dobson so kindly or indeed to read him at all, this seems a fair and perceptive assessment of his poetry. The key words are "refined," "tender," "delicate," "beautifully decorated." For Bridges and *Life*, these were the distinguishing marks of good poetry. These critics saw poetry as something to be read in a hammock on a drowsy summer afternoon; something that a man of substance would give his attention to only sporadically, for a few moments, to ease the pressure of affairs; something that a woman could read when bored. They saw it as comparable to a cool drink, pleasant and refreshing, from which it would be folly to expect nourishment, as a delightful accessory to a proper life, as important as a good horse or a well-brushed hat, an insignia of gentility. Therefore the genteel became for them the *sine qua non* of all verse, and the genteel poets the only ones with whom they had no quarrel. They never overrated the importance of Dobson,[8] or of their American favorite, Thomas Bailey Aldrich, unless such poets are automatically over-rated when they are ranked above Tennyson, Browning, Poe, or Whitman. Rather, *Life*'s fault was that it consistently underrated any poet who de-parted from genteel tradition. Bridges did not claim Dobson as an im-mortal, but recognized his fragility and lightness. *Life* assumed that fragility and lightness, if combined with gentility, were preferable to any solidity that lacked it.

I have said that *Life* found the genteel tradition optimistic. This is a matter that goes to the very roots of difference between the ordinary critical views of *Life* and those of the twentieth century. Optimism was a matter of principle with *Life*. But the whole critical attitude of the twentieth century is based on a pervasive pessimism. We demand that a poet present life either as it is but ought not to be, or as it ought to be but is not. We have assumed that the poet's function is to see through heaven, not to celebrate the kings of earth. The genteel poets are in effect optimis-tic court poets, praising the virtues and delights of the life around them. Court poets seem to us to have abdicated their responsibility to art. While they are surely no more subject to error of fact than any other poets, we are likely to declare them discredited when their flattery proves false. *Life* and Bridges based their judgments on an optimism so profound that beside it Whitman's is a shallow dish. They believed, not just that America could and would be great, but that she had achieved greatness in their own time by the efforts of their own kind. They believed that the society to and for whom they and the genteel poets spoke needed only a bigger dose of the same medicine to be perfect.

Therefore they admired American poets before Britons and genteel poets before all others. Aldrich, said Bridges, had earned "a proud place among the poets of the century." Henry Cuyler Bunner's poems were regularly and enthusiastically reviewed. In the spring of 1896, Martin recommended a list of poets for summer reading—a variety of reading, to be sure, that even by *Life*'s standards was naturally frothy. The list, com-plete, names Clinton Scollard, Bliss Carman, William Watson, Samuel M. Peck, Charles Leonard Moore, Zitella Cocke, Alice Brown, Alice Meynell, and Mary Berri Chapman. All are refined, tender, delicate, and winsome. Some are totally lost to posterity. The list demonstrates both the con-sistency of *Life*'s taste and the persistent primacy of the male on any roster *Life* made up.

Far from fighting a rear-guard action in its poetic preferences, *Life* was in a way a leader of public acceptance of what was, to the 1880's and 1890's, modernity. Inspired by another list chosen by Charles Dana of the *Sun* in April of 1897, *Life* polled its readers to discover the ten most popular short poems in English. The winners included Gray's "Elegy," Bryant's "Thanatopsis," Longfellow's "Psalm of Life," Poe's "The Raven," Tennyson's "Charge of the Light Brigade," Shelley's "To a Skylark," Holmes' "Chambered Nautilus," Whittier's "Maud Muller," Hood's "Bridge of Sighs," and Charles Wolfe's "Burial of Sir John Moore."[9] The list demonstrates that the public occupied itself with gloomy sentiments culled from an elder generation and spiced them occasionally with inspirational exhortation. *Life* apparently tried, with some success, to educate its readers in up-to-date poetic schools. At all events, *Life* published quantities of genteel poetry. Public taste in poetry has not kept pace with poetic experimentation since the turn of the century. If the poets whom *Life* favored spoke neither for the great public nor for the highbrows, they came as close to the former as any poets since Longfellow.

Bridges' reaction to Poe, Whitman, and Stephen Crane, the nineteenth century American poets who departed most drastically from gentility, follows the pre-determined course. He admired Crane as a writer of prose, but said of *The Black Riders* that the poems were not intended to be read: they existed to fill out a little space in the middle of a fine page, and balance it nicely. G. E. Woodberry's biography of Poe confirmed his suspicion that the poet, "highly endowed, well-bred, well-educated, with brilliant and favoring opportunities, wrecked his own career by opium and drink."[10] Bridges, although gentility's champion, did not seem to understand or care how much Poe's private aspirations to gentility contributed to the wreckage, how painful must have been the dilemma of a man who knew that he could choose only to be an abstainer or a sot, yet wanted desperately to be accepted as a *bona fide* Virginia gentleman. Whitman, neither so new a phenomenon as Crane nor so historically sanctioned as Poe, was a subject for comment outside the book columns of *Life* as well as inside. *Life* believed, with some justification, that the shaggy Whitman line was the result of sheer gaseous expansion of words, planless, artless, vulgar, and anything but genteel:

> Compose and write, all inside on 10 minutes, seven poems like Walt Whitman's best, and eight chapters of a novel like E. P. Roe's. This is not a literary test, but is simply to indicate the rapidity with which you move the pen.[11]

And it had the lowest opinion of Whitman's effect:

> It is rumored that Mr. Whitman once turned a pitcher of milk sour by reading a poem aloud in the same room with it. The milk was partially restored by an application of quick-lime and the poem taken out with a pair of tongs.[12]

Bridges' obituary notice of Whitman is less amusing but more revealing. From the gentleman's point of view he saw in Whitman many of the things that Whitman's defenders see and admire, but he saw them as anti-poetic and reprehensible:

> Green fields, bright sunlight, flashing waters, the movement and color of
> crowds—all those things which produce grunts of satisfaction in a well-
> constituted savage—gave him that sort of pleasure which ejaculates sonorous
> phrases. It is a fine thing to live and finer to enjoy it, and if you want to call
> the expression of it poetry, then Whitman was a poet.[13]

We may find this a dense attitude toward the poet now generally conceded
to be America's most original, but *Life*'s first duty was to hit at what was
funny about a public figure. Whitman made a splendid target, whiskers
and slouch hat, excited self-praise and woolly mysticism, peculiarities of
diction and all. One anonymous contributor composed a successful burlesque of Whitman's verse. It caught in a few lines his reiterated *I*, his
prophetic tone, his provincialism and his mixture of the ultra-aesthetical-
super-poetical with the deliberately coarse. These lines are the conclusion
of the "Whitman poem" on a proposed visit to New York by the actress
Mary Anderson:

> O thou parallax! thou heaven-born multiplication-table! thou mysterious
> grindstone!! I, the unspeakable Ego., the sublimated parenthesis of catas-
> trophic Force—I, the Ego., from the depths of my absolute and inalienable self—I
> holler forth a rejoicing at thy coming (not to say thy metaphysical approach).
> My voice quakes like a hurricane in a beegum; I fire myself off like an old
> musket loaded with buckshot!
> I shout, I yawp, I gallop around on all-fours and kick at horse-flies; I slap the
> cat off the rug; I unbutton my suspenders and climb a lamp-post; I roar like a
> sewing-machine till the whole earth (likewise the other side of the river) is
> filled with the reverberant echo of thy commendation.[14]

Although *Life* did not have a comprehensive grasp of Whitman's virtues,
it was not far off when it remarked his faults.

James Whitcomb Riley, who occasionally contributed to *Life*, can be
called genteel only by stretching the definition of that word. But *Life*'s
comments on Riley link its ideas of gentility to its ideas of American perfection. Riley was so well-known in 1883 that the reviewer of *The Old
Swimmin'-Hole and 'Leven More Poems* (not Bridges) recognized him
behind the pseudonym, Benj. F. Johnson. At that time *Life* wrote, "The
homely music . . . struck from his lyre is fresh and quaint and full of
sweetness."[15] Whatever his limitations, Bridges never wrote about anything "struck from his lyre." He did write of Riley fifteen years afterwards that:

> There is a pretty sound core of hero-worship and big-heartedness in the back
> country that people, who live in cities and talk of the "coming social revolu-
> tion," and the "alarming ignorance of the rural regions," never suspect.[16]

Riley, then, represented for *Life* both those things that were beautiful about rural America and those that were characteristic of the genteel
tradition—freshness, quaintness, sweetness, hero-worship and big-hearted-
ness. One wonders how a group of men so thoroughly steeped in city life
and so frankly approving of the outward forms of civilization could wallow

in nostalgia for the simplistic, sentimental "Life of Riley." But the American myth that *Life* took without salt was in itself sufficiently optimistic that the staff saw no contradiction between it and the gentility toward which they saw the country moving.

When *Life* considered women, however, its optimism vanished. The fear of the growing power of women forced the magazine to adopt a posture of defensive masculinity. The theme—What Sort of Horror Would Overtake the World If Women Took Over Men's Place?—is perhaps the nearest thing to a recurrent *motif* in all of *Life*, repeated time and again in the literary columns, and in the comments on high society, on politics, on trusts and unions, on business and pleasure: the point of hundreds of cartoons and anecdotes. Sooner or later it crept into *Life*'s judgments of the relative merits of books, cities, politicians, parties, art, prisons—nearly everything. In general, if women as a group were for something, *Life* was against it. When *Life* saw no immediate threat to its masculinity in some organized activity of womankind, it assumed a cruelly patronizing attitude which was more insulting than its outright attacks.

In its immediate application to literature, this attitude toward women accounted for one of *Life*'s most damaging faults. Though *Life* deplored the fact, it admitted that reading and talking of literature were amusements for ladies. Since *Life* posed as a gentleman, it had to deprecate its own interest in letters. In its cartoons an effeminate and lisping Fweddie might occasionally mention books, but no solid man of affairs would stoop to it. Even *Life* itself, in its own drawings, was shown being read by women more than by men. In the world of *Life*'s jokes and drawings ladies and gentlemen never mentioned literature in one another's company, women readers never got their teeth into anything tougher than suet, and whenever conversation in clubs got around to books, it was because some relic of a past generation insisted on forcing the subject down the throats of his audience.

Such was *Life*'s view of its audience, and it is no wonder that its reviewers suffered some embarrassment when caught out with books in their hands. Both Bridges and Martin repeatedly insisted that fiction, written or read, was not quite a manly occupation, but that no one was likely to be seriously hurt by it.

Life worked off its shame by deprecating the American woman whenever it could. It liked to tell her what her real place was, as understood by masculine possessors of horse sense. The words "American woman" would not have been used by *Life*. *Life* did not recognize such a person. It believed rather in "The American Girl." This mythological piece of native florodora bloomed at sixteen, matured at nineteen, and withered quite away as soon as she reached majority. On the one hand, she was a non-utilitarian but desirable property, and in this role she was likely to be called upon to represent all that was worthy in America's prospective future. On the other hand, she was subject to severe regional aberrations. A Chicago girl had enormous feet. A Philadelphia girl had twenty grandfathers. A Boston girl had a long nose and read too much. Not even the New York girl was exempt from insult, although Bridges backed New York girls against those from any other city. She had a name, then, but no local habitation, and *Life*'s inability to find her no matter where it sought her suggests that she did not exist in the real world.

But unreality never dampened *Life*'s enthusiasm. *Life* went right on glorifying The Girl and paying scant attention to woman in any other state. Almost all married women in *Life*'s pages had daughters of their own aged sixteen to twenty. Unmarried women over twenty-one were still considered good copy for a few years, because it was amusing to see the poor superannuated crones trying to compete for husbands against the delicate charms of the adolescents. Unmarried women over thirty in *Life*'s cartoons looked fifty and behaved twenty years older. All this showed most in cartoons and other illustrations, but Bridges' literary columns never lost an opportunity to mention it. Bridges wrote of The American Girl in 1888:

> For her, society, literature, and art exist. She is the flower of American liberty, the inspiration of American competition.

She achieved this eminence while she was still, as it were, larval.

The adult form did not inspire the same rhapsodies. When Charles Dudley Warner said, in a speech at Hartford in 1890, that women bid fair to corner the culture market in America, Martin rushed to the defense of his sex. He argued editorially that a woman "gets up literature because she likes clubs," not vice versa, and pointed out that a ladies' club buys one book for fifteen women, whereas a man buys fifteen books for the same number. This accountant's view of culture is no dimmer, certainly, than that of Bridges, who found it "hard to believe that a really strong writer can be hurt by any amount of culture."[17] In *Life*'s view, whatever women attended to was cheapened; whatever they appropriated was made useless to man forever. Culture was to be defended from them.

This smacks of the primitive tabus of the cannibal isles rather than of a highly successful publication issuing from the largest city of America in the late nineteenth century. The comparison was noted and pointed out in 1899 by Thorstein Veblen, in *The Theory of The Leisure Class*, in saying that "women and other slaves are highly valued, both as evidence of wealth and as a means of accumulating wealth."[18]

In Veblen's "primitive world" and "quasi-peaceable culture," woman is a slave, but a slave whose ever-more-important function it is to publish her master's opulence. When the world sees that even the master's slave has leisure, the world will realize the extent of his wealth. When a woman, one might say, has time to read novels and attend lectures, rather than shine her husband's boots, then her husband has proved himself a potent provider. The husband, however, carefully refrains from any such frivolity in his own person. The myth of his communal usefulness must be kept up.

It has been argued that Veblen's anthropology is fanciful, that his theory is no cultural parallel but an elaborate metaphor for his own society. This argument only reinforces the point in question. Veblen saw the man-woman relationship of the American 1890's as one of master and chattel slave. *Life* saw it exactly the same way, and wanted to keep it that way.

The trading in women, while it is discreetly and genteely ignored by *Life*, is one of the more important plot devices of Thackeray's novels. Thackeray deplores it. He wishes that every woman could marry for love. But the dear things have such a way of marrying beneath themselves— that is, of depriving themselves of their principal function by choosing a master who has no opulence to publish. What kind of life can they expect? *Life* thought the answer was obvious—a wretched one.

In the selection of verse and fiction for its own pages, *Life* followed with admirable consistency the fashions in taste which it applauded in its literary columns. From time to time *Life* collected its verse into books.[19] These books are difficult to find, and *Life*'s poetic content did not vary so much from year to year that successive books would show striking differences. So, the discussion is confined to the contents of one such book, *Rhymes & Roundelays from "Life"*, published in 1902.

The book contains one hundred and nineteen poems, some only four lines long, on one hundred and forty six pages of text. It is illustrated profusely by *Life*'s contributing artists. Thirty of the poems are unsigned. A few others are signed only with initials. All had appeared first in *Life*. The contributors, as might be suspected of writers of *vers de societe*, tend to sign three names to their works: Rufus Cyrene MacDonald, Willis Leonard Clanahan, Helen Hannah Clifford, Jennie Betts Hartswick, Grace MacGowan Cooke, Winifred Sackville-Stoner, William Wallace Whitelock, Albin Peddecord Ingram, and several more. The contributors are about equally divided by sex, which suggests that *Life* was indeed read and written for by women despite its defensive masculinity.

The contents of the book are almost universally concerned with the ironies of love among the upper middle class. There is no need for extensive quotation to demonstrate this—genteel verse deals inevitably with the upper middle class; *Life* dealt habitually with irony. Two of the shortest poems will show the drift of the remainder. The first, a take-off on Goldsmith's *The Vicar of Wakefield*, is by Dick Law, the second by M. E. W.

Lines to a Gray Sister

When lovely woman touches forty,
    And finds, too soon, her hair is gray,
What charm can make her blithe and sporty
    And hide the fact that she's passé?

There's but one way to make her pleasing
And bring back gladness to her eye,
So, fast the horns of Taurus seizing,
Her only refuge is—to dye!

His Home-Brought Luggage

Item: A battered dressing case,
   Items: A game bag and a gun.
Item: A girl's bright pictured face.
   Item: One dollar—and only one.[20]

But love's ironies in those verses are not seldom painful. Love is pictured as a passion more likely to wound than to soothe. This is not to say that none of the poems celebrates love's delights; but most aim their ironies to cut the tender heart:

Above and Below

She lives in the square below me there.
   Ah me! If she'd only love me!
She lives in the square below me there,
   But moves in a circle above me.

Dorothy

Dorothy doing crewel work,
   Ah, what a charming sight!
Needle that glances in and out,
   Eyes with a glance as bright.
Finished the work and thrown aside,
   Alas, for my heart so true!
Needle and glance have pierced alike,
   Dorothy's eyes do cruel work too!

The Truth That Hurts

Wisdom hath she beyond all other women
Who for a husband the lover indifferent chooseth,
She knoweth well that love of indifference born
Is better than love to indifference grown.

Foolish is she in her own generation
Who when she hath wedded her lover, cries,
   brokenhearted,
" 'Tis not the man I have loved! 'Tis another!"
Hath not love ever played mortals these tricks?

So, fair one, tarry and worry no longer
In choosing whom you shall marry. These
   teachings remember:
Love ever deceiveth; and, choose whom you may,
You will find you have wedded a stranger.[21]

The first two of these three poems are anonymous. The third is by Helen Hannah Clifford. They represent three distinct moods, but the painful irony of love is their mutual message. The pain represented was as a rule the sort that only the refined soul would feel. In "The Blot on Polly's Bonnet," by John R. Rathom, the beautiful Polly wears a beautiful feathered hat. Her suitor begins to think about the hat, and the poem's concluding stanzas are these:

> But what is this, with azure wing
>   Upon the sunshine borne?
> A little bird, a beauteous thing,
>   Trills gayly to the morn;
> I watch him bend his graceful head,
>   As flitting blithely by,
> He darts away in merry play
>   Beneath the summer sky.
>
> A shot rings out; the leaden rain
>   Sheds darkness all around,
> And writhing in its cruel pain,
>   The bird lies on the ground;
> A stream of blood its body yields,
>   It quivers and is still;
> And murder stains the yellow fields,
>   And fashion pays the bill.
>
> So, suddenly my fancy stays,
>   No beauty can I see;
> Gone all the charming daintiness,
>   The sham simplicity;
> And Polly's face seems grown less fair
>   Beneath her dainty bonnet,
> For a little mangled body there
>   Has set death's seal upon it.[22]

But there were occasions when the pain descended abruptly from the ironic to the brutal. The tenderhearted wooer whose ardor died with the "mangled" bird on Polly's bonnet was not intended to be laughed at. The hero-victim of "A Bourgeois Ballade" by J. H. Halliday inhabited a less genteel world. The poem, though obviously a burlesque tall tale, has the pain of love still there. Only now it has turned into something very like sadism. The poem concerns a moony bakeshop boy, a "puppy," who woos his lady in her father's butcher shop. These are the three climactic stanzas:

> "Lovely fairy," cried he loudly,
>   "Take a trusting pieboy's heart.
> I will guard you, O so proudly!
>   Let us never, never part!"
>
> But—the while our hero's cup is
>   Running o'er with rapture sweet—

> "Let him join the other puppies,"
> Smiled his Doris; "It is meet!"

> Then the rash, tempestuous tyrant
> (Never was a man so mean!)
> Thrust the overbold aspirant
> In his sausage meat machine.23

Doris, to finish off the pleasantries, skips rope with the linked remains. *Life*'s poets found pain in love, and they found the pain amusing. Perhaps it is no great wonder that the elaboration of the theme extended to the sausage machine.

Among the poets represented in *Rhymes & Roundelays from "Life"*, Guy Wetmore Carryl has made by far the longest-lived reputation. Carryl contributed two poems to this anthology—"The Facts in The Case of Bluebeard" and "Cinderella." Both have been widely reprinted, and they were by no means Carryl's only contributions to *Life*. Carryl's humor is considerably more energetic than that of most of the poets represented. His double rhythms and trisyllabic rhymes were beyond the technical competence of most of them, and where they were content to expend an entire poem on a single observed irony or a play on one word, Carryl crammed both into his verse until they spilled over the sides. Compare the opening stanza of "Bluebeard" to the opening stanzas of "The Gourmet of the Table D'Hote," a better-than-*Life*'s-average satire on the airs of a gentleman *manqué*:

The Facts in The Case of Bluebeard

A maiden from the Bosphorus, with eyes as bright as phosphorus,
Once wed the wealthy bailiff of the caliph of Kelat.
Though diligent and zealous, he became a slave to jealousy:
Considering her beauty 'twas his duty to be that.
When business would necessitate a journey he would hesitate,
But fearing to disgust her, he would trust her with his keys,
Remarking to her prayerfully: "I beg you'll use them carefully.
Don't look what I deposit in that closet, if you please!"24

The Gourmet of The Table D'Hote

When *Res Angustae makes you dine*
For fifty cents, including wine,
Rail not at Fortune, curse not Fate.
Let Laughter on Digestion wait.
Assist your appetite and note
The *gourmet* of the table d'hote.

Items: a full dress satin tie,
A polished shirt, a silker high,
A heavily-embroidered vest
(It's sweller if it's double-breast),
A just-marked-down Tuxedo coat,
The *gourmet* of the table d'hote.25

"The Gourmet" is by Wilton Lackaye, better known as an actor than as a poet. Nevertheless it is by no means a bad example. Both fragments depend for humor on clever rhyme and an ironical view of a well-known character. Carryl's simply has more of everything.

Moreover, Carryl's ironies characteristically avoid the clichés of thwarted romance on which so many of the others concentrated. His Cinderella won her prince by being the prettiest and liveliest dancer at the ball and wearing the most expensive dress—and a snap of the fingers for demure virtue.

As for prose, increasingly after the turn of the century Life published prose fiction as well as jokes and verse, anecdotes, sketches, and its regular columns. Life had printed short stories in special issues, such as Christmas or Easter issues, even earlier, but these stories were nearly all written by staff members. As the magazine's bulk increased, however, more pages were devoted to fiction. The idea seems to have sprung from the success of two contests run in 1898 and 1901, respectively. Life offered two-hundred dollar first prizes in both contests. The response was so great that the editors continued to look for short fiction from that time on.

Perhaps the most direct way to give the flavor of Life's short stories is to work with the contest winners.[26] First prize in the 1898 contest went to "Our James," by Robert Alston Stevenson. First prize in the 1901 contest went to "Miss Gay's Diplomacy," by Kate Jordan (Mrs. F. M. Vermilye). A later contest, the 1915-1916 contest, titled "How Short Can A Story Be and Still Be A Short Story?" was won by Ralph Henry Barbour. The prize was one thousand dollars this time. Ralph Henry Barbour was one of the judges. He had collaborated with Ralph Osborne on a story titled "Thicker Than Water." The second prize of five hundred dollars went to Harry Stillwell Edwards for a story titled "The Answer." The third prize of two-hundred-and-fifty dollars was divided by Dwight M. Wiley, whose story was titled "Her Memory," and Redfield Ingalls, whose story was titled "Business and Ethics."

When Life announced the winners of the 1898 contest, it added that the editors had rejected some good stories because they were not "suitable for Life." "Suitability for Life" was a prime criterion for prizewinners in all of the contests.

"Our James" is the story of a man of means who marries a lovely girl with a social conscience. The bride, Kitty, investigates slums and gathers information on the discontented poor. She is less easily gulled by fraudulent beggars than her husband is, but she spends what seems to him an inordinate amount of time with persons who do not deserve her attentions. One day she hires a tramp as a man of all work. The man, James, turns out to be a paragon. After about a year, he simply walks out one morning and never returns. Kitty is hurt, not because she has not had her money's worth, but because she has become fond of James. Some time

later a sociological friend invites the couple to dinner, promising to intro-
duce them to some interesting guests.   They meet Dr. J. Mortimer
Stubbs, whose book on social classes has just been published.   Dr. Stubbs
is James.   He and Kitty fall into conversation, while the husband steams.
Later the husband buttonholes Stubbs and demands an explanation.
Stubbs says:

> "I had lived with tramps, beggars, thieves, and all the other discontented classes,
> when it occurred to me that it would be an original idea to make a study of the
> fairly contented man—the man who didn't steal, beg, or want society done
> over.   Fortunately, I obtained a position with you, and I may say the chapter
> there written I consider my best."
>
> "Thank you," I replied; "you found the right place. I am contented."
>
> "You have a very good reason to be," said the Doctor, which showed he was a
> man of correct observation.[17]

"Our James" is an unpretentious story, and a good one on its own
terms.   The neat little compliment to the American Girl, slipped in at the
end of the story that demonstrates the futility of her efforts to mix into
matters that she cannot understand, is especially well done.   It is also
especially in line with *Life*'s attitude toward women.   The sentiments
about the importance of the contented man are *Life*'s very own, too.
Stevenson's story suggests that the gentleman deserves more consideration
than he has received from investigators into society.   It is indeed "suitable
for *Life*."

"Miss Gay's Diplomacy" is the story of a woman correspondent in
Cuba after the Spanish-American War.   Her landlady's niece, Rosita, wants
to marry an American.   The aunt, Doña Maria, hates Americans and has
threatened to send Rosita to a convent.   Her husband was Spanish, and was
killed in the war.   She tells Miss Gay of her own romance, and of how she
ran away to Key West to be married because her Cuban family hated the
Spanish.   Rosita does the same thing.   Doña Maria is hysterical until Miss
Gay points out the parallel to her.   Miss Gay pleads with her to understand
true lovers and not let their happiness and hers be blighted by her hatred
for an impersonal country.   She capitulates.

"Our James" is an effective story, but "Miss Gay's Diplomacy" is
not.   It depends on the most banal sentimentality.   Its reference to the
convent is gratuitous anti-Catholicism.   Its rhetoric speaks for itself.   When
Miss Gay confronts Doña Maria with her arguments, before a portrait of
Doña Maria's late husband, she speaks to her as follows:

> "Will it please him to see how you cast off this motherless girl because she loves
> your enemy as you once loved him? Down on your knees—down, I say, Doña
> Maria—as you ask that question of your dead love!"[28]

Even such is Miss Gay's diplomacy.   But a story that deals with the pain
of love, that has a word of censure for the Catholic church and a word of
pity for the motherless—such a story, whatever its defects of sentimental-

ity or style, is eminently "suitable for *Life*."

The contest of 1915-1916 was rather special. Mitchell himself had laid down the rules to be followed, and his ideas will be discussed presently. The prizewinning stories, in accordance with the rules of the contest, were so compact that they are difficult to condense.

Barbour and Osborne's first place story concerns a young girl who has been badly cut in a shop accident. A doctor persuades her brother that only a transfusion will save her life. The brother volunteers. Obviously abject and mentally tense, he submits to the operation. When the transfusion is completed. he asks how long it will be before he dies. The doctor had not told him that he was in no danger. He was willingly giving up his life for his sister.

Harry Stillwell Edwards' second place story concerns a young Irishman in New York, desperate to the point of suicide, who pawns his coat on Christmas Eve for enough to buy fare for his wife and baby to where "They'll take her, without me." A prosperous Jew who is standing by asks what he is doing. The Irishman says bitterly that he is looking for the Christ Child. The Jew says he has come to the wrong city for that, but he adds that if the young man prefers a job to suicide he can come to work at the Jew's billiard room. He says that he needs an honest man, and that any man who will pawn his coat and consider suicide for his family will not steal billiard balls. He gives the Irishman five dollars in advance and tells him to come to work Monday morning. The grateful Irishman buys gifts for his wife and baby and takes them home. He asks his wife if she remembers telling him that if he looked hard enough he would find the Christ Child. She does. He says that he has found Him. She asks where. He says, "In the heart of a Jew."

Dwight M. Wiley's story is about a gay-deceiver type who is playing the field at a resort. He literally stumbles onto a beautiful girl seated in the shadows of a porch. They flirt and he is captivated. Quickly they pass from flirtation to kisses, and he is having the time of his life. Then her mother appears. They are introduced. The mother excuses herself and her daughter—and wheels the girl away. She is hopelessly paralyzed. The man is embarrassed and revolted, but the girl is radiant. She has a memory to cherish.

Redfield Ingalls' story tells of A. Slivovitz, a manufacturer of dyes. He calls in his private secretary one day and tells the young man that he is fired. But he adds that he wants him to go to work for Slivovitz's rivals, the Domestic Dye Works, learn one of their secret formulas, and return with seventy-five dollars' bonus. The secretary refuses. Slivovitz raises the bonus by degrees until he reaches one hundred and fifteen dollars. The secretary still refuses. Then Slivovitz has a tantrum. He fires the young man on the spot and threatens to blacklist him. The secretary says he does not mind. He says that he only wanted to work for Slivovitz long enough to learn the formula for his "royal purple" anyway. Now, he says, he can go back to the Domestic Dye Works.

Of these four stories, that by Edwards has the most content per word, but it is at least twice as long as the one by Barbour and Osborne, and brevity was the first consideration in the judging. All four of the stories are written well, although the first two prizewinners are better than the winners of the third prize. But the content of the stories is the important consideration here. All, either by design or by accident, are freighted with material "suitable for *Life*."

The first story is of the incompetence of physicians in human matters and of self-sacrificing love displayed by members of a family. The second story is of self-sacrifice and honesty rewarded, of the human touch discoverable in the vast impersonality of New York, and of the surprising decency of a Jew. The third is about flirtation at a summer resort and the impossibility of a gentleman's becoming seriously involved with a woman who is not physically sound, however beautiful and charming she may be. The fourth is about the amusing convolutions of Jewish rapacity. Every one of these ideas was a staple of *Life*.

Mitchell's rules for the "How Short Can A Story Be and Still Be A Short Story?" contest reveal something of *Life*'s criteria for fiction, even though they are intended to apply only to the contest. The object of the contest was to write a story that was not a mere anecdote and could be classified as literature. The rules laid down Mitchell's minimum requirements for literature. We are justified in taking them to be his *essential* requirements for literature, also.

> A short story must contain at least two characters, for otherwise there would be no contrast or struggle. A situation must be depicted in which there are two opposing forces.
>
> A short story must be a picture out of real life which gives the reader a definite sensation, such as he gets upon looking at a masterpiece of painting. While it must be complete in itself, the art of it lies in what it suggests to the reader beyond its own limits. That is to say, it must convey an idea much larger than itself. It is the open sesame to a golden principle.
>
> Every short story must of necessity deal with human beings, either directly or indirectly. It must reveal in the briefest possible manner—as it were, like a flash—a situation which carries the reader beyond it. It is, therefore, inevitable that the supreme test of a short story lies in its climax. This climax must gather up everything that has gone before, and perhaps by only one word epitomize the whole situation in such a way as to produce in the reader a sense of revelation—just as if he were the sole spectator to a supremely interesting human mystery now suddenly made plain.[29]

No one can quarrel with Mitchell's point in the first paragraph. As for the second, Mitchell begins by demanding real life. While none of the situations in the prizewinning stories is so fantastic as to be impossible, "The Answer," Edwards' story, is too carefully constructed to be realistic, and Wiley's "Her Memory" is too patly sentimental. Nor is either one of

OLUME X.   **NEW YORK, JULY 7, 1887.**   NUMBER 236.

Entered at New York Post Office as Second-Class Mail Matter.
Copyright, 1887, by Mitchell & Miller.

A PATRIOT.

Younger: I should like to go abroad this summer and see the world.

Fond Parent: I do not object to your going; you would be a valuable accession to the world's society.

the other two particularly probable. To *Life*, truth was identical with *Life*'s own opinions.

Mitchell's next point is that of sensation. Each one of these stories appeals to sentiment, and produces a sensation in anyone vulnerable to such an appeal. The comparison Mitchell makes to painting is interesting. Painting in the twentieth century has moved away from the representational toward the abstract. "Modern painting" does not narrate. It seeks to impress or express. Mitchell, always an artist at bottom, was perhaps feeling the tenor of the times in his own first-chosen art more than he realized.

The rest of Mitchell's description of the minimum short story aims at a concept that he found hard to put into words. He calls it a golden principle revealed in a flash, which carries the reader beyond the boundaries of the story. This is nothing more than the point made by Thackeray at the beginning of *The Newcomes*: sometimes satire leads you to expect one thing and then hands you its opposite number.

In Barbour and Osborne's story the reader is led to expect that the young man is reluctant to help his sister, only to discover that he believes himself to be sacrificing his life to save hers. In Edwards' story the reader finds the spirit of Christmas in an unexpected quarter and also a reversal of the Jewish stereotype. In the story by Wiley the clichés of summer romance are abruptly shattered. In the story by Ingalls the stereotyped conniving Jew is discovered to have been outdone at his own game. There are *two* golden principles revealed by these stories. The first is that the clichés are untrustworthy. The second is that they were very handy tools for an author who wanted to write for *Life*.

There is of course a defense for these stories other than that Thackeray had recommended just such reversals of clichés. Brevity was the first aim of all four stories, and the only ideas which the public is likely to accept at very short notice are ideas which the public already entertains. The four authors had to exploit received ideas if they hoped to reach the public.

The same defense can be used to justify *Life*. As a commentator on current events *Life* always worked at the shortest notice. Its best device to obtain popular approval and therefore profitable circulation was to work entirely within the framework of ideas already familiar to the public. At the same time it had to adopt a pose of superior tastefulness and insight or—as Thackeray himself wrote—who would care about its opinions? Its belief in itself as an arbiter of human nature, its certainty that its favorite clichés were great truths, is suspicious and sometimes annoying. But no gentleman is a cynic. To save itself from cynicism, the humorist's great pitfall, *Life* had to believe that it "knew" that the ludicrous could be reversed and that nothing human is permanently bad. Given its self-imposed limitations, *Life* chose well when it chose its literary standards.

NOTES

[1]*Life*, III, 1884, p. 215.   [2]*Life*, IV, 1884, p. 186.

[3]*Life*, XI, 1888, p. 103.

[4]Frank Luther Mott, *A History of American Magazines*, III (Cambridge, Mass.: Harvard University Press, 1957), p. 268.

[5]Mitchell edited three of the four collections of verse from *Life*. Masson edited one.

[6]*Life*, VIII, 1886, p. 318.   [7]*Life*, V, 1885, p. 174.

[8]Another Non-American admired by *Life* was the Scot Andrew Lang. His *Ballades in Blue China* appeared in 1880. Martin's *Slye Ballades in Harvard China* appeared in 1882.

[9]*Life*, XXX, 1897, p. 67.   [10]*Life*, V, 1885, p. 90.

[11]*Life*, II, 1883, p. 83.   [12]*Life*, V, 1885, p. 356.

[13]*Life*, XX, 1892, p. 251.   [14]*Life*, VI, 1885, p. 262.

[15]*Life*, II, 1883, p. 71.   [16]*Life*, XXXI, 1898, p. 6.

[17]*Life*, XXIX, 1897, p. 108.

[18]Thorstein Veblen, *The Theory of The Leisure Class* (New York: The Modern Library, 1934), pp. 53-54.

[19]Four titles: *Life's Verses*, 1885; *Life's Verses, Second Series*, 1886; *Rhymes & Roundelays from "Life"*, 1902; *Taken from Life*, 1897.

[20]*Rhymes & Roundelays from "Life"* (New York: Doubleday, Page & Co., 1902), pp. 53, 16.

[21]*Ibid.*, pp. 111, 10, 53.   [22]*Ibid.*, p. 52.

[23]*Ibid.*, p. 84.   [24]*Ibid.*, p. 69.

[25]*Ibid.*, p. 125.

[26]*Life's* contests were open to all entrants. Of the seven writers named here, Barbour, Edwards, and Mrs. Vermilye were established authors with books to their credit. The others have left no discoverable record.

[27]*Life*, XXXII, 1898, p. 457.   [28]*Life*, XXXVIII, 1901, p. 457

[29]*Life*, LIV, 1915, p. 274.

CHAPTER VI

AMERICANUS SUM

Bridges was *Life*'s literary banner-bearer. It was no accident that his seventeen-year tenure as *Life*'s book reviewer corresponded exactly to the period of *Life*'s only genuine interest in literary questions. *Life*'s apotheosis of Thackeray, its commitment to gentility, and its misogyny were the joint responsibilities of Mitchell, Martin, and Bridges. The ideas continued to dominate *Life*'s literary opinions after Bridges quit his post in 1900. But while the same ideas ruled after his departure, the number of opportunities to exercise them dwindled away. John B. Kerfoot was more than competent as a book reviewer, but he was no replacement for Bridges. His ideas and *Life*'s did not fuse. Bridges and *Life* thought exactly alike.

While Bridges contributed heavily to the development of the ideas discussed in the previous chapter, he also modified them and fused them into a set of personal ideas. From Thackeray he took the "gentleman's" set of mind, skeptical and aloof. In the genteel tradition he found a mandate to delicacy. As a true believer in man's superiority to woman he preached the necessity of virility, independence, and expansiveness in literature. When he put all of these together, he called the result Americanism.

Mitchell's belief in the almost magical powers of Americanism has been demonstrated. Martin's is less easy to demonstrate, but it was as real as Mitchell's or Bridges'. His duties as editorialist made him adduce somewhat more specific arguments than theirs, since one who comments on generalities must avoid generalities in his arguments whenever possible. Thus his attack on the suffragettes rested finally on their offenses against motherhood, a somewhat more specific idea than Americanism. But Martin publicly deplored the alien influences in American life, and he invariably seconded Bridges' statements about manliness, purity, and independence, the specifics of Bridges' Americanism.

In 1886, relatively early in his career with *Life*, Bridges reviewed a milky-socialistic novel, *Face to Face*, published anonymously by Charles Scribner's Sons. Of it he wrote:

This novel exaggerates the importance of the American "leisure class" and the element of discontented and despairing workman.   Recent events have caused even more learned and weighty writers to overestimate the gravity of the present crisis.   They lose sight of the strong, pure, contented American life which abounds in all of our smaller cities and towns, where wealth is well distributed and the poorest boy may yet hope to be independent.   The old Puritan qualities of thrift and integrity are not so obsolete as the alarmists would have us believe.   There is a tremendous area of our country where Anglomania and Socialism are alike unknown, and peace and good will to men sway the hearts and lives of a happy people.   New York and Newport . . . don't tip up the continent to any alarming extent.[1]

This paragraph will serve as a point of departure for the discussion of most of Bridges' literary ideas.   The first noteworthy thing about it is its beautiful harmony with *Life*'s personality—Thackerayan skepticism leading inevitably to middle-of-the-road optimism.   Not Martin nor Mitchell himself could have turned out a paragraph more perfectly in accord with *Life*'s character.   This is so obvious as to require no further comment.   The second noteworthy thing, and the first to deserve investigation, is that at least two references in the paragraph contradict Bridges' very strong opinions expressed elsewhere.   He had no use, as a rule, for Puritans or Puritan influences, and both he and *Life* definitely believed that New York did tip up the continent.   These two contradictions are evidence of the mythical qualities of Bridges' Americanism.   He believed in a fictional America which not only had no real existence in his own time but which differed in some of its most important particulars from things which he observed to be true.   When "Puritanism" and "New York" were dissociated from the collective idea, "America," Bridges approached them in an entirely different manner.

Bridges was, if anything, more than ordinarily belligerent about New York's worth, for a member of *Life*'s staff.   *Life* as a rule placidly accepted its home city's central place in the universe.   Bridges wanted to defend it. His partiality to New York girls over girls of any other origin has been noted.   He championed New York writers and New York society with the same vigor.

Books about New York, if they had any merit at all, were certain to receive at least a muted cheer from Bridges.   Two pseudonymous writers, Sidney Luska and Ivory Black, each received Bridges' high praise for "a distinct and faithful picture of certain interesting sections of this great city."   Later the two men, using their real names, departed New York and made reputations elsewhere.   "Luska" was Henry Harland, who went to England and became editor of "The Yellow Book."   "Black" was Thomas A. Janvier, who became an author of popular Westerns, notably *Santa Fe's Partner*.   In both men's cases, their stories of New York have been thoroughly forgotten.   But *Life* and Bridges were happy to encourage anyone who gave faithful pictures of their city, provided that the pictures were like those which *Life* itself published and approved.   Henry Cuyler

Bunner, a mild satirist of New York's working-class life, a progenitor of O. Henry, a some-time contributor to *Life* and editor of its rival, *Puck*, enjoyed Bridges' extravagant praise for *Midge*, his novel of the French quarter.   Henry James, on the other hand, when he wrote of New Yorkers in "Two Countries," was publicly rebuked by Bridges. Bridges wrote that James's characters were relics of more than a decade past, "before the sensitive Puritan conscience had been made more robust by the broader and, perhaps, coarser life which material prosperity has promoted."[2] Bunner's mind was sufficiently like *Life*'s own, while James's was not. Bridges was aware of no need for subtlety in the delineation of the New Yorker's character.   He hugely admired E. W. Townsend's *Chimmie Fadden*, dialect and all. His whole attitude toward New York in fiction was Thackeray's foxy-sheepsy-crowsy story over again. He believed that "the real" meant not "that which is searching," but "that which is gently, decently amusing."

Bridges' dislike for Puritanism was linked to his municipal chauvinism, as can be seen in his remark about James. More specifically, he despised New England, root and branch. He struggled to convince the public that New England was a literary dead issue, and that the intellectual history of the Midwest and South was as important and illuminating as anything that had been written by or about the Puritans and Transcendentalists. He embraced the American local color movement, already reaching its apex when he began to write for *Life*, as a hero come to lead American letters out of the desert of New England, despite the fact that his high regard for independence usually made him look askance at "movements" of any sort. He thought of local color less as regionalism than as expansion.   He believed that a single region had represented America far too long, and that at last, by means of Southern and Western and Midwestern local color literature, the country would be able to pull itself away from this withered and juiceless root. He gave no credit to Howells or other New England editors who were lending support to and buying stories from local color writers. Neither did he comment on the fact that the early books of such local colorists as Mary Noailles Murfree, Constance Fenimore Woolson, and Edgar Watson Howe were published by the Boston firms of Houghton Mifflin and J. R. Osgood.   Bridges could be downright violent about New England. He held it responsible for the Civil War.

No particular origin of Bridges' antipathy for New England can be found, but perhaps the war is the key. Shippensburg, Pennsylvania, where he was born and grew up, is just ten miles from Chambersburg, which was raided by Stuart's cavalry in 1862. More than that, it lies directly in Lee's line of march up the Cumberland Valley to Gettysburg. The war might indeed have brought hardship and bitterness to Bridges and his family and friends. Southern Pennsylvania was never strong for abolition. When the Pennsylvanians had to stand off an invasion while New England's abolitionists slept in peaceful security, their deep resentment might have had an incalculable effect on a five-year-old boy.

The more pugnacious side of Bridges' personal quarrel with New England took the form of gleeful demolition of a series of novels, called by him "Boston Novels," that began to appear early in his career with *Life*. The more thoughtful side concerned local color. These Boston Novels were in fact nearly uniform, treating of the superiority of nineteenth century Boston to seventeenth century Boston in particular and everywhere else in general. Their plots came from factory molds. *Life* held up John L. Sullivan as an example of Boston's gift to the world of the mind. Following *Life*'s lead, Bridges pounced on such novels as *For A Woman*, by Nora Perry, *Roses of Shadow*, by T. R. Sullivan, and the anonymous *The Dawning*.

There were of course excellent reasons for New York to gloat over New England at this period in American literary history. New York was replacing Boston as America's center of mind and sensibility. Whitman and some minor poets had been in New York since before the war, and when William Dean Howells surrendered and came down from Boston in 1889, the last literary tie was cut. During *Life*'s flourishing period, New England culture as preserved at Harvard and Yale continued to diverge from American culture as embodied in New York City and in the Southern and Western states. Howells himself was the last outlander to head for Boston when the urge to civilization overwhelmed him. Bret Harte, in 1871, went straight for New York. *Life* had the strongest of sentimental ties to Harvard, but the sentiment only abetted its scoffing.

But Bridges treated the Boston Novels as personal insults over and above his admiration for New York. He made up a formula for a Boston Novel in 1885. The stock characters were to include a Commonplace Young Man with a Fortune; an Imperious Beauty with a Mission; a Precious Little Goose; an Eccentric Artist or Literary Man, suited to be either the good or the bad angel of the story, always an atheist; and "job lots of spinsters with eyeglasses, Unitarian ministers, decayed aristocrats, Harvard professors, and blasé club men." He characterized the Boston novelists' attitude as a "Pharisaism more intense and illiberal than that of their fathers whom they affect to despise." He fairly revelled in his self-appointed role as Boston's scourge, calling himself:

> The critic, with his flashing knife,
> Your novels seem to freeze,
> The savage "Droch" who writes for *Life*,
> And stabs all Bostonese.[3]

The Boston Novels and their authors played their game and vanished —almost. Their heyday was in 1885, when Bridges attacked Boston almost as often as he reviewed books. Yet somehow the names of James and Howells, Boston novelists only by accident of proximity, were connected with the "school" by *Life*. Possibly the reason was the Boston novelists' concentration on restrained manners or their proclamations of mystery and drama where mystery and drama did not exist. Whatever it was, as late as 1891 Tom Masson considered this joke so apposite that he gave it room on the first page of an issue of *Life*:

> Mr. Howeljames: Emerson, I fear that I have
> detected you in an untruth.
> Emerson Howeljames: (hanging his head) Yes,
> father.
> Mr. Howeljames: What a disgrace, Emerson! To
> think that you, the son of a Boston novelist,
> should be caught telling a story![4]

Bridges, for all his rant over Boston Novels, never accused either James or Howells of being among the guilty authors. He did conceive a violent dislike for Imperious Beauties with Missions, though, and for Precious Little Geese, and it led him forever afterward to consider all literary characters who reminded him of one or the other as Boston Girls, bluestockinged and brainless.

While Bridges' reaction to Boston Novels was as much emotional as intellectual, his admiration for local color was more reasoned and originated in recognizable principles. He believed first of all that America needed a true American literature. He wanted to crush New England, but in a more positive way he wanted a literature that represented all of America, not just her northeastern corner. He believed with Whitman that American literature should be panoramic, although he might have been a little ashamed to find himself agreeing with Whitman. Local color seemed just the panoramic genre that would fulfill his requirements.

Another of his critical principles, although possibly not a conscious one, was that prose tales of whatever length were more worthy of attention if they dealt with a settled community rather than a frontier. The principle is one that all of his contemporaries believed, and one that can claim a much stronger validity than mere custom. A recognizable social scheme is of highest importance to the action of almost all prose fiction, and one of the faults of exoticism is that it wastes time setting the social scene. Because Bridges applied this principle he never became so enthusiastic over stories of the Far West as he did over stories of the Kentucky-Tennessee country, the Deep South and the Midwest. In this he set independently a pattern of thought that persists to this day.

Basing his reviews on these two ideas, Bridges began shortly after he went to work for *Life* to cry up any writer who made his home southwest of the Housatonic. He read books, not magazine serials, and therefore was sometimes a year or more behind the earliest publications of local colorists. Charles Egbert Craddock (Mary Noailles Murfree), whose first book of tales appeared in 1884, was the first of the writers now called

A LITERARY COMBINATION.

Mr. H—w—lls: ARE YOU THE TALLEST NOW, MR. J—MES?
Mr. J—mes (ignoring the question): BE SO UNCOMMONLY KIND, H—W—LLS, AS TO LET ME DOWN EASY; IT MAY BE WE HAVE BOTH GOT TO GROW.

local colorists to come to his attention. He liked her work. He continued to like it and praise it for its "depth of sympathy with a narrow existence which brings . . . Tennessee Mountain characters within the circle of our pity and affection"[5] even after he had concluded that her prose was padded. Then he wrote that with the "weather reports" taken out, her novels would be about one-fifth as long as they are, and *Life* added that "Craddock writes with the feather end of a quill."[6] Two Kentucky novelists, John Fox, Jr. and James Lane Allen, both received Bridges' praise too, and less for their merits than for their championship of Scotch-Irish culture as opposed to that of New England. S. Weir Mitchell, Bridges' fellow Pennsylvanian, does not exactly belong in a list of local colorists. However, it was for his local interests that Bridges admired him. Mitchell insisted that some of the patriots in the Revolution were not from Massachusetts, but from the Scotch-Irish stock of the Philadelphia area. Bridges turned his praise northward once, for Sarah Orne Jewett of Maine. He praised Constance F. Woolson, who wrote of the Great Lakes region and of the South. He believed that the American short story was as a rule a story of domestic drama, and that women were naturally more talented in such matters than were men.

He discovered Edgar Watson Howe of Kansas when Howe's second novel, *The Mystery of the Locks,* was published in 1885, and he immediately read *The Story of a Country Town* and devoted three weeks' work to explaining Howe's talents and apologizing to *Life*'s readers for not having introduced them to Howe two years before. He found little to cavil at even among the Southern local colorists, much of whose work does not approach the quality of Howe's or Miss Jewett's. Joel Chandler Harris's "Uncle Remus" tales were more popular than his realistic novels, and Bridges liked them better. George Washington Cable's favorite subjects were simply not "American" enough by Bridges' standards; Louisiana's Creoles and Cajuns had a distinct alien flavor for him. Therefore he reviewed Cable politely but without enthusiasm. In the work of Thomas Nelson Page of Virginia, however, Bridges found a mirror image of *Life*'s views of the proper relation between gentlemen and the lower classes. He approved mightily of Page's *Befo' de War,* of which he wrote:

> If you sift the motive of these poems, you will find only kindly feeling, and even admiration for the negro. He is singing the praises of his old master, lamenting the end of the old days, risking his life for "young marster," longing for return to the plantation, and, in short, is an humble but persistent optimist—happy, contented, appreciative.[7]

This cements Bridges firmly to that side of *Life*'s thought dominated by Martin. Mitchell, whose sympathy and anger were so quickly aroused, could work himself to the point of suggesting a new American revolution. Martin, conversely, was himself a persistent optimist and saw no reason for anyone to be less optimistic than he was. He was always disturbed by

the obstinate refusal of the poor to see the beautiful symmetry of civilization's pyramid and the exquisite balance of time's pendulum.   He
would have appreciated a world populated by such men as the ex-slaves
described by Page.   But what neither Martin nor Bridges realized was that
Page's charming picture is almost devoid of truth.   It is painted in exactly
the false, sentimental colors that *Life* used to depict America, and it contains an even deeper falsehood.   It calls upon the Negroes, in effect, to
cater to the hurt vanity of the impotent, dying Old South.   It asks them
to set aside any constructive or useful endeavor and sit idly at the in-
valid's side, soothing him with flattery.   *Life* understood the plea, but it
understood only Page's side of it.   It used essentially the same arguments
against women's suffrage, immigration, and in Bridges' specific case, rough-
hewn poetry and realistic fiction.

Happily, *Life*'s sense of humor sometimes saved it from total commitment to bathos.   In 1891, when the Old South nostalgia was running
strong, a short sketch appeared in *Life* over the signature of Walker
Kennedy.   It told how the author accosted a venerable Negro working in
a field.   The old man refused to talk in dialect, denied that the old master
had ever told him to take care of the young master, said that his young
mistress was married before the war to an elderly widower and lived in
England while the fight was going on, said he would not care to return to
the good old days, made no sage aphorisms, manifested no desire to spend
all day talking, and finally asked whether his questioner was a census taker.
Life cherished quaintness and the picturesque, but too much of a good
thing was too much.

Thus it is demonstrable that Bridges supported New York as a rule
against all challengers, and that his feelings against New England ran so
high that he attacked her himself and supported other writers whose greatest merit, in his eyes, was that they were not New Englanders.   Indeed,
the local colorists had the distinction of being the only group of American
writers who were American enough, by Bridges' standards, to earn his
unstinting praise.   And yet there is more than an implied contradiction
here.   In that paragraph quoted above Bridges specifically stated that two
of America's great virtues were her Puritan heritage and her difference,
in essence, from New York City.   The answer is that when he was in an
"American" frame of mind, all things virtuous were to him typical of
America.   When he was more observing he could see that at least a few
American institutions were not absolutely faultless.

In the paragraph just referred to, Bridges lists, as the attributes of
American life, strength, purity, contentment, well-distributed wealth,
equality of opportunity, thrift, integrity, peace and good will, and
happiness.   As reinforcement let us look at another paragraph taken from
one of his defenses of New York:

> With our eye on *Life*'s motto, *Americanus Sum*, we loyally add that New York
> has received most of the follies satirized from its large foreign population; and,
> more than this, that throughout our broad country, and even in this city, there
> exists a solid, pure, and progressive American life which centres around homes of
> culture and happiness, and on it we appeal to our critics for judgment.8

Here Bridges asserts his willingness to be judged by his picture of American
life.

But the elements are so intertwined that the picture becomes confused. Some sorting out of Bridges' ideas is called for. First, he believed
wholly in the *reality* of his vision. But the most active literary movement
of his time called itself *Realism*, and its view of reality, specifically American reality, was in many ways diametrically opposed to Bridges'. Therefore, Bridges had to deny that Realists understood reality. In his view,
Realism dealt with unreal matters.

Secondly, the writers contemporary with Bridges were not all
Realists. Some, notably Robert Louis Stevenson and Rudyard Kipling,
were what we would today call writers of romances. But since Stevenson's
and Kipling's world views corresponded more closely to *Life*'s than did
those of the Realists, *Life* and Bridges praised Stevenson and Kipling for
their realism while censuring Howells, James, and Thomas Hardy for their
unreality.

Thirdly, *Life* equated its optimistic view of reality with a courageous
view. It believed that optimism and courage were complementary virtues,
and that no fact was so bad that it could not be faced by a man possessed
of such a combination. As a result, it had to deny the factuality of anything it did not wish to face.

As corollary to this third idea, Bridges believed that optimism and
courage bred good fellowship, and that the three were the hallmarks of
manliness. Manliness, virility, was a virtual fetish with Bridges. It was
obviously a result of *Life*'s suspicious misogyny. It colored Bridges'
judgments of Realists and romantics alike. The heroics of a Stevensonian
character like Alan Breck are too evidently more optimistic, more courageous, more comradely, more "manly" than the introspections of a
Jamesian character. Therefore, for Bridges, they were more real.

Fourthly, since purity is high on his list of real American virtues,
Bridges concluded that whatever was impure was unreal and un-American.
It did not strike him as odd that a foreigner like Ibsen should deal with
hallucinatory matters unfit for the young person. It did seem strange to
him that any American should want to read it, let alone imitate it. Again,
this idea of purity is linked to manliness by Bridges and *Life*. Comradeship, the "manly" virtue, could not lead to improprieties, as *Life* saw
it, whereas relations between persons of opposite sexes might. Therefore
the most "manly" authors were credited by *Life* with being the purest, and
by an easy twist of logic the "impure" writers were judged unmanly.

Fifthly, Americanism meant independence to Bridges. Therefore he deplored the American Realists' patterning themselves after European models. The local color writers, although in a sense realists, impressed Bridges as independent both of Europe and of previous American tradition. Whenever Bridges thought he discerned a trend in fiction he set himself squarely against it. In the 1890's two separate "trends" came under his guns. The first was a rash of Scottish novels, beginning with Ian Maclaren's *Beside The Bonnie Briar Bush* in 1894. For four or five years afterward Maclaren, James Barrie, and other canny Scots authors assaulted the American reading public with canned Scots dialect and canted Scots sentiment until many a more patient man than Bridges must have wished them out of his life. The second was a series of what Bridges called novels of gore, and it included the works of Anthony Hope, Arthur Conan Doyle, and their imitators. When any American authors showed signs of the influence of such trends, Bridges was merciless. When, in 1896, Brander Matthews deplored the imitative bent of American writers, Bridges took it as affirmation of what he had been saying for years. Occasionally his dislike of trends caught him short. More than once he dismissed an author, on the basis of a first novel, as a mere follower in the wake of a trend, then, later, had to change his mind.

Finally, Bridges believed in bulk, not so much for itself as for the opportunities that sheer size gave for expansiveness. He believed with some reason that writers of exquisite literature were likely to be ingrown, and therefore unmanly and unwholesome. He praised Hall Caine without seeing any particular merit in his style or his content, simply because Caine wrote big books. A later and less sympathetic commentator in *Life* dismissed the Manx rhapsodist with "Hall Caines look alike to me."

In one notable case the majority of Bridges' ideas concentrated in his opinion of a novel, George Du Maurier's *Trilby*. He praised *Trilby* to the skies on the grounds that it was a book about friendship and its heroine brimful of camaraderie, gaiety of heart, and good fellowship. In short, she was more a man than a woman. *Trilby* satisfied all of Bridges' requirements for truth, optimism, manliness, courage, comradeship, and purity. He was so taken by its story of jolly times in old Montmartre that he failed to see the emptiness, mental, emotional, and moral, behind the jollity. The men in the novel, and Trilby herself, behaved as Bridges thought men ought to behave; and Bridges' judgment was exactly that of the public, although perhaps it sprang from sources other than those from which the public drew. By the end of the century the Camille story had assumed almost mythic proportions among that segment of the reading public to which Bridges and *Life* spoke. While Bridges was able to see that it descended to bathos at the drop of a blood-stained handkerchief, he was as blind as his readers to many of its implications. Particularly, he was blind if the forlorn heroine laughed, rather than coughed, her life away. *Trilby* taught that art was a disease of youth, that The Woman Always Pays, that young men's wild oats are sown in more orderly rows when their companions are strictly male and that properly constituted young men prefer their companions that way, that Mother knows best, and that God cancels all debts for the lamebrained and weak hearted. This abdication of responsibility and praise of the infantile life might have been a considerable comfort to those members of *Life*'s middle-class audience who suspected that Victorian life had withheld something from them but who had no means of discovering what it might be. It might, particularly, have been a comfort to those women whom *Life* was willing to shelve forever once they had been wooed and won. It confirmed the nobility of boredom. However, the whole matter points to an enormous gap in *Life*'s intellectual armor. Bridges and *Life* really believed that men should live without thinking, gaining whatever they gained from the willing and natural sacrifices of their women. This view of the world was one of the firmest bases of their optimism. It is no wonder that Bridges approved of Thomas Nelson Page's sentimentally demeaning pictures of freed slaves.

Let us turn next to the American practitioners of capital-R Realism, and to their shifting fortunes in *Life*'s pages. In the main, *Life* continued to admire Howells even while it deplored his work, and the severity of its remarks about him was determined by whether it was the man or his books that was foremost in *Life*'s mind. In James's case the opposite was true. Howells as Realism's most vocal champion, and James as the shiniest example of a promising artist corrupted by it, took the brunt of *Life*'s attacks during Bridges' term as reviewer. Howells, in the long run, escaped with fewer bruises than did James. Howells was substantial and respected and one could understand everything he wrote. James's opacity was easy to deplore or to burlesque, and he was an adopted New Englander and an expatriate. Even before Bridges took over the book column *Life* printed a cartoon by Kendrick which showed James standing on Howells's shoulders. Their combined height was just enough to reach to the knot in the necktie of a majestic figure labeled "Thackeray." In 1888, Martin wrote of the two:

> It will be a proud day for *Life* when both these gifted gentlemen, scourged from their maleficent theories, are found humbly putting in their sturdiest licks for the entertainment of their brethren.[9]

Life's first complaint against the two was that they were un-American, sycophantic, importers of European dirt to besmear American truth. The second was insufficient plotting and the third was excessive triviality.

Life saw Realism as originating with Tolstoy and Ibsen. Bridges actually liked the writings of Tolstoy, and saw some good in Ibsen. Martin found them both loathsome. But Bridges would not admit that a good American should allow a foreign writer, however great, to influence him. Nor could he see that the influence of the Russian on the American was anything but pernicious. Martin never lost an opportunity to attack Tolstoy, and when Max Nordau called Tolstoy and Ibsen "degenerates" Martin quoted it with applause. Only a few weeks later, Bridges called them geniuses. *Life*'s treatment of these two men is more than usually equivocal, then, and will be discussed later. Presently, the important thing is that they represented to *Life* the bad company that American Realists were keeping.

Life believed thin plots and trivia to be inseparable from Realism. It wished that American writers had the good sense to avoid them. A cartoon of 1886 by W. A. Rogers shows several characters from stories by Howells and James. They are trudging on a treadmill while the authors look on at their ease. The little cupid figure who represents *Life* asks the Muse where they are going, what is the action of the story, what happens, what is the plot? The Muse replies, "Nothing, as usual." An editorial suggested that Howells admired Tolstoy "because Tolstoy was even more concerned with trivia than Howells is." Another editorial considered Howells's statement that "The true realist cannot look upon human life and declare this thing or that thing unworthy of notice." It asked:

> Is this not rank literary communism? If this be the true theory of literary art, then journalism should rank higher than the best novel writing, for it thinks no detail too insignificant for its chronicles; neither does it stop at any barrier of decency and self-respect in "working up" those details.[10]

Bridges added to this:

> True it is that life is the resultant of many forces, some of them trivial. But after all, men, like planets, are kept in their orbits by a few primary forces. It is the error of the Howells school that they devote their energies to studying the perturbations.
>
> They miss the grand sweep of the curve, while measuring with a micrometer its petty inequalities.
>
> And the school of American realists can never add a dignity to life until they grasp the truth of this new gospel of materialism.[11]

This seems inadequate as criticism of Howells. *Life* was nearer the mark when it accused him of pseudo-scientific folderol:

> The apostle of realism will pardon the suggestion that a scientist is not worthy of the name who cannot classify the fruits of his observations, and separate the significant from the insignificant.[12]

It was nearer still when it caricatured him as a pitchman peddling Realistic, Intoxicating—milk. But it erred when it substituted its own science for that of Howells:

> Do not we, in the light of what is "newest in science," look for a finer type of man than our brother today? If fiction writing means anything to an earnest, intelligent man, it should find its noblest object in helping forward the great work of development.[13]

Life's most perceptive criticism of Howells accused him and his school of snobbery. To ridicule vulgarity, *Life* argued, was to crush the ambition of the vulgar to rise. Surely, it said, material success offered more noble targets to the satirist—living examples of its demoralization were to be found everywhere—than unmannerly *nouveaux riches* eating with the wrong fork. *Life* wondered why Howells wasted time on eccentricities that *Life* saw as good only to make false distinctions in class and rank.

Since *Life* believed that men were "kept in their orbits by a few primary forces," one would guess that it would find Henry James's ideas of Realism more congenial than those of Howells. But *Life* continued to pillory James's theories even while it appreciated his books. It ran lengthy and repetitive parodies of point-of-view style, and once it suggested that somebody should sharpen James's point of view "and stick it into him." *Life* raised mild eyebrows when a New York paper reported that Julia Ward Howe, lecturing to the Concord School of Philadelphia, had said that James's style "is minute and mean and does immense damage to the character." This was in the late summer of 1885, and James's latest novel was *Portrait of a Lady*, although *The Bostonians* was running in the *Century*; the full-blown Jamesian style was barely in rompers. But *Life* suggested to Mrs. Howe that "it must be recognized that the process of getting through any of his later novels necessitates the possession of patient, plodding endurance and self-control, qualities, the exercise of which ought rather to elevate than debase the moral tone."[14]

Parodies of James were legion, as might be expected. The best one came late. It was the announcement of his intention to assume British citizenship, in 1915:

> The intelligence, or should we say adumbration of certain rumors, that the no less celebrated author, because he is an American—strange to say, we are mentioning Henry James—should have signified his intention to become a British subject, thus abjuring his allegiance to this country is, or will be, undoubtedly instigated by certain tergiversations.
>
> These would be, most naturally, we are to assume, because Mr. James undoubtedly will conceive it his duty to explain why he is taking this step. But inasmuch and wherefore or be that as it may, he will, perforce, consider it his duty to explain, in his own manner, himself, and as nobody, after reading what he has to say, will or can possibly understand what he is driving at, therefore nobody will be the wiser.[15]

But *Life* and Bridges spoke highly of James's books, singling out his books of short stories, and the only work by James that it thoroughly disliked was *What Maisie Knew*, which Bridges called vague, disagreeable, enigmatic, "intelligently, artistically, analytically dull." This criticism is further evidence of *Life*'s automatic rejection of anything like difficult reading. It is evidence of something else, too, if one places it side by side with an earlier review of Bridges' that called Frank Stockton's *The Late Mrs. Null* "monotonously clever." It suggests that a good oxymoron is worth more to a magazine of humor than any amount of criticism. More important, it suggests that Bridges and *Life* looked for and missed just those things in James that they looked for and missed in Stockton—speed, the heroic gesture, and the issues of the time that struck *Life* as important.

From *Life*'s sniping at Ibsen and Tolstoy it is evident that those issues did not include the things the newly lionized writers of Europe wrote about. *Life* lumped Ibsen and Tolstoy with unnecessary imports. In the 1880's and 1890's everything Europe did not want, from spirit-rappers to bogus statuary, seemed to *Life* to get crated and shipped west across the Atlantic, where it was received with wonderment and pious cheers. All too quickly for *Life*'s taste, admirers of European writers became cultists, and the cults seemed always to fasten on the least attractive characteristics of their heroes' work. It had happened to Browning and to Marie Bashkirtseff, and it was to happen later to D'Annunzio. Now it was happening to Ibsen and Tolstoy. Their admirers called them Realists, but *Life* insisted that their "reality" was sordid, tasteless, and, worst of all, untrue. Bridges, it is true, admired Tolstoy, but for a curious reason. He thought it praiseworthy that the aristocratic count should wear peasant clothing and work in the fields. He did not praise these acts as a furthering of democratic precepts. He praised them because they showed that Tolstoy was at heart not a mere writer, but a doer.

Ibsen was rather more in the news during the 1890's than the great Russian. Also, his flying mane and Norse eyebrows appealed to *Life*'s artists more than Tolstoy's peasant costume. He was caricatured first by F. G. Attwood, who enthroned him on an Olympus built of discarded books by previous idols, surrounded by gaunt and worshipping Boston Girls. The next year W. A. Rogers caricatured him as a gardener, crushing lilies and roses with his booted feet while cultivating toadstools.

Bridges saw artistic truth in Ibsen. He hoped that his readers perceived "the tremendous truth behind the somber mask" of *John Gabriel Borkman*. But he suspected the subject matter and the general reliability of the playwright's information about life and, in particular, science. He believed that the sensible American audience would find the end of *A Doll's House* too drastic. Surely, he wrote, something could be worked out if Nora and Helmer stayed together. He wrote of George Bernard Shaw, whom he admired rather more than Ibsen as an artist:

> The recipe for an Ibsenized play is simple: Choose a well-accepted principle of life as held by most decent people; then show that most decent people use it as a cloak for all manner of meanness and selfishness. The result will shatter a host of illusions, and give play to dialogue that fairly sputters with epigrams.[16]

Thus it appears that Bridges understood the value of the revival of moral dialectic as a dramatic device by Ibsen and his followers. But he could not see that Ibsen criticised the fundamental structure of contemporary society. Rather, he believed that Ibsen chose only to make entertaining fireworks by exposing some of society's worst products. But in this, Bridges was no farther from the truth than far more solemn critics of the time. He was troubled most by a habit of Ibsen's that critics of our own time shrug off, perhaps too easily. He found the Norwegian's ideas about science half-baked. The twentieth century is likely to find them so, too, but the twentieth century dismisses whatever imprecision of scientific particulars it finds in the plays. Today, we point out that Ibsen used science less as a subject for exploration than as a symbol of the irresistible facts that Victorian convention chose to ignore. This, however, is exactly what Bridges objected to:

> The man of science always knows enough to know the compensations Nature has up its sleeve, but the dabbler in science who converts it into fiction sees only the dire and implacable fact.[17]

It is only fair to say that on this question, perhaps a minor one, *Life*'s reviewer was ahead of Ibsen rather than behind him. Finally, Bridges never made the common error of damning Ibsen on moral grounds. As early as 1891 he wrote of *Hedda Gabler*:

> While firmly convinced that there are inadequate reasons why people should write or read books of this kind, we can have no sympathy with the howl against this book that it is immoral.[18]

There is *Life*'s vaunted common sense speaking. While firmly convinced that cynicism, despair,. and suicide had no place in the reality expressible in literature, Bridges could see that *Hedda Gabler* was unlikely to entice anyone to emulate the actions of its heroine.

Bridges' good sense in this instance distinguished him from other members of *Life*'s staff, and especially from Martin, the apostle of good sense. Immorality or trumped-up immorality in Realistic fiction infuriated Martin. Bridges was able to preserve a professional detachment even when his colleague sank to the most outrageous arguments *ad hominem*. *Life*'s whole attitude toward letters was in fact moralistic. Martin positively gloated when an alleged corruptor of literary morals fell onto evil days. He wrote in 1892:

> Poor De Maupassant has gone mad, and Tolstoi (sic) is ill at ease in his intellectuals. If authors hope to live peaceful lives and die pleasantly they cannot be too careful about the morals of their literature.[19]

Oscar Wilde's trial was undoubtedly the age's most celebrated mixture of literature and morals. When the case broke into headlines, Martin proposed that *Life*'s readers should:

> . . . make our acknowledgments to our lively London contemporary, the Marquis of Queensberry, for the service he has done to all sane people in obliterating Oscar Wilde. Sport as represented by the Marquis . . . has won a signal victory over aestheticism.[20]

We no longer see the Wilde case as a victory for "decency, fresh air, and honorable behavior," as Martin did. Martin and *Life*, though, were consistent in their anti-aestheticism. A magazine that saw manliness threatened on all sides could hardly help siding with the codifier of pugilistic

GLIMPSES INTO THE FUTURE.

GLIMPSE VIII.

THE STAGE IN THE TWENTIETH CENTURY, AS PROMISED BY PRESENT INDICATIONS.

science against the velvet collared posybearer. *Life* had seen the comic side of Wilde in its first issue and had lampooned his long hair and soulful eyes ever since. Even had Wilde been more conventionally masculine, the chances are that his artistic theories and practices would have cost him *Life*'s good will. Bridges himself wrote, after the trial:

> Any kind of a pose is bad enough, but the worst of them is the Bohemian pose. It is generally merely the excuse for a half-formed, shiftless ambition, that is afraid to do its work earnestly because it knows its weakness will be revealed.[21]

The variance between Bridges' opinion of bohemianism here expressed and his opinion of *Trilby* is less than appears. Everyone in *Trilby* who amounted to anything dropped Bohemia and returned to solidity as soon as ripeness and wisdom and Mother taught them that they should. Bridges saw the Realists and the aesthetes as all of a piece, morally. He predicted more than once and sometimes a little wistfully that a conservative revival was coming. It was going to cater neither to the sordid nor the fantastic. It would erase the man of twisted life from the roster of characters and replace him with the solid citizen. It would concern itself neither with Wilde's languors nor with the "brutality" of writers like Hamlin Garland, of whom Bridges wrote, "talented, but decent people take some things for granted." Bridges' new conservatism was to consider "the things that used to make life genuine, if not beautiful."

For all of this, Bridges was ready to admit that the morals of fictional characters need not necessarily cling to the codes set for living persons. He insisted, for example, that Rudolph Rassendyll of Anthony Hope's *Prisoner of Zenda* should have run away with the new bride of the weakling prince, his cousin. It should be understood, though, that he recognized *Zenda* as out-and-out hokum. Ruritania, the fictional nation in which *Zenda* is set, has become a generic term for the kind of Balkan fairyland most often found in operettas. For anyone else besides Bridges, such an idea would be perfectly consistent. But since it is Bridges' idea, he must stand convicted of setting aside his principles at least for the moment, because as a rule Bridges saw no difference at all between reality and Ruritania. He believed that Ruritania was the proper setting for fiction, but he also believed it to be the true state of American affairs. No real, living people ever bore nearly so close a resemblance to Bridges' idea of Americans as do the optimistic, cheerful, dauntless Ruritanian peasants as they gather in the public square to dance.

There is still one word to be said in Bridges' favor over this question of Realism, and one final irony. It was his fate to read through the offerings of the Realists, not years after they had been picked over and judged, but at the time of their publication. The messages of Tolstoy and Howells were also carried by a legion of writers with far more conscience than talent. Many of their books were crude or sickly sentimental or tasteless. To do this at all he had to find an unswerving set of principles, and certainly he might have found worse ones than "American reality is beautiful and good." Apparently his readers were happy to be reassured that all was well with the country.

The irony is that Bridges once complained with some bitterness of how little the home appeared in current American fiction, Realistic and otherwise. But if any publication ever spread more thousands of pages over more decades and included fewer references to the home or to anything in it than *Life* did, it would be little short of miraculous. *Life* simply ignored all human activity remotely connected with home life. It played the irreverent man-about-town, and there is reason to believe that the members of its staff *thought* of themselves as sharing the magazine's pose, although it is difficult to prove that they did. Mitchell, childless, dedicated to his paper and devoted to his clubs, still managed to maintain summer and winter houses and seems to have enjoyed living in them. Still, he was a man of habit and could have spared only a minimum of time to devote to his home and the enjoyment of the America he wrote of so lovingly. Martin was a far less methodical man than Mitchell but a far more public one. He reared three children, and the nature of his work for *Life* and *Harper's Weekly* might have made it possible for him to work at home. But he, too, was a clubman and frequent after-dinner speaker, and he was in the city most of the time. Bridges himself does not appear to have traveled much outside of New York, although he never severed himself completely from Shippensburg, Pennsylvania. All of these men could indeed look back without self-delusion to childhood hours spent in the country, but in each case "the country" meant an establishment of some opulence and not the old whitewashed farmhouse to which *Life* yearned to return. It is fair to say that *Life*'s staff wore their city clothes when they worked for the magazine. They separated their professional lives from their home lives almost completely.

I am at a loss for a proper terminology to discuss Bridges' and *Life*'s opinions of Stevenson and Kipling. First of all Bridges was an Anglophobe. He distrusted British poetry, and his contempt for British Realism was such that when he reviewed Thomas Hardy's novels he wrote first that no *American* jury would have convicted Tess, and then that had Jude lived in an *American* small town his fellow townsmen would have helped him out of his difficulties. Yet here are two of his favorites, both British. More important, the improbable distinction he made between the real and the unreal makes it impossible to put a name to the kind of novels that Stevenson and Kipling wrote. This distinction was unclear even to Bridges. At one point he linked Charles Dickens, Victor Hugo, Alexandre Dumas the elder, and George Meredith, calling them all "Romancists." But he and *Life* had high praise for all of these men, and a cartoon in 1890 by F. G. Attwood leagues Dickens, Thackeray, Sir

Walter Scott, and Samuel Johnson into a vigilante committee, armed to repel the hapless Howells as he tries to land on the far side of the Styx.[22] Well and good; but another time Bridges wrote, "Meredith is the best delineator of the reality of our generation." There can be no doubt that Meredith and Thackeray belong in the same category, discounting questions of skill. In Meredith's world of meddlesome baronets and idealistic politicians, and in his hypertrophied biographical investigations into romantic newspaper stories, one can see Thackeray's world reflected much more clearly than anything that Bridges could possibly have experienced himself. Yet to Bridges this was "the reality of our generation." To him and to *Life*, romance was reality and facts were merely confusing.

From Bridges' review of *Dr. Jekyll and Mr. Hyde* in 1886 to Martin's final word—"He wrote classics"—in January, 1895, Robert Louis Stevenson's reception by *Life* was never less than Martin's summary indicates: "There have been greater novelists than he in this century, but no storyteller of equal merit."[23] *Life* commended and admired Stevenson for his storytelling, his romance, his mesmeric evocation of far-off times and places. Martin more than Bridges was caught up in the Stevensonian web. He even resolved, once, to believe that there must be some good in Whitman, since Stevenson admired him. In 1889 *Life* ran a double-page cartoon personifying various rival magazines, among them *Scribner's* and *Puck*. The former was caricatured as a lace-pants youth, the latter as a Teutonic, oafish child riding a goat. The editors of *Puck*, whether or not they were stung by the caricature of their paper, objected publicly to the *Scribner's* symbol as an attack on the masculinity of Stevenson, whose work frequently appeared there. *Puck* was wrong at least three ways. First, *Life* would never have attacked Stevenson under any circumstances. Secondly, at the time *Life*'s book reviewer was an assistant editor of *Scribner's Magazine*, and a great admirer of Stevenson. Thirdly, masculinity was exactly what *Life* admired Stevenson for. Stevenson's tales were adventurous, pure, comradely and filled with courage. *Life* had waited too long for a writer so irreproachably masculine, by *Life*'s standards. Any slur on Stevenson's masculinity would have been a slur on *Life*'s.

For Bridges as well as for Martin every review of a book by Stevenson was an encomium. When Henry James wrote in the April, 1888, *Century* that all Stevenson had to talk about was the joy of youth, Bridges took him to task for imagining that the "enormous range of Stevenson's subject matter" could possibly be included in such a statement. Just what the enormous range was, and wherein James erred, Bridges did not say. He spoke feelingly in another column of the "realism" of *Kidnapped*. Realism meant romance to Bridges. Little wonder that he quarreled with the realism of James and Howells.

Martin, too, suggested Stevenson to Howells as a model. Howells had been campaigning for wider recognition of the literary merit of his friend, Mark Twain. Martin wrote:

> If Mr. Howells has not passed the teachable age he ought to read Stevenson.
> There's a writer for you, William, and one that makes literature.[24]

This was in 1887, when Howells was doing some of his most frequent
public theorizing about Realistic literature and *Life* was firing back almost
weekly. Hard as it would be today to find any grounds, let alone grounds
of realism, upon which to prefer Stevenson to Twain, we can test the
grounds for Martin's choice in a moment. We have only to set David
Balfour beside Huckleberry Finn and ask which is the sturdy, well-
spoken, upright, courageous youth and which the vulgarian with his eye
on the main chance—which, in short, would do for the hero of a novel
by Thackeray and which would not—and we can see why Martin chose as
he did. By *Life*'s standards, Stevenson's boy was more real, more typically
American than Twain's.

Most of Rudyard Kipling's characters would cut no better figure
than Huck Finn among Thackeray's lordlings, climbers, and proudly
dignified poor relations. Yet *Life* approved Kipling as heartily as it
approved Stevenson. Not, though, as readily. *Dr. Jekyll and Mr. Hyde*
was the first of Stevenson's books to make much impression on America,
and Bridges had heaped praises on it. This was most unusual, for Bridges
was not one to excite himself over a new writer, regardless of that
writer's ideas or style. Stevenson had been one of the few exceptions.
Francis Marion Crawford's case is sufficiently like Kipling's to be quoted.
Bridges first called Crawford "a fish spawning novelist," and said that his
characters behaved with predictable asininity. Within five years Bridges
was using Crawford to argue against Howells in the fight over Realism.
Ten years after Bridges first discovered Crawford, he reviewed *Don Orsino*
and compared the title character to Clive Newcome, an accolade as high
as any *Life* offered. It was just so with Kipling.

Bridges first reviewed Kipling's work after *Departmental Ditties*,
Plain Tales From the Hills, *In Black and White*, and *Soldiers Three*, and
concluded that "In both prose and verse he seems to be the Bret Harte
of India." Harte had come home from England by this time. Five years
before, a comparison to Harte by *Life* would have been an insult for
Kipling. But Harte's repatriation had reinstated him in *Life*'s good graces,
and the comparison was friendly but unenthusiastic. In 1891, reviewing
The Light That Failed, Bridges discovered that Kipling's virtues approached
those that *Life* demanded of an author. "With all his worldly cynicism,
his brutality if you please," Bridges wrote, Kipling's heart was in the right
place. He made love and friendship the enduring values. He was an
optimist under it all, and "is this not the optimism of a man whose eyes
are open, and who sees clear?"[25]

Having discovered optimism in Kipling's work, *Life* went on to find
that his most salient characteristic was "manliness." Kipling delighted in

swashbuckling, and Bridges admiration for it was such that he would praise a writer whose characters swaggered through adventures, whatever faults he found in that writer's work. He had recognized H. Rider Haggard as a romantic fraud, but he had praised Haggard's "virility" all the same. Kipling insisted that heroism erases all records of irresponsibility. Bridges' admiration for *Trilby*, which does approximately the same thing, has been noted. Kipling enjoyed playing tricks on his readers; he preached the gospel of the stiff upper lip; he was careless about probability; and he was willing to please the public even at the expense of destroying his original conception of *The Light That Failed*. All of these things except possibly the last qualified him in *Life*'s view as a manly writer.

Today we count every one of the traits here named as a mark of Kipling's *boyishness*, not his *manliness*. It is hard to believe that the culture's whole attitude toward maturity has been reversed since the 1890's. The alternative conclusion is that *Life* confused boyish ideas with mature ideas. *Life*'s undeniable good sense seemed to it sufficient proof of its own maturity. But when Kipling's romantic outlook is touted as a real man's cleareyed vision of the world, that opinion is wrong. Edmund Wilson has referred to Thackeray's "inextinguishable boyishness."26 Even *Life*'s heroes were subject to its critical scourge. When Bridges reviewed *Stalky & Co.* he recoiled from Kipling's indignant picture of unhappy childhood. He offered William Allen White's *The Court of Boyville* as "nearer the truth" than *Stalky's* "unrelieved brutalities."

Although *Life* missed the point of Kipling's world view, it appreciated and even overrated his detailed realistic presentation. Bridges saw the secret of Kipling's method in Captain Disko Troop's remark, "*The* most interesting thing in the world is to find out how the next man gets his vittles," and he commented on how much effort Kipling expends describing men at work. Bridges also wrote that he knew a man who read "McAndrew's Hymn" to a ship's engineer and his assistants while on a transatlantic voyage, and that they said it was good. This assertion functions as a sort of minor premise in a syllogism all Bridges' own. The conclusion is, "Kipling is a good writer." The major premise is, "A good writer is one whose grasp of the facts is such that when he writes a poem about ship's engineers, then ship's engineers will appreciate the factuality of that poem." The extension of such logic can only lead to the conclusion that a well-written manual of directions—a good cookbook—is a better poem than *The Iliad*. Bridges never pursued it so far, of course, but his belief in the literal fact as a critical criterion and the literal mind as a source of criticism already carries appreciation of detail too far.

Bridges saw that Kipling could describe vividly the sights and sounds of a Gloucester fishing boat or the executive offices of a railroad or the cab of a steam engine. He saw that Kipling could describe a job, a job that someone had to get up and go to every day, and could make that job seem as remote and romantic as the life of a white king in a Himalayan tribe. He saw further that this was an almost unique achievement among English writers, who are notoriously shy of describing work for money. He caught glimpses of the possible social importance of such a talent in an age when jobs were becoming increasingly humdrum and unrewarding. But rather than content himself with these excellencies he sought an absolute judge, and he found one in absolute literalness.

The names of two more American writers must be mentioned before the discussion of Bridges' and *Life*'s Americanism is concluded—Stephen Crane and Mark Twain. Neither fits properly into Bridges' theories of reality and manliness, but both are too important to overlook. Crane was a favorite with Bridges despite his alliance with Realism. Doubtless the fact that his stories are both more violent and more sentimental than those of James or Howells helped raise his stock with Bridges. Specifically, Bridges agreed with and praised Crane's abhorrence of war. Elsewhere in *Life* Crane was frequently parodied, most often during the Cuban war, and once *Life* wrote that Crane "writes with a chameleon on his desk. The chameleon supplies the adjectives."

Twain was one author whom *Life* found neither realistic nor manly. He was not optimistic, nor pure, nor comradely, nor did he believe that the true America was a Utopia. *Life* never recognized him as anything more than a deft and successful humorist, and as such it caricatured him— white flannels, bushy brows, mane and cigar. As for parodying his style, though, *Life* just could not do it. It found him inimitable. This might have suggested to *Life* another, closer look at Twain's works. But no, when Howells suggested Twain as a genuine writer *Life* laughed and offered Stevenson. *Life* even paid little attention to his publications, although Bridges reviewed *Huckleberry Finn*. The review went as far astray as anything he ever wrote.

Bridges found *Huckleberry Finn* insufficiently funny and too gory. He objected to the literal description of Pap Finn's delirium. He objected to the loving care with which Twain followed the details of Huck's feigned murder. He objected to the bloody violence of the Grangerford-Shepherdson feud, to the King's Camelopard, and to the very idea that a fictional undertaker could "slide off" during a funeral sermon to beat a noisy dog who "had a rat." He called the incident of the King's Camelopard "a good chapter for lenten parlor entertainment and church festivals."27

Bridges' convictions about the purity of American life militated against his ever having a clear view of Twain. But there were limits of *Life*'s moral indignation. When it was reported that the Concord Library Committee banned *Huckleberry Finn* shortly after its publication, *Life* snickered up its sleeve at them. It suggested that as long as they were in the banning mood they should attend to the Concord School of Philosophy. Bridges did find one thing in Twain's book to praise. He liked the illustrations by E. W. Kemble, *Life*'s long-established contributor. Kemble did one hundred and seventy-four drawings for the first edition of *Huckleberry Finn*, and Bridges called attention to their "wonderful variety of laughable expressions, attitudes, and costumes."28 There are not many great books published during any reviewer's lifetime. Bridges had a chance to borrow glory from Twain at no interest, and he turned it into an advertisement for one of his co-workers on *Life*. It seems almost too stagily ironic that the writer of the period whose work Bridges and *Life* assessed with the least accuracy should have been, like *Life*, a humorist.

Bridges was by no means a man of ungenerous sentiments. Due credit was a shining principle with him. He was capable of extending charitable opinion in the unlikeliest directions. He was willing to admit that Howells had been "broadened" by dabbling in socialism.29 He wrote of John Brown:

> An orderly way of doing things is the foundation for prosperity. A rich country is unlikely to love its fanatics.30

And yet he concluded that Brown would be considered one of America's great heroes some day. On occasion Bridges could be patronizing in an adverse review, especially when the book under review offended his Americanism, but he was never pompous or arrogant. While he upheld purity, his ideas of purity were entirely consistent with his and *Life*'s picture of themselves—that is, he thought that purity included all topics suitable for gentlemen. He was never guilty of Comstockery. Perhaps best of all, he knew the literature of his own time as few men knew it. He knew it infinitely better than Martin, who pretended to be expert. Also, he knew the literature of the age just past at least as well as Mitchell or Martin knew it, and he showed excellent taste in choosing models from it.

He worked under one very serious handicap for a book reviewer. To give him credit, he did not often show it. But it was there, and whenever he was backed into a corner he let it interfere with his ordinary good sense and moderation: he did not like fiction, or books, or authors. In 1886 he wrote:

> When the land is teeming with opportunities for men of brains and acuteness to reap great material advantages, why should they sit down and dream of things immaterial and unreal? The philosophy of development has given to life as we live it from day to day a deeper meaning, and for men who really think, dreaming has become a synonym for mental weakness.
>
> The day will probably come when scientists will classify novel writing as a degree of emotional insanity, and novel-reading as a premonitory symptom.31

He hoped in 1888 that Howells would some day realize that "a novel is one of the toys of manhood." He advised a "typical American Girl" who asked him for a list of books for summer reading to turn her beautiful eyes to the scenery past which her yacht sailed rather than to waste them on books. He turned a jaundiced eye on the notion that fiction stimulates its devotees:

> Port, strong cigars, or a hundred yards (sic) dash will do as much to increase heart action and rush blood to the head.

At the same time that he begged Howells to understand the nonutilitarian childishness of writing novels, he quoted Francis Marion Crawford's philosophy of the novel with immense approval:

> A little laughter, a little sadness, and, when it is done, the comfortable assurance that you have been amused and not bored.[32]

He considered authors decorative at best. We have seen his appreciation for Tolstoy's theories of the author-as-peasant and his praise of the "new doctrine of materialism." Authors who accepted neither, and this included almost all authors, seemed to him unmanly. He wrote of the "spiritual abasement of the pious and the feverish money-hunger of the worldly," and he called upon both camps to brace up and be men. We have also seen his dislike of "the Bohemian pose." At bottom, he suspected all authors of striking such a pose.

This mistrust of introspection, this delight in conformity, this belief in a brave New York that was to be places Bridges directly in the main stream of *Life*'s thought. He believed in belief, in materialism, in the useful and the literal. He looked forward to the day when the human race would have developed to the point where not even authors wanted to be eccentric and smoke "long-stem" pipes. He was ashamed to waste on books the precious effort that might help to bring that day closer. He was an expert on fiction, but he did not want to be. He wanted to be an expert on manly American virtue with short hair and no interests beyond the material. He outlived the Gilded Age, and doubtless he changed with the times. But he was a perfect representative of the minds that made and supported *Life. Americanus erat.*

NOTES

1*Life*, VII, 1886, p. 314. The "recent events" are probably the Chicago Haymarket bombing and its attendant public discussion.

2*Life*, XI, 1888, p. 322.

3*Life*, VI, 1885, p. 300.

4*Life*, XVIII, 1891, p. 286.

5*Life*, VII, 1886, p. 34.

6*Life*, XI, 1888, p. 12.

7*Life*, XI, 1888, p. 237.

8*Life*, VI, 1885, p. 287.

9*Life*, XII, 1888, p. 81.

10*Life,* VIII, 1886, p. 30.

11*Life*, VIII, 1886, p. 118.

12*Life*, VIII, 1886, p. 118.

13*Life*, VII, 1886, p. 20.

14*Life*, VI, 1885, p. 108.

15*Life*, LXVI, 1915, p. 334.

16*Life*, XXXI, 1898, p. 522.

17*Life*, XXXIII, 1899, p. 129.

18*Life*, XVII, 1891, p. 384.

19*Life*, XIX, 1892, p. 32.

20*Life*, XXV, 1895, p. 254.

21*Life*, XXIX, 1897, p. 46.

22*Life*, XV, 1890, pp. 228-29.

23*Life*, XXV, 1895, p. 4.

24*Life*, IX, 1887, p. 144.

25*Life*, XVII, 1891, p. 38.

26Edmund Wilson, *Classics and Commercials* (New York: Farrar, Straus and Co., 1950), p. 353.

27*Life*, V, 1885, p. 119.

28*Life*, V, 1885, p. 146.

29*Life*, XIV, 1889, p. 358.

30*Life*, XIII, 1889, p. 106.

31*Life*, VIII, 1886, p. 48.

32*Life,* XI, 1888, p. 20.

CHAPTER VII

PHILISTINE, N., THEAT. ENEMY OF THE CHOSEN PEOPLE

Life's pronouncements on the drama are less concerned with plays and players than with the business methods of those responsible for the selection and production of plays in New York City from 1883 to 1918. *Life* maintained artistic standards by which to judge plays but they are like *Life*'s literary standards. They are also remarkably like the standards of *Life*'s adversaries, the merchant-managers. *Life* believed that contrivance was the soul of action and sought for the reversal of clichés and characters on stage as patiently as it sought it in printed fiction. It believed further that the public was the last arbiter of the worth of a play. It believed that a good play would be popular and that a popular play was probably a good one. This is almost to the letter the opinion of the Theatrical Syndicate, the group against whom *Life* struggled through libel suits, threats of violence, advertising boycotts, and the banishment from New York theaters of its reviewer.

It must be recognized that first, *Life*'s criticism of the drama adhered closely to the standards of excellence set by *Life*'s literary criticism. It believed in Americanism, virility, purity, and the gentleman's point of view; and secondly, *Life*'s quarrel with the Theatrical Syndicate, a quarrel which was without doubt the bitterest it ever engaged in, was marked by injustices done to both sides. *Life* justified its complaints that the Syndicate was guilty of unethical practices, and the Syndicate justified its complaint that *Life* was guilty of anti-Semitism.

Two men supplied *Life*'s dramatic criticism, Alan Dale and James Stetson Metcalfe. For *Life*'s first five years, no one writer contributed a regular column, nor did the dramatic column appear regularly. From 1885 to 1887 the bulk of *Life*'s dramatic criticism was done by Dale, who was born Alfred J. Cohen in Birmingham, England, in 1861. He must have made the change of name legal at some time in his life, since his will mentions a daughter and a sister, both named Dale. Dale came to America in 1885, and must have begun to contribute to *Life* almost immediately. He joined Pulitzer's *World* as critic of the drama in 1887 and moved to Hearst's *Journal* in 1895. This habitual employment by publications which *Life* abhorred may be only accident, or it may show an affinity of Dale's for the yellow journals. At all events, after he left *Life* there was no love lost between them.

When Dale's play, *The Madonna of the Future*, earned Dale and his producer an arraignment on indecency charges in 1918, *Life* attacked it savagely.[1] The play was an Ibsenesque melodrama about an unduly emancipated woman who seduces an innocent youth and then will not marry him. It was supposed to herald the New Woman, and the heroine, among other affronts to *Life*, was given the line, "My highest standard of motherhood is a cow." The *Life* which battled against women's suffrage because votes demeaned motherhood could not stand for that. But the police magistrate, when the case came before him, only ordered that the name of the play be changed to *The Woman of the Future*, thereby erasing any hint of blasphemy. He did not say one word for motherhood. However, this happened three months before Mitchell's death. *Life*'s age was passing. Dale had moved from the *Journal* to the *American* in 1915, and he continued there until he died in 1928. He was the author of at least ten books of humorous prose, none of whose titles means anything at this distance.[2] In his obituary he was called "the dean of New York critics."

Dale's three-year employment as a regular *Life* contributor added little of significance to *Life*'s personality. The fact that he imitated Ibsen, even though he did it twenty-five years after Ibsen had ceased to be scandalous, demonstrates that his tastes were more "advanced" than those of *Life*'s policy makers. His most evident dislikes were affectation and quackery. He thought Shakespeare was florid and overblown, at least as performed by Edwin Booth specifically and actors of the period generally. He was not excitable. *Life* gained in vigor when it replaced him with James S. Metcalfe.

Metcalfe's ideas on the drama were *Life*'s from 1888 on. For two weeks he worked hard at being literate—his first column was written in imitation of Pepys, his second in imitation of Montaigne. After that, for thirty years, he never repeated the effort. By the time his column was four weeks old, it contained strong hints of anti-Semitism. Despite his unoriginal mind and strong prejudices, though, Metcalfe was a lively writer and his critiques stung. He aligned himself with *Life*'s regular policies. Metcalfe, Martin, and Bridges fitted into *Life* as comfortably as toes into an old shoe.

In the main, Metcalfe believed that moderation was necessary in art, and he was prone to see any sort of excess as inartistic commercialization. Like Bridges and Martin he talked of virility when he meant "heroics." He once wrote that "melodrama is the most virile possession of the stage."[3] He admired *Trilby* on stage even more, if that were possible, than Bridges admired it in print. He had the same dislike of foreign writers that Martin had, and hope for a genuine American theater stirred in him every time a native playwright produced an even ordinarily good play. This wish for American play of merit was often father to the thought, and he was likely to go off the deep end in admiration for a play like James Herne's *Shore Acres*. Herne had attempted to inject realism into the melodramatic American rural-play tradition; it is certainly a cut or two above the dead level of that tradition. It was by no means the herald of an American Renaissance, though, and Metcalfe's enthusiasm for Americanism also extended to less deserving plays. Of *Senator Rivers*, a play whose author Metcalfe did not deign to name, he nevertheless wrote:

> It is grateful and refreshing to behold a purely American play, dealing with American scenes and people and acted by American actors, putting American dollars into American pockets.[4]

Metcalfe found extravagance impressive sometimes. He reported that Joseph Holland had to memorize three-hundred-and-ninety-one typewritten pages for the part of "Mark Harriman" in a play named *Settled Out of Court*. He considered the deed spectacular. More often, though, he counseled the middle of the road, particularly in style of acting. He questioned Henry Irving's delivery as insufficiently elocutionary and ridiculed James Owen O'Connor's as too much so.

Metcalfe wanted the theatergoing public to have the best, and he thought that he knew what was best. He also expected the public to agree with him. In his early columns he frequently registered surprise when a play for which he had predicted failure became popular. He never came to terms with the fact that the theater-goers did not always support the best theater. But he refused to blame the public for what he considered its lack of discrimination. Instead, he blamed the theater managers. Some of his cherished ideas about public preferences were directly contradicted by the practices of the managers, and specifically by Charles Frohman. Metcalfe believed that in the absence of a genuinely good play the public would prefer small-time farce to pretentious trash. But Frohman repeatedly urged prospective playwrights to give him "strong" or "dramatic" plays. Frohman continued to produce financially successful plays, and Metcalfe continued to deplore the corruption of theatergoers' tastes by managers.

Metcalfe's great ideal was that the stage was, and must be kept, a great force for good. He wanted to have a part in America's moral evolution, and he saw the money-making instincts of the theater managers as an obstacle to that evolution. *Life* saw humor in bad public taste, in jerry-built scenery, in borrowed or stolen stage-props, in stranded actors walking the railroad ties toward the next town, in hotel clerks eyeing an actor's luggage before registering him. So did Metcalfe, but he always insisted that behind all of these abuses lurked the greedy entrepreneur.

Metcalfe liked what he thought was wholesome, and that did not include imported plays that he believed were amoral or immoral. Like Bridges, he took seriously *Life*'s motto, *Americanus Sum*, and like Bridges he was devoted to the myth of pure and bucolic American life. He found the early Ibsen "an absurd fad," "petty," "trivial," "not playable," and "desolate." By 1903 he was willing to concede that Ibsen was not evanescent, but he insisted that an Ibsen play was not amusing, not moral, and not educational, and he wondered what good it was. He felt the same way about Strindberg when James Huneker praised *Miss Julie*, then called *Countess Julie*. He attacked Oscar Wilde less as a foreigner than as an immoralist. If one granted Metcalfe's major premise, one would have to admit that these germinal twentieth-century plays were bad. Ibsen is *not* amusing nor educational, nor specifically moralistic, and if one admits that these are the things a play must be, then he must admit that Ibsen's plays are bad plays. But twentieth-century criticism does not look only for these things, and the things it looks for—the dramatic statement of an idea, the artistic development of a theme, the poetic intensification of human experience—never entered *Life*'s mind. *Life* functioned in the darkness before the dawn of the first vigorous era of stage history since Racine. It resolutely averted its eyes from that dawn, but it had other contributions to make.

While Metcalfe disliked foreign writers and was too easily persuaded of the value of homegrown plays, he was not stampeded by low-level appeals to Americanism. He intensely disliked George M. Cohan's Yankee Doodle pose. He called Cohan a "vulgar, cheap, ill-mannered, flashily dressed, insolent, smart Aleck," and said that his music was "several bars of well-known patriotic or sentimental songs strung together with connecting links of lively and more or less original musical trash." Later he demanded that Cohan be prosecuted for using the American flag draped over his own portrait for advertising. But Cohan was in the employ of the Theatrical Syndicate. Some of Metcalfe's strong convictions of the Syndicate's "vulgarity" certainly colored his opinion of Cohan.

Perhaps Metcalfe's opinion of *Trilby* indicates as well as anything his ideas of wholesomeness and purity in the drama. Of it he wrote:

> Suffragettes, feminists, Socialists, anarchists, Shavians, Highbrows, Ibsenites, Hauptmannites, Sudermannites, Granville-Barkerites and other improvers and elevators of the drams are respectfully invited to . . . find any more legitimate use of the stage in its various functions than . . . in this presentation of *Trilby*.[5]

The "legitimacy" of *Trilby* bears investigation. Certainly it created dramatic tension on stage. Everyone in the audience wanted to know how it would end. But beyond this its legitimacy and morality are both questionable. It left eroticism to the imagination, but it spared no pains to keep the imagination lively. It preached homely virtues, but it set its sermon in an atmosphere of exotic Parisian Bohemia and urged its patrons to believe that figurative Sodoms and Gomorrahs were somewhere just off stage. It was for good fellowship and motherhood and against odd characters, geniuses, and Jews with heavy accents. The first two may be reasonable candidates for universally recognized virtues, but the last three are recognized villains only in the eyes of a very special audience. *Life* and Metcalfe were a part of that audience. They were pleased to be told that the world could do perfectly well without intellect. Metcalfe's blast at all possible newfangled ideas in the passage just quoted convicts him of Philistinism. The anti-intellectual fervor that is willing to lump all new ideas together and call the lump useless burns in Metcalfe as it does in no other contributor to *Life*. Doubtless anyone who fires shotgun blasts into a crowd of "advanced thinkers" will wound a fool sooner or later. But Metcalfe obviously believed that the whole crowd was made up of fools.

Metcalfe was not hopeful for the future of morality on stage even at the beginning of his career with *Life*. Reviewing one of Edward Harrigan's musical farragoes in 1888, he wrote sarcastically that Harrigan was too loud, too American, too vulgar, not depressing enough, included no drunk scenes in the play, and overlooked vice and immorality as dramatic motives. "On the whole," he concluded, "he must reform from everything but the coarseness of his plays, if he wishes to be considered a dramatist in the present acceptation of the term." This was the season during which Metcalfe's vote for the best play went to *Little Lord Fauntleroy*. Twelve years later, when someone publicly criticized a play's "cheap morality," Metcalfe wrote wistfully, "Morality on stage is too rare to be called 'cheap' by its detractors." All the same, he did not want censorship. He believed that a censor would be an evil more insidious than any immorality the stage was likely to offer. When in 1902 a bill was introduced into the New York legislature at Albany to establish an official stage censor, both Metcalfe and Mitchell wrote against it.

Metcalfe wrote in 1893 of Arthur Wing Pinero's *The Second Mrs. Tanqueray*:

> *Life* believes in looking at things as they are. It believes that the stage should hold the mirror up to nature. It detests prudery and mock modesty. But it does not believe that loathsome diseases should be paraded in public. Do our best, and vice and its consequences are bound to show themselves in plain view. We are not doing our best when we allow them to strut triumphant on the stage. We are very far from doing our best when we let our sons and daughters have the opportunity to witness such plays as "The Second Mrs. Tanqueray."[6]

Pinero's play deals with a woman whose pre-marital liaison ruins her chance to be respectable and finally drives her to suicide. What this has to do with "loathsome diseases" escapes me, but *Ghosts* had been published in America in 1890, and possibly Metcalfe saw no reason to distinguish one sort of nastiness from another. Here, as in *Life*'s literary opinions, "real" to *Life* means "pure, and the vehicle of a proper moral lesson." But this review of Pinero's half-hearted protest against cruelty to castoff mistresses appeared during the same season when Brandon Thomas's *Charley's Aunt* won Metcalfe's warmest praise. Now *Charley's Aunt* is not specifically immoral, but its humor seldom rises above the level of slapstick and the entire action of its plot concerns transvestitism in a men's college. It has remained popular, and perhaps it is better farce than *Mrs. Tanqueray* is serious drama. But a play that asks its audience to laugh at suggested perversion is no more moral, nor does it "hold the mirror up to nature" any better, than a play which asks forgiveness for a fallen woman.

Metcalfe's moral indignation against Oscar Wilde's *A Woman of No Importance* reached such a pitch that, besides calling the play a "filth heap" and a "running sore," he added that "anyone who observes the crowd dispersing from one of Mr. Wilde's matinees can determine quickly the class of women to whom his plays appeal most strongly." He "naturally supposed" that decent women would be disgusted by references to sex. His temper, then, occasionally got the better of him, even to the point of insulting the audience. It furnishes a clue to the bitterness of his attacks on the managers. When Wilde had fallen to another foe, and the Empire Theater, which was Charles Frohman's headquarters, opened *The Importance of Being Earnest* without so much as printing the author's name on the playbill, Metcalfe's disgust with the management's pusillanimity nearly equalled his disgust with Wilde. He said it was "a lovely tribute to the moral cowardice of the Anglo-Saxon race" that the show should have any patrons.

The ease with which Metcalfe moved from moral criticism of the play to moral criticism of the producers and the audience helps to explain why abuses rather than plays took up the bulk of his critical energies. He was easily angered. Most often, he was angered by the managers, but ticket speculators, newspapers, and the public followed close behind. He objected to whispering box-holders. He insisted that the rowdies who disrupted the New York opening of *The Playboy of the Western World* should have been fined more heavily than they were, and would have been if the judge who tried them had not been Irish. But he defended the right of the audience to hiss a play, or to shout "Boo!"—this last a form of criticism that was imported from England in the late 1890's. He said that he had attended plays during which the gallery put on a better show than the cast.

He objected to the hats that ladies wore to the theater. In January, 1896, he began to run a regular notice in his column: "The size of the hat a woman wears on her head in the theater is in inverse proportion to her breeding." When in 1895 several city ordinances against theater hats were considered, he sneered at any woman who wore such a thing, and then felt constrained to add, "If she happens to be a Jewess, she probably thinks that any reflections on her vulgarity are simply evidence of race prejudice." This apparently groundless insult demonstrates that even in a matter so trivial as hats, Metcalfe could not keep "racial" issues out of the argument.

In the late spring of 1891, Metcalfe published a three-part manifesto titled "Theatre-Goers' Enemies." The first part deals with speculators, the second with false advertisement, and the third with less-than-honest newspaper reviewers. The speculators were *Life*'s first targets and remained to be sniped at after the larger battles had been fought. The first move against theaters by *Life* had been a cover picture by H. A. Ogden on May 1, 1884, which showed a hydra-like, three-headed speculator attacking theater patrons while a manager looked on complacently. The collusion between managers and speculators, or the conviction that such collusion existed, had been discussed in *Life* ever since.

In April of 1894, an incident occurred at Daniel Frohman's *Lyceum* that inspired Metcalfe's column to verse. The verse was unsigned, and may not be by Metcalfe himself.

The Ballade of Danne and The Speculator

Now glory be to Danne Frohmanne,
   And laurels everywhere.
For is he not a doughty manne
   And gallant manageaire?

A knavish speculator came
   His patrons to annoy,
When Daniel hied him forth and hired
   A plucky colored boy.

And to the boy, both fore and aft,
   He placards did affix,
To tell that tickets bought upon the pave
   Were worth exactly nix.

The knave shassayed both up and down,
   The boy did shassay too,
And for his tickets bought with cash
   The knave received no sou.

Then hied he to a Tammany judge,
   A special friend of his'n,
And begged that doughty Danne be jugged
   Within some nearby prison.

But Danne was out for gore, he was,
   And looking for a fight,
And made the judge confess the corn,
   And rule that he was right.

So glory be to Danne Frohmanne
   And every manageaire
Who follows up the ticket knave
   And downs him everywhere.[7]

Life had published an anti-scalper manifesto in 1892. Since then, the city had licensed speculators in the hope that they could be controlled in this way and the really piratical element kept out. The speculator whom Frohman and his sandwich-man dispossessed was a licensee, and when the city magistrate ruled against him he threatened Supreme Court action, but dropped it immediately. The speculators as described by *Life* were a ragtag collection of men who could make enough in an hour before curtain time every night to keep themselves in drink until the next day. Their retailing practices were none the gentlest—foul language was a staple and threats to prospective customers who refused their wares were by no means uncommon. After the licensing began, the only change noticeable to *Life* was that some of the old theater loafers were replaced by other loafers with better Tammany connections. The man who wanted to spend an evening at the theater with a woman whom he did not care to have insulted had every right to complain vigorously. The profits from the enterprise, when it was organized as tightly as Ned Harrigan's plan exposed in *Life*'s manifesto, could have been considerable. Every good seat in the house was in the speculator's hands, and the manager's brother oversaw the speculators and their one-third markup. The theater was in effect selling every ticket twice.

A second item on *Life*'s manifesto, the business of false advertisements and advertisements that are printed in the newspapers as though they were news, is more pertinent to a number of later cases during *Life*'s fight with the Syndicate, and belongs in the story of that fight. Because of its declared hatred of sensational journalism and its pride in its own integrity, *Life* suspected all newspapers on principle. Metcalfe went beyond suspicion and openly accused the New York press of conspiring with theater managers to mislead the public.

Along with his blanket accusation, Metcalfe had a way of taking jabs at specific papers for specific abuses. In the 1892-93 season a burlesque called *1492* was popular. Metcalfe liked it, but James Gordon Bennett's *Telegram* did not. Metcalfe mentioned this, following it with, "Haven't the '1492' people 'seen' its business department?" On the same page he accused the New York *Sun* of "personal malice and favoritism." But while he believed the newspapers to be one of the "theatre-goers' enemies," he believed the critics who worked for them to be rather worse.

A fourth enemy of theater-goers which *Life* assailed repeatedly was fire. Metcalfe urged New York fire inspectors to greater diligence, objected time and again to overcrowding, and suggested every summer that the managers use the closed season to remodel and fireproof the theaters. It was a fire—the Iroquois Theatre fire in Chicago in December of 1903— that began the really violent phase of *Life*'s struggle against the Syndicate. Metcalfe held the managers responsible for firetrap conditions as well as for speculators and newspaper payoffs.

The Theatrical Syndicate had so many enemies and so many legal battles that it is impossible to tell how much *Life*'s pugnacity harmed it. The magazine certainly gave the Syndicate an enormous amount of adverse publicity, both in its own pages during its years of widest circulation and in the newspapers when the clash came to a head. The Syndicate was entirely a commercial venture, and quite possibly its members never cared enough for *Life*'s critical standards to investigate them. They insisted that *Life*'s opposition to their organization was dictated not by differences of taste nor even by indignation at their business tactics, but simply by the fact that they were Jews.

Let us dwell momentarily on *Life*'s whole attitude toward "alien" minorities. *Life* took the white Protestant native American to be the norm. Therefore it embraced national or racial stereotypes as automatic laugh-producers. Its Jews are uniformly unshaven, heavy lidded, sporting such enormous noses that their burial calls for extra-deep graves; its Negroes are all ragged, razor-toting, and slap-happy; its Irishmen are apes in laborer's clothing; its Germans are obese, yellow-mustached, and stuffed with sausage. It did not occur to the editors that anyone should find these slurs offensive. These caricatures were abnormal and the abnormal was funny. Why not point out the joke?

Moreover, *Life* with its habitual preference for myth over fact insisted that the stereotype was true.

To Metcalfe and to *Life*, then, it was *the American way* to find humor in such stereotypes. *Life* would not deliberately swerve an inch from what it believed to be the American way.

Life flourished during the period of emerging anti-Semitism in America. A Jewish social historian, writing in 1957, said of the period:

> The dominant Protestant Anglo-Saxon group differentiated between the "old" and worthy immigrants, and the "new" unworthy ones. The last quarter of the nineteenth century was also the period in which the beginnings of overt anti-Semitism and discrimination became observable, and when the American image of the Jew began to take the form of a stereotyped immigrant-peddler or old-clothes dealer, of a Shylock or parasite "producing nothing, fattened on the produce of land and labor and living on it" who was out somehow to subjugate the world financially.[8]

Life was only following the times in conceiving its stereotyping to be the American way. It had something else to follow, too. Thackeray, *Life*'s great model, seldom mentioned Jews without a smirk. *Life* needed no stronger justification. The Jews in *Life*'s cartoons and stories spoke with the accents of the Jews in Thackeray's novels. Surely the facts were otherwise. The speech of the Jews in New York at the time was much closer to that recorded by Montague Glass, whose cloak-and-suit partnership, Potash and Perlmutter, demonstrates that funny stories about Jews need not be insulting. There are few better examples of *Life*'s literary distance from reality than its assumption that the English corruptions attributed by Thackeray to London Jews seventy years before, still held good for New York Jews in 1910.

Metcalfe was at once more conscious of the Jewish stereotype and less careful about applying it than most of *Life*'s contributors. In 1897, after the Theatrical Syndicate had been formed but before it had begun to make itself felt, he announced in his column that with two exceptions all the theater managers in New York were Jews. Certainly he would have taken no notice if all but two had been Presbyterians. Shortly before that he had written a condemnation of immorality on stage and stated flatly, "Our Semitic managers are to blame." In 1893, long before the Syndicate existed, he wrote of one of Harrigan's plays, *The Woollen Stocking*, which presented a Jewish lawyer sympathetically: "It may be that he has sacrificed truth to a fear of hurting the sensibilities of his Hebrew patrons." Obviously he was so steeped in *Life*'s stereotyped "truth" that he rejected any other sort. In 1901 he wrote, "There is little sympathy here in America for the Jew. He has contaminated everything in American life that he has touched." His suspicion of Jews sometimes reached almost paranoiac intensity. He wrote of a character in Pinero's *Iris*:

> (Frederick Maldonado) is a Jew with the money and vulgarity of the objectionable members of his race, and also with the curious passion for the Gentile woman so much in evidence among his kind in gay centers of the world.[9]

Given the social beliefs that *Life* held, Metcalfe's proprietary interest in women comes as no surprise. But the belief that "those strangers" are lusting after women "that ought to be mine" is familiar enough to the psychology of race hatred.

To insist that *Life* and Metcalfe were anti-Semitic, though, is not to grant that the Theatrical Syndicate was faultless. The story of its beginning and the purposes for which it was founded is very much a matter of which side the observer stands on. *Life* insisted that it was formed by profiteers, for profit, at the expense of everything good in the theater. Charles Frohman's biographer, who is predictably in sympathy with the Syndicate, claims that the monopoly in theatrical booking

> marked a real epoch in the history of the American theater because within a year a complete revolution had been effected in the business. The booking of attractions was emancipated from curb and cafe; a theatrical contract became an accredited and licensed instrument.[10]

The same movement, though, and its aftermath, when recounted by a disinterested historian, was called "an intolerable situation":

> The triumph of the Syndicate meant the end of honest competition, the degradation of the art of acting, the lowering of the standard of the drama, the subjugation of the playwright and the actor to the capricious whims and sordid necessities of a few men who set themselves up as theatrical despots.[11]

Life obliquely accused Frohman of freezing out other and better men quite early in the fall of 1896, calling him "America's only surviving manager." It was well aware of the Syndicate's existence early in 1897, and vociferous about Frohman's part in it. It pictured him as a would-be Caesar whose thirst for personal aggrandizement was surpassed only by his appalling ignorance of all good things and his love of pelf. The first accusation was fairly well deserved. Even Frohman's friends called him "The Napoleon of the Theater," after his personal idol. But *Life* was being facetious when it reported that Frohman, when told that Maude Adams wanted to play in *Romeo and Juliet*, said, "Let me have the typewritten scenario, if he sent one, and I'll see if it will suit her." Frohman's office also contained "bound copies of the plays he had produced. Interspersed was a complete set of Lincoln's speeches and letters." This is not a comprehensive library for the czar of an artistic empire. Still, the man must have had a degree of judgment and enormous personal charm, and a list of Frohman-produced plays includes, among many that must indeed have been chosen for their immediate vulgar appeal, a fair number that could hardly have looked very promising to a producer with no motives other than a quick dollar—James Barrie's *Peter Pan* not the least among them.

Life accused him of packing first night houses with a private claque and catering to the lowest tastes. It predicted that he would soon rule the New York theater with an iron hand. When Frohman and Oscar Hammerstein had a brief vendetta in September of 1897, Frohman, so *Life* reported, connived to have the police raid Hammerstein's vaudeville house, the upshot of which was that beer was afterward prohibited at theaters. Metcalfe commented, "Mr. Frohman is made after the manner of his kind."12 What Hammerstein thought of this kind of aid and comfort is unrecorded.

That season, the Syndicate began to apply pressure in a number of directions, withdrawing theater advertising from newspapers and magazines which printed adverse criticisms of Syndicate plays. In warning the public, Metcalfe ended his statement by gratuitously declaring, again, that the "men who control the Trust are all Jews."

Metcalfe, on occasion, could make his point without overstating it if evidence was amply in his favor. Not long afterward, *A Ward of France*, by Franklin Fyles, opened, and to demonstrate the unnatural co-operation between certain papers and the Syndicate, *Life* predicted a long run for it, not because the public wanted to see it, but because "in the present dangerous condition of its affairs the Theatrical Trust cannot afford to let a play written by an employee of the New York *Sun* be considered a failure." Metcalfe then quoted opinions culled from the press about the play. The *Telegraph*, the *Herald*, the *World*, the *Journal*, the *Tribune*, the *Press*, the *Times*, and Metcalfe himself had attacked it unmercifully.

The sole friendly review was indeed from the *Sun*. "Abundant pictur-esqueness, color and spirit," it ran. "Engrossing action and picturesque movement. The large audience received the play with enthusiastic favor." The *Sun*'s reviewer was Franklin Fyles.

Next *Life* attacked, not the methods, but the taste of the Syndicate. Where he had seen Jewish businessmen before, Metcalfe saw Jewish vulgarians now.

This was in the late spring of 1898, at the end of the first full season of Syndicate operation. The season was a particularly bad one, but Metcalfe offered no explanation as to why Jewish bad judgment rather than ordinary bad judgment had caused its artistic anemia. Some of *Life*'s Jewish subscribers finally took sufficient offense to complain. Metcalfe explained his position, as he was to do many times in the future:

> A Jewish gentleman—and his own letter, both in tenor and manner, bears out his own contention that there are Jews who are gentlemen—writes to *Life* in complaint of the tone used in this column towards people of his race. He holds that there are good Jews as well as bad Jews, in which *Life* agrees with him perfectly. . . . Unfortunately, Jews like our correspondent . . . are less in evidence in any walk of life than the bad and vulgar Jews against whom we write.
>
> * * * * * *
>
> That play and its manner of production answer fully our correspondent's complaint. Let him see it, and he will understand why *Life* fights strenuously against Jewish control of the American stage.[13]

As described by Frohman's biographers, *The Conquerors*, the play to which Metcalfe objected so strenuously, was indeed a triumph of managerial hokum. But there was nothing specifically Jewish in its loose-woman-with-a-heart-of-gold story. Frohman had been enthralled, while in Paris, by a Grand Guignol adaptation of de Maupassant's "Mademoiselle Fifi." He had persuaded Paul Potter to stretch the story to four acts. Then he had filled in with what he remembered of the Grand Guignol production and some scenes that had worked well in other plays. One of these scenes was taken entirely from *The Sporting Duchess*, which Frohman had produced at the Academy of Music in 1895, and now it was lashed by critics as a new low in salacity. Also it was charged that he made some direct appropriations from a Sardou play, *La Haine*. The whole thing was frankly sensational, and the customers flocked to be corrupted. It was one of Frohman's greatest successes.

For the next six years the Syndicate prospered and *Life* chipped away at it, always with Frohman the prime target. Klaw & Erlanger, who booked tours and produced few shows in New York, rated only a few mentions. When Daniel Frohman produced *Surprises of Love* in the 1899-1900 season, *Life* nearly went into mourning over his capitulation to Syndicate morals. Metcalfe called it "one of the plays that make it im-possible for unmarried women to go to the theatre in France." When

Charles Frohman opened the same season with a play called *The Girl From Maxim's*, written by himself, Metcalfe commented: "Having checked your sense of decency at the cloak-room, you will find the piece very funny. . . . We always like to help a budding genius who hopes to make a livelihood by debauching American morals."[14] When Mark Hanna exploded into American politics, Metcalfe suggested that Frohman team with Hanna and run *everything*. When Franklin Fyles, the *Sun* critic and erstwhile admirer of his own play, was dismissed at last from the paper, having switched abruptly from total inability to see merit in the acting of Mrs. Patrick Campbell to great admiration for her just when she finally signed on with a Syndicate company, *Life* was gleeful. In February of 1900, Metcalfe began to run a classified list of current plays along with his column, labeled "Clean" and "Not Clean." On May 3, of the same year, he issued his first "Bulletin of The Theatres," which recapitulated his opinions, particularly his moral judgments, on all of the shows currently running. This remained a regular *Life* feature. When the National Industrial Commission investigated the Syndicate, *Life* reported its findings with satisfaction. The Commission discovered all of the abuses that *Life* had been trumpeting, and at least one that was new to *Life*—Syndicate-run dramatic schools that turned out novices trained mainly to work for Syndicate salaries. Throughout it all, Metcalfe never stopped insisting that the theatre was being ruined by Jewish patrons, Jewish manners, Jewish morals, and Jewish dress. When George W. Lederer, with a gall amounting almost to charm, announced the imminent production of *The Gibson Girl* while Gibson and *Life* fumed, Metcalfe called it Jewish Plagiarism. When a play produced at Frohman's Empire Theatre used stage furniture that Metcalfe disliked, he called it Jewish scenery and said it looked as if it had been bought at Baxter Street second-hand stores.

On December 30, 1903, the Iroquois Theatre in Chicago caught fire during a performance of *Mr. Bluebeard*, and 571 patrons, mostly women and children, were killed, many of them crushed or suffocated when the panic-stricken crowd found all emergency exits padlocked, and tried to force the doors. A week afterward, *Life* ran a grisly drawing of a leering skeleton holding up a key. The skeleton grinned at the reader, and the key pointed to the locked doors of a burning theater, through which trapped patrons tried vainly to force their way. The caption read, "Messrs. Klaw and Erlanger present 'Mr. Bluebeard,' Late of the Iroquois Theatre." Agitation for enforcement of fire ordinances in New York began at once. Within a month, the wheels of New York politics had turned sufficiently so that Mayor McClellan and fire and building commissioners got busy. They had held secret investigations and made secret agreements with the theater managers. But the managers had failed to keep their promises. Indeed, they had failed to make even the pretense of keeping their promises, in spite of the Mayor's perhaps too generous protection. Now, *Life* hoped, in the interest of public safety, the mayor would take summary proceedings against them. On May 19, Proctor's Theatre in New York caught fire, but its 1800 patrons escaped unhurt. *Life* reported the incident with relief at the lack of casualties, but it demanded once and for all a complete cleanup of fire hazards before New York became the scene of a second Iroquois tragedy. On the same page, Metcalfe announced that Klaw & Erlanger had entered a libel suit against *Life* for $100,000 dollars.

It took almost a year to bring the suit to trial. In the meantime, the Syndicate was being attacked from several directions. David Belasco, who had remained independent of the Syndicate at first, found himself excluded from the nation's playhouses, and later tried to co-operate with Syndicate officials. He had discovered that co-operation meant nothing short of surrender. Now he wrote a series for the New York *Times*, full of peppery opinions about the Syndicate's honesty and the value of its contracts. *Life* applauded, but it pointed out with a sneer that the *Times* disclaimed responsibility for Belasco. With its own libel suit hanging fire, *Life* assumed a devil-may-care insouciance toward the Syndicate and all its power. It seemed to believe that everyone else should do the same. The Syndicate had run into some financial difficulties, too, and had cut its advertising expenditures in New York to $300 per week per theater. *Life* told it that it could not buy many newspapers at those prices.

Klaw & Erlanger vs. *Life* came to trial on the third of January, 1905. Judge Wallace presided in the United States Circuit Court, and the jury, according to Metcalfe, was made up of "representative business men." The contention was whether or not *Life* was justified in using the names of Klaw & Erlanger in the caption of the drawing concerning the Iroquois fire. *Life*'s attorneys, Ordway and Wierum, presented evidence of the fire hazards at the theater, the locked doors and the overcrowding. They proved that Klaw and Erlanger were on record as owners of a quarter interest in the Iroquois, that they were both booking agents for the theater and producers of Mr. Bluebeard. Within five minutes after the jury had retired for deliberation, it brought in a verdict in *Life*'s favor.

Metcalfe covered the trial. Besides the verdict, he reported a threat of mayhem by Abraham Erlanger "if you ever mention my name again." Erlanger then devised what he must have thought a subtle way to silence Metcalfe and *Life*. On January 12, a meeting of the Managers' Association was held. *Life* pointed out that since Klaw & Erlanger booked practically all the theaters and traveling attractions in the country, every other manager was dependent on them for his very existence in the theatrical business. Other managers might therefore be expected to vote as Klaw and Erlanger dictated. The Trust voted to exclude Metcalfe from all theaters under control of the Managers' Association.

Now Greek had met Greek. *Life* countered with a suit for conspiracy

MESSRS. KLAW AND ERLANGER PRESENT
"MR. BLUEBEARD," LATE OF THE
IROQUOIS THEATRE.

to restrain Metcalfe from the pursuit of a lawful calling. Belasco attacked the Syndicate's flank with another suit for restraint of trade, and the New York District Attorney, William T. Jerome, began to push investigation of fire hazards at New York theaters, suspecting that the special committee appointed by Mayor McClellan had purposely overlooked a number of abuses which might have cost the managers more to correct than they wished to pay.

Metcalfe, unable to review the productions in the theaters, used his column in *Life* for bitter denunciation of the Syndicate. He used his extra time for a program of harassment that amused the entire country, as a regular troop of reporters followed him each evening to watch him being ejected from the theaters. Within a week after he was debarred he had reached the unprecedented pinnacle of theater-going notoriety that allowed him to announce, a day in advance, which theater he would visit on a given evening, and be certain of attracting a crowd. *Life* printed letters and clippings from all around the country, cheering him on.

Belasco's suit was decided in favor of the Syndicate, despite Belasco's testimony that Erlanger had demanded fifty percent of the profits of the road company of *The Auctioneer*,[15] the show around which most of the controversy settled. Belasco maintained that Erlanger had told him, "I'll crush you out of business. I'll kick you out of this theatrical business, and hereafter you won't get another thing." He further claimed that Erlanger had tried some extortion on his own, attempting to circumvent the Syndicate, which demanded only five percent of the profits. Later Marc Klaw, Erlanger's partner, testified in successive sentences first that he got two-thirds of Joseph Brooks's fifty percent of the profits of *The Auctioneer*, and second that he never had any interest in the profits of that production. To these disclosures *Life* added a list of its own, including "the disappearance of witnesses and the destruction or concealment of important books and papers." Perhaps it was the concealment of books and papers that made the difference, because the Supreme Court of New York ruled that there was insufficient evidence of restraint of trade.

On May 31, 1904, at a preliminary hearing, Magistrate Joseph Pool decided that twenty-four New York managers should be held for trial on the presumption that they were guilty of conspiracy. "Under the penal code of the State," *Life* wrote,

> If two or more persons conspire to keep a person from the pursuit of a lawful calling, they are guilty of a misdemeanor, punishable by a fine of five hundred dollars or imprisonment for one year, or both. The courts have held that if a person who had not joined in the original act of combination which constituted the conspiracy, shows by any subsequent acts that he is acting in accordance with it, he also is guilty of the crime.[16]

Acting on the magistrate's decision, the police arrested the managers. Bond was posted for all except Charles M. Burnham, the "one member" who had instigated the boycott. He was held in Tombs for several hours, and released on a writ of habeas corpus which read, in part:

> . . . While a number of the members of said association were together your petitioner called their attention to scurrilous, libelous, and malicious attacks made by one James S. Metcalfe, upon some of the members of said association, affecting their personal integrity and holding their religion up to ridicule.[17]

The statement that Burnham had read to the association was as follows:

> A certain writer in a certain periodical has for the past ten years persistently and without just cause libeled in its columns a large portion of our theatergoers and attacked the personal integrity of members of this association. Its continued malicious, vile and unjustifiable attacks upon those of the Jewish faith are unwarranted, and as it may affect our business interests should receive attention from all managers.
>
> For their so-called criticism on plays or business methods we make no mention— that does not concern us and is without our province—but when they persistently and for no discernible just cause (but a personal feeling perhaps) make a butt of one's religion—be his faith what it may—then some action should be taken to give confidence and support and to take necessary steps to prevent our business interests being injured.
>
> I deem it but fair to say that this paper has been presented without the knowledge of Messrs. Klaw & Erlanger, and is for such individual action as managers may see fit to take.[18]

Burnham's statement raises two points. First, the "individual action" the managers chose to take was by a remarkable coincidence exactly the same action at exactly the same time, as an aftermath of the meeting. Secondly, as *Life* quite properly pointed out, neither Metcalfe nor anyone else on the magazine's staff had ever publicly criticized the Jewish religion. Probably Burnham's words regarding *Life*'s anti-Semitism were only ill-chosen, but it is quite true that nothing that could be remotely considered an article of the Jewish faith had ever been questioned in *Life*'s pages.

Metcalfe, of course, had never ceased to attack the managers as Jews, defending his actions with the usual complex logic.

> If the Theatrical Trust was composed entirely of Chinamen, or Senegambians, or Apaches, and indulged in high-binding, cannibalism, or scalping, *Life* would speak of them as Chinamen, or negroes, or savages, and caricature them with the worst features of those races. This would not imply that there were no decent Chinamen, or negroes, or Indians.[19]

Life did not offer to explain how that implication could be avoided. But Burnham's statement, not *Life*, brought the race prejudice question into the public fight, and *Life* saw a sinister motive in it. Many newspaper proprietors, many businessmen who bought advertising space, were Jewish. *Life* suspected the Syndicate of trying to seduce these men into the conspiracy. Could the Syndicate be hoping that some of the most economically powerful men in the country would see its fight with *Life* as a fight of the beleaguered Jews against another Sennacherib, and would join their forces with the Syndicate's? *Life* thought as much, but it suggested that the Pulitzers, Ochses, Strauses, Sterns and Altmans would hardly allow their influence to be used by the sort of men who made up the Syndicate, simply because they happened to be Jews.

Life found an unexpected ally in the *Jewish Daily News*, which did not necessarily defend Metcalfe, but wanted no part of the Syndicate. One of its editorials was reprinted in *Life:*

> Even if it should be established beyond contradiction that Mr. Metcalfe attacked the Frohmans and others solely because they are Jews, their righteous indignation would be laughed at by the Jewish community, and their attempt to shelter themselves beneath the folds of Judea's standard would be resented by the Jewish community. For they are not known as Jews, and some of them have not, until now, shown any desire to be identified as Jews. We doubt whether certain of them would come under the category of "Kaddish Jews"[20]— so far away are they from all things Jewish, and so anxious have they been (until now) to keep aloof from things Jewish.[21]

This seems like fair-mindedness to a fault. If it should be "established beyond contradiction" that Jews were abhorrent to *Life*, then *Life*'s heedlessness of theological distinctions would seem to be beside the point. Christian Anti-Semites seldom attack Judaism, or even bother to understand it. They simply do not care how their enemies observe their religion. Their only interest is in the myth of Jewish antagonism to all things Christian, which to them means all things virtuous. *Life* considered the editorial to be proof that it was not Anti-Semitic, but *Life*'s defense must be, not that the Syndicate members were not practicing Jews, but that they were guilty of ruthless monopoly and totally unethical exploitation of the worst public taste.

The suit dragged on through delay after delay—which *Life* blamed on the Syndicate—until 1907. In the meantime, Metcalfe managed to see a few plays, mostly in non-Syndicate theaters. Belasco, Fiske, and the Shuberts were now fighting the Syndicate, not in the courts but commercially, and making slow incursion into the booking business. The Syndicate won a suit of its own against the speculators, and with it the right to refuse to honor tickets purchased other than at the box-office. *Life* commented that now there was no excuse at all for a theater to allow speculators at its doorstep, and that a speculator on the outside could only mean a dishonest manager inside. In December, 1905, the twenty-three managers petitioned the New York Supreme court with the writ of *habeas corpus* procured by Burnham. Special district attorney the Honorable James W. Osborne presented a brief of charges to show why they should be held for trial. Justice James Fitzgerald dismissed the managers' petition and ordered them to readmit Metcalfe until the conspiracy suit was settled. *Life* immediately sued the Managers' Association for $270,000 damages incurred by Metcalfe's banishment from the theaters. Daniel Frohman, then managing Daly's Theater, just as immediately barred Metcalfe again. Klaw & Erlanger appealed the libel suit, but lost. "Metcalfe Bills" were introduced into the New York City Council by Assemblyman Kavanagh of Brooklyn and into the New York State Legislature by Frank J. Gardner and Charles E. Murphy. The bills provided fines for managers or owners of places of public entertainment who discriminated against any person or class of persons. The Albany bill passed the Assembly 81-17, but was defeated in the Senate 22-19 through the efforts of the Committee on Codes and its chairman, Nathaniel A. Elsberg. Elsberg, a Jew, told Metcalfe quite frankly that he fought the bill because he thought *Life* was opposed to Jews. That November, Elsberg lost his Senate seat. *Life* refused to admit that Elsberg's personal scruples had influenced his political decisions, and maintained that he deserved a better reward for having done Tammany's work so well on the Gardner Bill. *Life* also imposed upon itself an embargo on Jewish jokes, although it continued to exploit Irish, German, British and Negro stereotypes.

When it was finally brought to court, the suit was anti-climactic. *Life* lost. The court ruled on the basis of an English law governing race tracks, which established that privately owned places of public entertainment were not public places. *Life* appealed, and lost again. Rancor was the order of the day on both sides. *Life*'s "Confidential Guide to the Theaters" continued to heap its moral censures on "dirty" Syndicate plays, and in March of 1908 Metcalfe expanded it to include a separate list of shows "Not For The Young Person." The Syndicate struck back with a campaign of letters to Jews and others who had business with *Life*, advising them that by advertising in *Life* they would alienate Jewish trade, and urging Jewish newsdealers not to sell the magazine. *Life* countered by lifting its embargo on Jewish jokes. "*Life* sees no reason," the announcement said, "why he should discriminate in favor of the only people who are seeking to injure him."

But if *Life*'s private battle with the Syndicate appears to have ended in a tangle of unpleasant and underhanded mutual attempts to injure, the Syndicate had been notably weakened, and *Life*'s part in the weakening had been considerable. Frohman removed "objectionable" advertising from his programmes and improved their printing. Klaw & Erlanger lobbied for an anti-speculator bill, although *Life* suspected that they only wanted to turn out the small speculator and set up dummy agencies under their own control. The Shuberts continued to gain prestige and power. A wave of virtue struck the newspaper critics. Two, at least, became so virtuously anti-Syndicate that they lost their jobs.

The newspaper critics who were fired for anti-Syndicate sentiments were two of the leading American dramatic critics of the day, Walter P. Eaton and William Winter. Eaton, author of *The American Stage Today*, criticized the acting of Margaret Illington (Mrs. Daniel Frohman) rather caustically in the columns of the *Sun*. Klaw & Erlanger withdrew their advertising from the *Sun*; Eaton was dismissed, and Klaw & Erlanger immediately opened their account again. The sequence of events does not prove, as *Life* claimed it did, that the $151 per week which the *Sun* collected from Syndicate theater advertisements was the price of virtue, but *Life* can be pardoned for seeing a connection. William M. Laffan, the *Sun*'s publisher, considered *Life*'s logic libelous and sued for $100,000 dollars. The *Sun*, as a corporation, did the same. It might have developed into another knockdown fight and opened a few more windows on Syndicate methods; or it might have meant the financial ruin of *Life*. But Laffan died before his suit came to trial, and the *Sun* dropped suit. Winter's case, which did not involve *Life* directly, was a little more complicated. Winter, the author of several books on drama and generally considered the foremost American critic of the drama in his time, resigned in 1909 from the *Tribune* because his criticism had been censored. In April of 1915, when Alexander Woollcott, then the critic of the no-longer-pusillanimous *Times*, was barred by the Shuberts, *Life* gloated. Woollcott was readmitted before the fall season, though. The managers' iron grip had been broken.

By 1915 there was no real fight to keep up. When, in May, Charles Frohman's name appeared on the list of passengers who had gone down with the *Lusitania*, it marked the end of any organized warfare between *Life* and the Syndicate. Outside of New York, the Syndicate had never really meant much to Metcalfe and *Life*, anyway, and without Frohman the Syndicate in New York was just another businessmen's club. *Life*'s obituary notice for Frohman deserves to be reproduced, although it might be the part of charity not to comment too freely on it. Frohman was a man who loved flattery, and he had received little enough of it from *Life* during his lifetime. He whom *Life* had called the debaucher of youth and monarch of quick profit, the cornerstone of an edifice erected to corrupt art and dictate the huckster's terms to the artist, was transformed in death. It was not *Life*'s policy to speak ill of dead enemies, and the battle with the Syndicate was over, but even so it seems a shame that Frohman could not have seen *Life*'s last opinion of him:

> Often the subject of honest criticism that he never resented, he was a manager who cared more for what he accomplished than the profit that came from it, a manager who was generous and honest with his artists, and a manager who kept his word.[22]

Whether this description of Frohman is more accurate or less than the language of abuse that *Life* used to describe him when he was alive is neither here nor there. *Life* had called him its bold, bad enemy. Now he was dead, and *Life* eulogized him. It proclaimed him a paragon. The contradiction seems a kind of cowardice—exactly the kind that *Life* claimed to abhor.

NOTES

[1]*Life*, LXXI, 1918, p. 600. Dale's play does not appear to have any similarity beyond its name to the 1873 short story by Henry James, "The Madonna of the Future."

[2]Some Dale titles: *Jonathan's Home, A Marriage Below Zero, An Eerie He and She, My Footlight Husband, Miss Innocence, Familiar Chats with Queens of the Stage, An Old Maid Kindled, Conscience on the Ice, The Great Wet Way.*

[3]*Life*, LX, 1912, p. 1858.   [4]*Life*, XV, 1890, p. 96.

[5]*Life*, LXV, 1915, p. 668.   [6]*Life*, XXII, 1893, p. 252.

[7]*Life*, XXIII, 1894, p. 260.

[8]Bernard D. Weinryb, "Jewish Immigration and Accomodation to America," Publication of The American Jewish Historical Society, XLVI, No. 3-4 (May-June 1957). Reprinted in Marshall Sklare (ed.), *The Jews: Social Patterns of An American Group* (Glencoe, Illinois: The Free Press, 1958), p. 16.

[9]*Life*, XL, 1902, p. 308.

[10]Isaac Marcosson and Daniel Frohman, *Charles Frohman, Manager and Man* (New York & London: Harper & Bros., 1916), p. 186.

[11]Arthur Hornblow, *A History of the Theatre in America* (Philadelphia & London: J. B. Lippincott & Co., 1919), pp. 319-320.

[12]*Life*, XXX, 1897, p. 292.   [13]*Life*, XXXI, 1898, p. 52.

[14]*Life*, XXXIV, 1899, p. 312.

[15]Ironically, *The Auctioneer* starred David Warfield as a sympathetic Jewish character. Metcalfe had said (*Life*, XXXVIII, 1901, p. 272), "Warfield has made the stage Jew . . . a human being." It was one of the few concessions of the sort he ever made, and now Belasco's testimony had made the play the very symbol, for *Life*, of Jewish villainy.

[16]*Life*, XLV, 1905, p. 306.   [17]*Life*, XLV, 1905, p. 738.

[18]*Ibid.*   [19]*Life*, XLV, 1905, p. 199.

[20]Jews who observe no religious forms except the Kaddish, hence only deserving inclusion as Jews by the minimal margin.

[21]*Life*, XLV, 1905, p. 253.   [22]*Life*, LXV, 1915, p. 911.

CHAPTER VIII

LIFE AFTER DEATH

Life's apparent reversal of its freely stated convictions about Charles Frohman should not be difficult to understand by now. While it seems a kind of cowardice it also seems a sort of altruism. *Life* seldom offered harm, even to its enemies, when comfort was needed. It wore its heart on its sleeve.

What conclusion is to be drawn from all *Life*'s impulsive generosity, all its vindictiveness, all its posing, all its pride in ancestry and virility? Perhaps the only absolutely safe conclusion is that *Life* represented and did its best to perpetuate a certain level of thought in the America of its time which has proved to be less influential on subsequent events than have other levels of thought. That much is certainly true. When one tries to pursue the general conclusion into specifics, one finds the path strewn with imponderables. It is impossible to calculate how many persons in America thought as *Life* thought and how many were persuaded to change their minds to *Life*'s way of thinking. It is impossible to judge the degree of good or harm that *Life* did in taking any stand on any question. Nevertheless there are at least two speculative conclusions suggested, although not proved beyond doubt, by the history of John Ames Mitchell's *Life*. The first is that *Life* spoke with a child's voice to a childlike audience. The second is that *Life*'s audience and its attitudes were more widespread and more powerful than they have ordinarily been given credit for.

Let us attack these two in reverse order. The existence and even the great influence of such ideas as American ancestor-worship, the unreasoning hatred of aliens, and the genteel vogue have all been chronicled.[1] But it has been the common practice to treat them as historical aberrations which the nation has outgrown. They were not aberrations, however. They were the sacred convictions of men, like John Ames Mitchell and his associates, who were born to America's oldest traditions and educated in her finest universities. These men understood the minds of their fellow Americans well enough to catch and hold popular attention in a medium where the competition was strong and the records of past failures were ominous. There is little doubt that *Life* was *statistically* wrong when it claimed that the majority of Americans were blissfully contented with their pure and wholesome lives. But statistics are not the whole story. *Life*'s class was a minority, but it was a vocal and influential minority, and *Life* was among its most vocal members. Admittedly, *Life*'s influence cannot be measured. Unlike its two chief rivals, *Puck* and *Judge*, it was never credited with swaying a national election.[2] Yet the power it carried was enormous. It gave Americans a model citizen—itself. In an age given to hero-worship, it was a public hero.

Life's childishness and that of its audience is even less easy to prove conclusively, since any decision implies a judgment of *Life*'s values. Yet *Life* (and *Puck*) personified itself as a little child. Mitchell's childlike qualities, or rather those attributed to him by his closest friends, have been mentioned. Dixon Wecter, admittedly an unsympathetic critic, quotes with approval the sentiments of Henry James that childishness was the hallmark of James's America. The magazine, its editor, and its era reminded close observers of childlike things.

Life's most obvious characteristics suggest a childlike personality, too. Its impulses, its emotionalism, its quick sympathy for the hurt and its savage hysteria when it attacked an enemy, all are childlike qualities. Its genteel aspirations too often became nothing more than a device to avoid responsibility. Its "pure American" beliefs too often became an echo of "My father can lick your father." Its defensive masculinity does not suggest an adult's way of dealing with the opposite sex. It suggests preadolescent fears for the loss of manhood. The obscure link that *Life* always saw between virility and morality may well be found here. *Life* thought, as Freudian analysis tells us that most little boys think at some time, that all things evil were somehow emasculating. *Life*'s anti-Semitism might have been rooted here. One historian of anti-Semitism has argued that the anti-Semitic mind has traditionally perceived the Jew as a threatening, emasculating father-figure.[3] Even *Life*'s charity can be seen as a child's charity. Its generosity extended to pets and children, and not much farther. It wanted some return for its charity. It wanted to be loved.

Although the foregoing is speculative, it has a place here because the facts suggest so much more than they prove that some speculation is necessary. And if these conclusions are true, the history of *Life* is of considerably increased importance in the annals of America. As a spokesman for a lot of discredited ideas, *Life* demands little more than passing attention. As a spokesman for a state of mind that threatened to envelop the nation in the smothering folds of a *Peter Pan*-like refusal to grow up, encouraged by America's oldest citizens and most venerated institutions and equated with virtue and manliness, *Life* is a giant. And even if the truth is at neither extreme, but somewhere between, it is only fair to *Life* that the suggestion of its true importance be emphasized.

Mitchell was a great editor or a very near thing to it. He began with nothing, in a field strewn with the wreckage of former aspirants to public favor. He led his magazine through thirty-five years of constantly increasing prosperity, and in doing so he impressed his personality on the magazine, and the magazine's on the nation, to a degree and for a period of time unequalled by any other comparable American publication. He died with the age he had spoken to and for, without a professional enemy in the world. Childlike or no, his is the record of a successful life.

After Mitchell's death, momentum carried *Life* for a year or more. Miller was now the president of the company, and Metcalfe was the magazine's editor, and they collaborated on editorial duties. Metcalfe bought the art while Miller ran the show. Then Miller died in December of 1919, and Metcalfe carried on alone for a month. In February of 1920 there was a shuffle in *Life*'s executive offices, with the result that Martin became president, Metcalfe treasurer, Masson secretary, and LeRoy Miller, Andrew Miller's son, assistant treasurer. Late in March, Masson announced that the magazine had been sold to Gibson.

Fairfax Downey, Gibson's biographer, has given an account of the sale and of *Life*'s very gradual waning under Gibson and a series of editors until it was sold again and reorganized as a monthly.[4]   In the early twenties the "new" *Life* boasted such staff members as Robert Emmett Sherwood, Robert Benchley, and Dorothy Parker. Masson invented the slogan, "Obey that impulse—clip that coupon!" and circulation picked up momentarily. The new staff collaborated on the great "Burlesque Number" of 1921, which contained among other burlesques and parodies Benchley's parodies of Mencken and Nathan, still reprinted.[5] But Masson reported that the new members of the staff composed that number in secrecy, fearing that the older staff members would ruin it before it came to press.[6] The new and the old were trying to survive in harness, but they could not pull in the same direction. Downey wrote:

> Masson, Martin, Louis Evan Shipman, Sherwood and Norman Anthony succeeded each other in the editorial chair. None of them evolved a policy with the vital spark that would carry *Life* through, although each contributed something of value, and the magazine, though its income steadily dwindled, kept on the profit side of the ledger until the Depression.[7]
>
> For *Life*, as for countless other enterprises, the depression was a disastrous blow.
>
> In 1932, Gibson sold his entire interest to Clair Maxwell and Harry Richter who made *Life* into a monthly and commenced a gallant fight to restore its former prestige.[8]

Maxwell put out a good publication, but where Mitchell had been an artist and novelist with burning convictions about all sorts of subjects, Maxwell was an advertising man who knew how magazines were run.[9] After four years, Maxwell sold to Time, Incorporated. *Time* reported that "*Life*'s staff will be taken over by Time, Incorporated, intact. The only *Life* activity to be continued by Time, Incorporated, is its Fresh Air Fund." It also reported that Maxwell had made a profit during those last four years. Later the *New York Times* reported that Monte Bourjaily, who had recently purchased *Judge*, had bought *Life*'s subscription list and fixtures, and that the work of *Life*'s artists and writers would thereafter appear in *Judge*. All that Time, Incorporated really wanted was *Life*'s name.

Two more brief quotations will bring *Life*'s history to a close. The first is taken from an article by Alexander King in *Vanity Fair*, and quoted by Downey. King was writing of all three weekly humorous magazines, *Life*, *Puck*, and *Judge*, and of the reasons why they sank into obscurity after so many years of signal success:

> They became arrogant, conservative, and stuffy, and losing complete sight of their prime functions as humorous weeklies, they standardized their material until it lost all contact with the turbulent life and reality about them.[10]

The second quotation is from the last issue of *Life*, November, 1936. Martin, who had worked himself into a malarial relapse trying to pull *Life* through its critical infancy, presided over the obsequies. Unruffled as usual, he pronounced a benediction on the new photographic *Life* that was also a long farewell to his and Mitchell's *Life*, to the attitudes it had adopted, and to the world it flourished in:

> And as for me, I wish it all good fortune, grace, mercy and peace and usefulness to a distracted world that does not know which way to turn nor what will happen to it next. A wonderful time for a new voice to make a noise that needs to be heard.[11]

NOTES

1Examples: For ancestor-worship, see Grant Cochran Knight, "Americanismus and Americanism," *The Strenuous Age of American Literature* (Chapel Hill: The University of North Carolina Press, 1954), pp. 50-101. For anti-immigration see Barbara Miller Solomon, *Ancestors and Immigrants* (Cambridge, Massachusetts: Harvard University Press, 1956). For the genteel movement see Edwin Harrison Cady, *The Gentleman in America* (Syracuse, Syracuse University Press, 1949).

2Cf. Appendix.

3Norman Cohn, *The Pursuit of the Millenium* (London: Secker and Warburg, 1957), pp. 63-74.

4But the *New York Times* for March 22, 1920, p. 6, reported that the Miller estate was the seller. Perhaps both are right. So far as I can determine, Mitchell owned three-fourths of *Life*'s stock and Miller owned one-fourth.

5Last reprinted in Dwight MacDonald, *Parodies* (New York: Random House, 1960), p. 215.

6Masson, *Our American Humorists*, p. 389.

7Downey, *Portrait of an Era*, p. 357.

8*Ibid.*, p. 361.

9Maxwell went to work for the new *Life*, in 1936, as an advertising salesman. He ended his days as a distributor for Hiram Walker Distilleries. (*New York Times*, May 12, 1959, p. 35.) It is simply inconceivable that Mitchell could have accepted the collapse of *Life* in the same way.

10Quoted in Downey, *Portrait of an Era*, p. 355.

11*Life*, CIII, (November, 1936), p. 29.

APPENDIX

RELEVANT HISTORIES OF *PUCK* AND *JUDGE*

The rivalry among the three leading magazines of humor in America at the end of the nineteenth century was complex and lively, but it was seldom bitter except in presidential election years. Then *Puck* and *Judge*, who were violent political partisans, would mutually lambaste one another's candidates and policies, *Puck* on the side of the Democratic party, *Judge* for the Republicans. *Life*, as a political independent, would take advantage of their momentary preoccupation with one another and try to make their partisanship look ridiculous. *Life*, however, could be as violently opposed to a man's candidacy as either of the other two papers, and *Life*'s cartoons and editorials rivalled theirs in political influence. The events in the history of the three magazines which commentators have found most noteworthy were the two political campaigns of 1884 and 1896. In each of those one of the two politically-minded magazines had an enormous public influence. In the campaign of 1884, the political cartoon was new. Thomas Nast's drawings for *Harper's* earned the widest reputation as having been politically persuasive in that year, but Joseph Keppler's and Bernard Gillam's caricatures of James G. Blaine, for *Puck*, were at least as influential as those of Nast.[1] Twelve years later, *Judge* contributed the slogan, "the full dinner pail," to McKinley's campaign, and Mark Hanna himself gave *Judge* credit for having helped elect the Major.[2] *Life* had attacked Blaine almost as fiercely as *Puck* had done, and if it had not supported McKinley in 1896 it had certainly done its best to discredit Bryan. It is possible that if there was any thunder stolen, it was not *Life* who was guilty of stealing it.

The real three-way rivalry was in operation only from 1885 to about 1902. The reason for this was that *Judge*, although it predated 1885, was reorganized as a Republican spokesman in that year, and its vigorous period extended just beyond the turn of the century. During John Ames Mitchell's editorship of *Life*, *Puck* appeared to *Life*'s staff members to be their "real" rival. *Judge* was largely ignored.

Puck began as a German-language paper printed in St. Louis. Its founders were Keppler, a lithographic draftsman, and Adolf Schwarzmann, a lithographer. It was circulated almost entirely among the German-speaking theater-goers of St. Louis. In the 1870's it moved to New York, and was printed weekly, still in German, and with illustrations in color lithography. It borrowed heavily from the local German-language humorous papers. But it was noticed that many non-Germans read *Puck* for its cartoons. In 1876, *Puck*'s cartoons on the disputed Hayes-Tilden election won wide attention. Sydney Rosenfeld then approached Keppler and Schwarzmann with the idea of publishing *Puck* in English.[3] He persuaded them that the venture might succeed, and in March of 1877, *Puck*'s first English language edition appeared. Thereafter it was published weekly until September, 1918, when it ceased publication. It was a larger magazine than *Life*, an extra-large quarto, running approximately the same number of pages as *Life* ran and selling for ten cents, as *Life* did.[4]

The parallel between the three founders of the English-language *Puck* and the three founders of *Life* is very close. Schwarzmann, like Andrew Miller, was a business manager who never intruded into the editorial side of the publication. Rosenfeld, like Edward S. Martin, supplied witty commentary and editorial criticism. Keppler, like John Mitchell, was artist, overseer of artists, and inspiration for the magazine.

Rosenfeld gave up the editorship, after a year, to a twenty-two year old writer who had joined the staff when *Puck* began to publish in English —Henry Cuyler Bunner. Bunner remained in the editor's chair from 1878 until his death in 1896. He was Keppler's right hand, and even though it was Keppler (like Mitchell) who guided the magazine's policy, it was Bunner (like Martin) who was its public spokesman. Brander Matthews wrote:

> *Puck* was the earliest to succeed of all the many American attempts to establish a comic weekly; and in large measure its success was due to Bunner,— to his fertility, to his resourcefulness, to his insight and to his unfailing taste.[5]

Puck was not so gentle as *Life*, for all of Bunner's "unfailing taste." Keppler's cartoons, and those of such artists as Frederick Opper, Bernard Gillam, James Albert Wales, and F. Graetz left real wounds when they were turned against public figures. Ambrose Bierce, who certainly would never have approved anything namby-pamby, thought that Bunner's tastefulness was too great a drag on Keppler's genius.[6] Yet *Puck* gained a reputation for biting humor which indicates that Bunner's jokes were not weak-kneed. Tom Masson tried to sort out the differences between *Life*'s approach and *Puck*'s by differentiating between Mitchell's "comic spirit" and Bunner's:

> I purposely avoid using the word "comic" in connection with *Puck* because *Puck* was never a comic journal in the sense in which George Meredith uses the word comedy, and which I take to be the best sense. It was under the editorship of Mr. H. C. Bunner that *Puck* later achieved its preeminence as a purveyor of the very best American humor. Yet it cannot be said of Bunner, as

it might have been said, and indeed has been said of Mitchell, that he had the spirit of comedy. Bunner had a fine literary judgment, good taste, and editorial ability of a high order, and he made *Puck* an influential journal. Mitchell had within him quite strongly the spirit of true comedy. . . . In this sense then [intellectual laughter] *Life* was a more comic journal than *Puck*. Bunner had humor and sentiment. Mitchell undoubtedly had more of the comic spirit.[7]

What this finally means is that *Puck* was less gentle and more combative than was *Life*. This comparison is best made in the area of cartoon caricatures. Both magazines printed caricature, and both caricatured the same persons, but *Life*'s caricatures are far less grotesque than *Puck*'s. Joseph Pulitzer and William McKinley, for example, were caricatured in both magazines during the latter 1890's. *Life*'s Pulitzer is a scrawny man with an enormous nose. *Puck*'s Pulitzer is a species of stork. *Life*'s McKinley is a pompous little man dressed as Napoleon. *Puck*'s McKinley is a bulbous dwarf manipulated by strings of money.

Puck's use of color on its center-page drawings and sometimes elsewhere in the magazine made it an altogether gaudier production than *Life*. Many persons, *Life*'s staff not the least among them, considered *Life*'s black-and-white more chaste and tasteful. *Life* made much humorous capital out of the pejorative connotations of "colored" as applied to *Puck* and occasionally to *Judge*, which also printed in color.

Puck's motto, chosen in November of 1877, was "What fools these mortals be." Its emblem, like *Life*'s, was a child, in *Puck*'s case a top-hatted, cane-twirling child. Its social ideas were almost exactly *Life*'s, too. The significant difference between the magazines was not in their convictions, but in their expression. *Puck* was a rowdy railer. *Life* was a Thackerayan, and a Thackerayan who adopted the master's gentlest moods.

Bunner was replaced in 1896 by Harry Leon Wilson. In 1902, Wilson was succeeded by John Kendrick Bangs. In 1905, Arthur Hamilton Folwell succeeded Bangs, and in 1916 Karl Schmidt succeeded Folwell. Except for Schmidt these successive editors appear to have had little to do with any policy changes. In 1914, Nathan Straus, Jr. of Macy's department store in New York bought *Puck* from Schwarzmann and Keppler. He and Schmidt tried to make over the magazine to combat the high anti-German feeling running at large in the country. The attempt failed. *Puck* ran downhill quickly during World War I and stopped publication at last in September of 1918, less than four months after Mitchell's death.[8]   The era was over.

Judge was never considered by *Life* as a rival in *Puck*'s class. In the late 1890's *Judge*'s circulation surpassed *Life*'s[9] and *Judge* outlived *Life* by nearly a decade, but under Mitchell's administration, *Life* simply did not think of *Judge* as a direct rival. *Judge* was started as an imitator of *Puck*. *Life* thought itself outside the battle.

In 1881, James Albert Wales seceded from *Puck* to begin his own humorous weekly, and the first issue of *Judge* came out October 29, 1881. This early *Judge* was typographically like *Puck* (*Life* was not), but it was milder, less assertive, and simply did not muster the talent that *Puck* offered. It faltered and would have died early. But in 1885 the Republican party was stinging from the slap the humorous papers had given it during the Blaine-Cleveland campaign. *Judge* appeared to have potential as a Republican spokesman in the same medium, and W. J. Arkell bought the magazine, hired Bernard Gillam away from *Puck*, and set up as an outspoken Republican partisan. It reached its peak in the 1896 campaign. After that the partisanship that had brought it success drove it toward failure. The Republican party was so conspicuously dominant for sixteen years that the public began to think of *Judge* as ill-mannered. In 1889, *Judge* had bought *Leslie's Magazine*, and in 1910 the company reorganized so that *Judge* took over some of the features of *Leslie's* and became neither a Republican magazine nor a humorous magazine. After this it merely survived, although its survival might be attributed to its blandness. It absorbed much of *Life*'s editorial staff when *Life* finally succumbed in 1936. It continued to publish until the second World War finally killed it.

Judge and *Life* differed on too many basic points to be serious rivals for one another. *Life* was politically non-partisan; *Judge* was saved solely because it seemed to have a future as a political partisan. *Judge* imitated *Puck*'s format, and therefore bid for *Puck*'s customers; *Life* developed its own format, unlike that of the other two magazines. *Judge* was even a gentler humorist than *Life*, when non-political matters were involved. After the turn of the century, *Life* seldom mentioned *Judge*, although it continued to exchange gibes with *Puck*. After 1910, *Judge* was just another magazine.

NOTES

[1] Frank Luther Mott, *A History of American Magazines* (Cambridge, Massachusetts: Harvard University Press, 1957), vol. 3, p. 521.

[2] Mott, *A History of American Magazines*, vol. 3, p. 554.

[3] Masson, *Our American Humorists*, p. 35.

[4] Mott, *A History of American Magazines*, vol. 3, p. 520.

[5] Brander Matthews, introductory note *in* Henry Cuyler Bunner, *The Stories of Henry Cuyler Bunner, First Series*, (New York: Charles Scribner's Sons, 1916), p. x.

[6] Mott, *A History of American Magazines*, vol. 3, p. 523.

[7] Masson, *Our American Humorists*, pp. 28 and 30.

[8] Mott, *A History of American Magazines*, vol. 3, p. 528.

[9] Mott, *A History of American Magazines*, vol. 3. p. 556.